# NAVIGATION

Navigation can be a rewarding and fascinating study, no less for the amateur than for the professional student. It does not have to be the province of the specialist alone, and there is no reason whatever why a person of average intelligence, with a minimum of mathematical knowledge, should not be able to master the basic theory and principles of navigation from this book. The author, who has many years' experience of teaching navigation and practising it at sea and in the air, explains in simple language the techniques, instruments and calculations used in all kinds of navigation. He also includes a brief history of navigation, and gives many helpful examples and exercises.

# TEACH YOURSELF BOOKS

# NAVIGATION

**A. C. Gardner,** B.A.

Extra Master, Flight Navigator,
Fellow of the Royal Institute of Navigation

**TEACH YOURSELF BOOKS**
**HODDER & STOUGHTON**
ST PAUL'S HOUSE   WARWICK LANE   LONDON EC4P 4AH

*First printed 1958*
*Second edition 1973*
*Fourth impression 1975*

ISBN 0 340 05668 1

*Printed in Great Britain for*
*Teach Yourself Books, Hodder & Stoughton,*
*by Fletcher & Son Ltd, Norwich*

# Contents

# Introduction

Books on navigation are usually written for specialists—for navigating officers of the Royal or Merchant Navies, for navigators of the R.A.F. and civil airlines, and occasionally for yachtsmen.

The writer of this book has spent more than twenty years practising navigation at sea and in the air; he has spent ten years teaching the subject; and if he is not yet a real yachtsman, he nevertheless likes to spend his spare time 'messing about in small boats' . . . provided that he is allowed to act as navigator.

For navigation can be a rewarding and fascinating study, no less for the amateur than for the professional student. And there is no need for it to be the province of the specialist alone.

It is true that professional navigators at sea and in the air require complicated and expensive instruments with which to navigate great ships and fast aircraft. They also need Nautical or Air Almanacs and sets of nautical tables. But the uses of these instruments can be easily described in a book for the general reader, and extracts from almanacs and tables can be given as required.

In fact, there is no reason whatever why a person of average intelligence, with a minimum of mathematical knowledge, cannot master all the basic theory and principles of navigation from a short book, such as this one. If he should then wish to study more advanced works that have been written for specialists, or even wish to buy himself a second-hand sextant, with which to practise the theory that he has so readily mastered . . . then that will be all to the good.

In this book, most of the examples that are given refer to the navigation of ships, but reference is also made to air navigation, particularly when the methods used in the air differ from those used at sea.

The writer wishes to express his appreciation of the help given him by his friends, Captain J. W. Stephen and Dr. D. Emslie-Smith, in checking the MS. and proofs; but if any errors in calculation are found in the book, the writer himself is entirely responsible for them.

DUNDEE.                                              A. C. G.

# CHAPTER 1

# The Early Navigators

If, as is generally believed, the earliest habitations of men were on the banks of rivers, such as the Euphrates, the Tigris and the Nile, then it may be assumed that navigation began as the simple art of conning a small boat or coracle from one bank of a river to the other.

Even this comparatively simple operation required a certain amount of knowledge and skill. The whereabouts of sandbanks and other submerged, or partially submerged, hazards had to be known. And if the crossing of the river was to be made without undue waste of time, suitable allowance would have to be made for the effect of tide or current.

From the beginning, therefore, navigation could be defined as the art of taking a craft from place *A* to place *B* as safely and as quickly as possible. And for all ordinary purposes that definition still holds good today. For when an ocean greyhound crosses the Atlantic in three days, or an airliner flies round the world in two, both are navigated according to the principle of the greatest possible speed combined with the greatest possible safety. If the latter part of this principle is neglected, accidents can, and do, happen.

But although the basic principle remains the same, the modern navigator's job is more complicated than it was in ancient times, because of the great distances that must now be covered at ever-increasing speeds.

To help him with his more complicated task, however, the navigator has at his disposal today the mathematical and scientific discoveries of centuries which have been applied to navigation in many different ways.

The first science to be applied to navigation was astronomy. When a few small vessels began to venture out from river estuaries into the open sea, their navigators were not slow to make use of a phenomenon that was already known to travellers on land; namely, that the bearings of certain stars near the Northern and Southern Poles remain the same, or vary only slightly, throughout the night. By keeping one of these stars on a certain bearing relative to the ship's head, it was possible to keep the ship on the same course from dusk until dawn. In daylight hours the coastline could be seen, and empirical methods were soon devised whereby the distance from prominent landmarks could be estimated. When visibility was poor, a billet of lead, made fast to a line, was cast overboard in order to find out if the ship were approaching shallow water.

The Pole Star method of keeping a vessel's head in a given direction, however, was not available in daylight or in cloudy weather, and this difficulty was not overcome until the advent of the magnetic compass. Nobody appears to know exactly when or where this invaluable instrument was invented, but there is reason to believe that it may have been known in the West during the Viking period, and its use was well established in the Middle Ages.

By its use, which will be described more fully in the next chapter, a ship can be kept heading in the same direction indefinitely without any reference to stars or landmarks except as a means of obtaining periodic checks on the ship's position and on the performance of the compass.

The invention of the compass, however, resulted in longer and more ambitious voyages being attempted; and this in turn resulted in seamen feeling the need for accurate maps and charts on which the routes of past voyages could be traced and those of future ones projected.

This need raised a fundamental difficulty which was not easily solved. By this time in the world's history most navigators knew that the earth was round and not flat, as primitive man had apparently believed. Early priestly astronomers had observed that the shadow cast by the earth during an eclipse of the moon was circular in shape; and watchers on Mediterranean shores had observed that a ship's masts slowly 'dipped' below the horizon as she sailed farther and farther away.

The earth, then, was a sphere. But if one wanted to make a chart, it had to be made on a flat piece of parchment or vellum.

Have you ever tried to stick a square label, or even a large postage stamp, on to the surface of a sphere? If so, you will know what happens. The paper cannot be made to stick properly. If it can be made to stick at all, it develops the most unsightly wrinkles. In other words, it becomes distorted.

And that is what happens, and has always happened, when men have tried to make a chart of the curved surface of the earth out of a flat piece of paper. It simply cannot be done exactly. There is always some distortion, and the distortion becomes greater as the area to be charted is increased.

But that was not the only difficulty that faced the early cartographers.

If we draw a straight line between two points, $A$ and $B$, on a flat piece of paper, we have been taught to accept two facts: (i) that the line from $A$ to $B$, if it is straight, is heading in a constant direction relative to the edge of the paper or some other datum line, and (ii) that the distance from $A$ to $B$, measured along the straight line joining them, is the shortest possible distance between the two points.

We shall see, however, in due course, that these facts do *not* hold good when $A$ and $B$ are two widely separated points on the surface of a sphere, such as the earth, which is represented in Fig. 1.

The horizontal curved lines in Fig. 1 are parallels of latitude spaced 15° apart. They are called 'parallels' because they are parallel to the Equator, which extends right round the earth midway between the Poles. If the earth were cut in half by a knife cutting along the line of the Equator, the blade of the knife would pass through

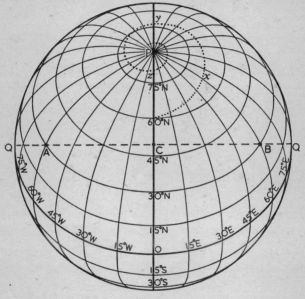

Fig. 1

the centre of the earth. For this reason the Equator is called a 'great circle', i.e. a circle on a sphere, the plane of which passes through the sphere's centre. The parallels of latitude, however, are called 'small circles' because their planes do not pass through the centre of the sphere.

The curved lines in the up-and-down direction, which meet at the poles and are spaced 15° apart along the Equator, are called meridians of longitude, and these are arcs of great circles, because their planes also pass through the centre of the sphere. The Zero meridian (or 'Prime meridian', as it is sometimes called) is the meridian of Greenwich, from which all other meridians are numbered from 0° to 180° in an easterly and westerly direction.

The parallels of latitude are numbered from 0° to 90° North and South of the Equator; and these are important in another sense, because the distance separating them, measured along any meridian, is used to measure distance on the earth's surface in nautical miles.

One minute of latitude, measured along a meridian, equals one nautical mile, of which the average length is 6080 feet. This is the accepted length of the United Kingdom nautical mile and is equal to 1·8532 kilometres. The International nautical mile is 1·8520 kilometres in length. The United Kingdom nautical mile is used throughout this book. Therefore the distance due North along any meridian, from the Equator to 15° N, or from 15° N to 30° N, equals $15 \times 60 = 900$ n. miles (1667·9 km). Similarly, from 65° N to 75° N equals 600 n. miles (1111·9 km), and so on.

It has been mentioned that 6080 feet (1·8532 km) is the *average* length of a nautical mile. This is because the earth is not an exact sphere. It is in fact an 'oblate spheroid', which means that its polar diameter is slightly less than its equatorial diameter, and this accounts for the variation in the length of the nautical mile, although 6080 feet (1·8532 km) is good enough for most practical purposes. For the same reason, the length of one minute of longitude, measured along the Equator, which is known as a 'geographical mile', is a little more than 6080 feet (1·8532 km); but, in practice, we can use this figure without causing any serious error in our work.

If one wishes to be precise, the term 'one minute of latitude' can be expressed more exactly as 'the length of the arc of a meridian which subtends an angle of one minute at the centre of the earth'. Also, the term 'one minute of longitude' can be expressed more exactly as 'the length of the arc of the Equator which subtends an angle of one minute at the centre of the earth'.

Now let us consider $A$ and $B$, which are two points on the earth's surface illustrated in Fig. 1. They are both on the parallel of latitude of 30° N, but $A$ is in longitude 60° W and $B$ is in longitude 60° E.

If you have a sphere of any kind—even a large ball will do—you should now draw lines on it to represent the Equator, the parallel of 30° N and the meridians of 60° W and 60° E respectively.

Mark the points $A$ and $B$, and then take a piece of string and measure its length when it is made to lie along the parallel of 30° N between $A$ and $B$. You will find that the string is quite slack. If, however, you continue to make it pass through $A$ and $B$, but tighten it as much as possible, you will now find that it lies along the pecked line $ACB$. In other words, the length $ACB$ is the shortest possible distance between $A$ and $B$ on the surface of the sphere. The distance along the parallel of latitude is quite appreciably more.

But if a ship has to go from $A$ to $B$, the easiest thing for her navigator to do is to set course due East along the parallel of latitude. This course makes an angle of 90° with every meridian that it crosses, so that the ship remains on the same course all the time. That is to say, she is heading in a constant direction from $A$ to $B$. But, as we have seen, she is not going by the shortest possible route.

A line on the earth's surface which crosses every meridian at the same angle is called a 'rhumb line' by seamen and a 'loxodrome' by mathematicians. A parallel of latitude is only one particular example of a rhumb line, i.e. it is one which crosses successive meridians at an angle of 90°. A rhumb line can cross the meridians at any angle. The dotted line $xyz$ in Fig. 1 is a rhumb line which crosses successive meridians at an angle of about 70°. It is a spiral which approaches, but never reaches, the Pole. An aircraft which left latitude 60° N longitude 0° and steered a constant course of 070° would follow the path *xyz*.

Returning again to the question of the distance between *A* and *B*, we have seen that *ACB* is the shortest possible distance. But if we produce *ACB* right round the earth, we shall find that it divides the world into two halves. In other words, *ACB* is the arc of a great circle.

From this we conclude that, on the surface of a sphere or spheroid, such as the earth, the shortest possible distance between two points is *along the arc of a great circle*.

But we must also observe that to travel along such an arc (along the arc *ACB*, for instance) we do *not* proceed in a constant direction. The line *ACB* crosses each meridian at a slightly different angle, and a ship which follows this route must keep altering her course all the time.

To follow a great circle course across the earth's surface, therefore, is a tedious process. And, in practice, the saving of distance, compared with following a rhumb line route, is very small, unless the total distance to be covered is very great. Later on we shall work some numerical examples to illustrate this point.

From what has been said already, however, it can be appreciated that the rhumb line course is by far the easier to follow. At *A*, one sets the ship's head in a given direction, and by steering in that same direction continuously, one should arrive at *B*—provided that the rhumb line course has been worked out correctly beforehand, and that no currents or strong winds deflect the ship from her predetermined track. The ship travels a little farther than she would if she followed the great circle course, but over short distances the difference is not worth taking into account.

We can presume that the navigators and cartographers of the sixteenth century knew a great deal about the matters that we have been discussing here. They must have done so, because it was at the end of that century that the Mercator's chart first appeared; and the Mercator's chart was probably the most important contribution to the art of navigation since the invention of the magnetic compass.

'Mercator' is Latin for 'merchant'. Most shipmasters were merchants in the sixteenth century, so it is possible that the name given to the chart simply meant 'the merchant's (or shipmaster's) chart'. Some authorities, however, say that the chart was invented by a German named Kremer or Kaufman. 'Kaufman' is the German variant of the Old English 'Cheapman' (modern 'Chapman'), which also means 'merchant'—and thence 'mercator'. You can take your pick of these explanations; but if you happen to have read Shakespeare's *Twelfth Night*, or seen it performed, you will recollect that Maria describes Malvolio's behaviour to Sir Toby Belch in these words: 'He does smile his face into more lines than are in the new map with the augmentation of the Indies'. Shakespeare was nothing if not topical in his plays, and in all probability he was referring to the newly published Mercator's chart of the Indies; and some of the lines that he mentions would be the parallels of latitude and meridians of longitude on that chart.

For these had really quite an extraordinary appearance when compared with those on the earth. They were, in fact, very much distorted—but distorted with a purpose. And the purpose was that a rhumb line course from place *A* to place *B* could be drawn on the chart as a straight line with an ordinary ruler or straight edge. A shipmaster could thus rule a line from *A* to *B* and read off the rhumb line course. He was able to do this because on a Mercator's chart the meridians of longitude do not converge towards the Poles as they do on the earth. On the chart they are represented as equally spaced parallel lines at right angles to the parallels of latitude, which are themselves represented as straight lines. And therefore a straight line on the chart is a rhumb line by definition—because it crosses every meridian at the same angle. The great circle course from $A$ to $B$ on such a chart, however, is a curved line bent towards the nearer Pole.

Fig. 2 ($a$) is a sketch which shows the parallels and meridians as they appear on the earth—no attempt has been made at perspective. The important points to notice are: (i) that the meridians are equally spaced at the Equator and converge towards the Poles, and (ii) that the parallels of latitude are equally spaced North and South of the Equator.

Fig. 2 ($b$) is another sketch which shows how the same meridians and parallels of latitude appear on a Mercator's chart. Obviously, the essential differences are that (i) the meridians do *not* converge and (ii) that the parallels of latitude are *not* equally spaced, but the distance between them increases as the latitude increases.

In fact, on a Mercator's chart the lines on the earth's surface, like those on Malvolio's face, have been considerably distorted—but to some useful purpose. For the curved rhumb line $AmB$ on the earth has become the straight rhumb line $A_1m_1B_1$ on the chart, and can now be drawn with a ruler. This is such a great advantage to the navigator that it far outweighs some of the slight disadvantages of the Mercator's chart, which will be mentioned later.

The great circle course from $A$ to $B$ (the pecked line $AnB$ on the earth) becomes $A_1n_1B_1$ on the chart, curved towards the nearer Pole. Note that, although this is really the shortest route from $A$ to $B$, it doesn't seem to be so on the Mercator's chart, because the chart is distorted in comparison with the earth. But this really doesn't matter; for except in very long-distance navigation, a navigator prefers to follow the rhumb line, so that he can steer in a constant direction and draw his course on the chart as a straight line.

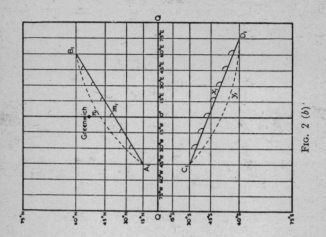

Fig. 2 (b)

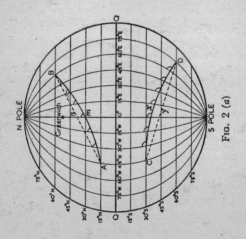

Fig. 2 (a)

$CxD$ and $CyD$ are the rhumb line and great circle courses, respectively, from $C$ to $D$ on the earth. $C_1x_1D_1$ and $C_1y_1D_1$ are the same courses as they appear on the Mercator's chart. The rhumb line course from $C$ to $D$ is about 120° or about 60° East of South. The rhumb line course from $A$ to $B$, on the other hand, is about 060°, or 60° East of North.

Having seen what a Mercator's chart looks like, we must now describe the principles upon which it is constructed. These principles are mathematical, so we must digress for a moment and discuss a little elementary

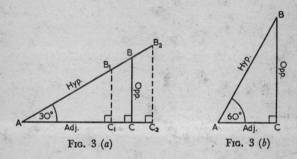

FIG. 3 (a)          FIG. 3 (b)

trigonometry. There is no need to be alarmed if you are not good at mathematics, because the trigonometry that we require is very simple indeed.

In Fig. 3 (a), $ABC$ is a triangle right-angled at $C$. Angle $A$ is 30°, and if we consider angle $A$ with relation to the other parts of the triangle, we say that $BC$ is the opposite side (opposite to the angle that we are considering) and $AC$ is the adjacent side (adjacent to the angle that we are considering). $AB$ is the hypotenuse no matter what angle we are considering.

Now, depending upon the value of angle $A$, the sides of the triangle bear certain relationships to each other. The side $BC$ bears a certain relationship to the side $AB$, and another relationship to the side $AC$. There are six such relationships, or 'ratios' as they are called. They are as follows:

$$\frac{BC}{AB} = \frac{\text{opp}}{\text{hyp}} = \text{sine } A \qquad \frac{AB}{BC} = \frac{\text{hyp}}{\text{opp}} = \text{cosecant } A$$

$$\frac{AC}{AB} = \frac{\text{adj}}{\text{hyp}} = \text{cosine } A \qquad \frac{AB}{AC} = \frac{\text{hyp}}{\text{adj}} = \text{secant } A$$

$$\frac{BC}{AC} = \frac{\text{opp}}{\text{adj}} = \text{tangent } A \qquad \frac{AC}{BC} = \frac{\text{adj}}{\text{opp}} = \text{cotangent } A$$

Note that the ratios on the right are the reverse or 'reciprocals' of those on the left.

You can find out the values of any of these ratios for any given angle by simple measurement. For instance, if you construct a triangle like the one in Fig. 3 (a), making $A$ exactly 30° and $BC$ exactly perpendicular to $AC$, you can make the triangle any size you like (such as $AB_1C_1$ or $AB_2C_2$), but you will always find that the length of side $BC$ divided by the length of side $AB = 0\cdot5$. Try it and see.

It is much easier, however, to look in the Table of Natural Sines at the end of this book, and take out the value of sine 30° from there.

If, perhaps, you have forgotten the trigonometry that you learnt at school, you should find, by measurement, the values of the other ratios of angle 30° and verify your results from the Tables.

The ratios, of course, are different for every different angle, and you should study the Tables in order to see how the ratios change as the angle changes. The important points to notice, at the moment, are as follows:

For angle 0°, the *cosine* is 1, and it *de*creases as the angle increases until, for an angle of 90°, it is NIL.

For angle 0°, the *secant* is 1, and it *in*creases as the angle increases until, for an angle of 90°, it is infinity.

As an example of this, in Fig. 3 (b), angle $A$ is 60°, and you will find by measurement or from the Tables that whereas cosine 30° = 0·866, cosine 60° = 0·5, and whereas secant 30° = 1·1547, secant 60° = 2.

Having drawn attention to these few important mathematical points, let us now return to our discussion of the Mercator's chart.

In Fig. 2 (a), the meridians of longitude on the earth are spaced 15° apart. Now, for most practical purposes, 15 degrees of longitude, measured along the Equator, is 60 × 15 = 900 nautical miles (1667·9 km).

But, as you can see on the diagram, the meridians converge towards the Poles, and in latitude 60° N or 60° S, if you could measure the distance between the meridians exactly, you would find that they were only 450 nautical miles (834 km) apart. If you have a globe or sphere to represent the earth, you can verify this for yourself.

But 450 is half 900 and 834 is half 1667·9—and the cosine of 60° is 0·5.

This simple example serves to illustrate the important principle that *the distance apart of meridians on the earth varies as the cosine of the latitude.*

This agrees, of course, with what we know about the cosine. It is maximum for an angle of 0° and nil for an angle of 90°. Similarly, therefore, the distance apart of meridians on the earth is maximum at the Equator (latitude 0°) and nil at the Poles (latitude 90°). In any intermediate latitude of $x°$ North or South we can find the distance apart of the meridians by the formula:

Distance apart of meridians in lat. $x°$ = distance apart at Equator multiplied by cosine $x°$.

Thus, if two meridians are 1° (60 n. miles or 111·12 km) apart at the Equator, then in lat. 45° N or S they will be 60 × cosine 45° = 60 × 0·707 = 42·42 n. miles apart, or 111·12 × cosine 45° = 111·12 × 0·707 = 78·56 km apart, measured along the parallel of 45° N or 45° S. In lat. 80° N or S they will be 60 × cosine 80° = 60 × 0·1736

= 10·416 n. miles or 111·12 × cosine 80° = 111·12 × 0·1736 = 19·29 km apart.

So much, then, for the state of affairs on the earth itself.

But let us now consider what happens when the meridians and parallels are drawn on a Mercator's chart, as in Fig. 2 (b).

As we have seen before, the meridians on the chart do not converge towards the poles as they do on the earth. In fact, in lat. 60° N or S the meridians on the chart are twice as far apart as they are on the earth. But the secant of 60° is 2, and the secant is the reciprocal ratio of the cosine. We may thus infer the following formula for the distance apart of meridians on a Mercator's chart in latitude $x°$ N or S:

Distance between meridians in lat. $x°$ on a Mercator's chart = Distance between meridians in lat. $x°$ on the earth multiplied by secant $x°$.

In other words, on a Mercator's chart the distance between places, measured in an East-West direction, is distorted. It is in fact expanded, and the rate of expansion varies as the secant of the latitude.

But if we wish to keep directions constant on a map, and if we wish to show the shapes of land formations correctly, we cannot expand the scale of the map, compared with that of the earth, in an East-West direction only. We must expand it in a North-South direction in the same proportion. This is clearly shown in Fig. 4.

In Fig. 4, $ABCD$ is the map of a rectangular piece of land which measures 200 miles by 100 miles, the scale being $\frac{1}{2}$ inch to 100 miles.

Thus, $DC = 1$ inch and $BC = \frac{1}{2}$ inch.

$BGFE$ is the map of an adjoining piece of land which is also rectangular in shape and also measures 200 miles by 100 miles; but here the scale is $\frac{3}{4}$ inch to 100 miles.

Thus, $BE = 1\frac{1}{2}$ inches and $BG = \frac{3}{4}$ inch.

Similarly, using metric units, if *ABCD* measures 200 km by 100 km and the scale is 1 cm to 100 km, then *DC* = 2 cm and *BC* = 1 cm. Suppose *BGEF* also measures 200 km by 100 km, but here the scale is 1·5 cm to 100 km. Then *BE* = 3 cm and *BG* = 1·5 cm.

Note that, using either system of measurement, the scale of the area *BGFE*, compared with that of *ABCD*, has been expanded 50 per cent. in both the North-South and East-West directions. As a result of this equal expansion of scale along both parallels and meridians, directions

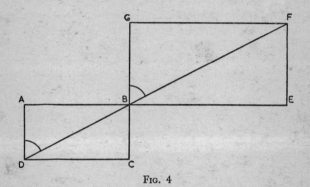

Fig. 4

and shapes on both maps remain the same. The direction *DBF* is constant (about 063½°) and the shape of the two areas is unchanged, because they are both rectangles. The only feature that gives a false impression is the size of *BGFE* compared with *ABCD*. The former looks much larger in area, but it nevertheless represents the same number of square miles or square kilometres as the latter.

The Mercator's chart, however, was invented for the use of navigators—and navigators don't worry themselves unduly about areas. It doesn't upset a navigator if Borneo appears to be the same size as Iceland on a Mercator's chart of the world. (It is, of course, much larger.) A navigator is principally interested, as we have seen, in having a chart on which a straight line represents a constant direction and on which the shapes (not relative sizes) of coastlines and islands are shown correctly.

Therefore, since the distance between meridians on a Mercator's chart, compared with the distance on the earth, is expanded in an East-West direction, the distance between the parallels in a North-South direction is expanded in exactly the same proportion. And that proportion, or ratio, is that of the secant of the latitude.

This explains why, on a Mercator's chart, as in Fig. 2 (b), the distance between parallels of latitude becomes greater and greater as one goes North and South from the Equator. At the Equator, the distance between parallels is the same as the distance between meridians. But as one approaches the Poles, on a Mercator's chart, the distance between meridians remains the same as it is at the Equator, but the distance between parallels becomes infinitely large—because the secant of 90° is infinity. This simply means that the polar regions cannot be shown on a Mercator's chart. If one wishes to navigate in polar regions, one must use some other kind of chart, as we shall see later.

Finally, then, we arrive at the following conclusions:

(i) The distance between parallels on a Mercator's chart in lat. $x°$ N or S equals the distance between parallels at the Equator multiplied by secant $x°$.

But the distance between parallels at the Equator on the chart, as on the earth, equals the distance between the meridians. The distance between meridians, however, on the chart does not change. Therefore:

(ii) The distance between parallels on a Mercator's chart in lat. $x°$ N or S equals the distance between meridians on the chart multiplied by secant $x°$.

In this last very important formula the distance between meridians on the chart, which is constant, depends on the *Natural Scale* of the chart.

As an example of what is meant by this expression, let us suppose that a length of 1 inch on a given chart represents a distance of 10 000 inches on the surface of the earth. Then the natural scale of the chart in question is $\frac{1}{10\,000}$. Similarly, if 1 cm on a given chart represents 10 000 cm on the surface of the earth, the natural scale of the chart is again $\frac{1}{10\,000}$.

In Fig. 2 (*b*), the distance on the earth between meridians 180° apart at the Equator is represented by a line 2 inches (5·08 cm) long. Therefore, the natural scale of the chart in the diagram is arrived at as follows:

$$\text{Natural scale} = \frac{\text{Chart length}}{\text{Earth distance}}$$

$$= \frac{2 \text{ inches}}{180° \text{ of longitude expressed in inches}}$$

$$= \frac{2}{180 \times 60 \times 6080 \times 12*}$$

$$= \frac{2}{787\,968\,000}$$

$$= \frac{1}{393\,984\,000} \text{ (approx.)}.$$

If the above calculation is done in metric units the working is as follows:

$$\text{Natural scale} = \frac{\text{Chart length}}{\text{Earth distance}}$$

* See footnote to page 26.

$$= \frac{5 \cdot 08}{180° \text{ of longitude expressed in cm}}$$

$$= \frac{5 \cdot 08}{180 \times 60 \times 185\ 320*}$$

$$= \frac{1}{393\ 987\ 000} \text{ (approx.)}.$$

A chart drawn to such a small scale as this is, of course, quite useless for navigation; but the method of finding its natural scale is quite correct, except for the very slight error that may be caused by the variation in the length of the nautical mile.

It is usual, in practice, for the natural scale of a chart to be stated for a given latitude: i.e. if the natural scale of a chart is stated to be $\frac{1}{1\ 000\ 000}$ at 50° N, it means that the distance between meridians on the chart is $\frac{1}{1\ 000\ 000}$ of the distance between the same meridians on the earth in latitude 50° N.

The reader is now in a position to construct his own Mercator's chart, on which he will be able to work the chartwork problems given in Chapter 3. For this purpose he will require a piece of stout drawing-paper, size 22 inches (56 cm) by 30 inches (76 cm) (drawing-paper is sold in this size). He will also require a pen and pencil, a long ruler, a pair of compasses and some Indian ink. The specifications for the chart are as follows:

'Construct a Mercator's chart to a natural scale of $\frac{1}{500\ 000}$ at lat. 60° N, to represent an area bounded by the parallels of 58° N and 61° N and by the meridians of

* Each degree of longitude contains 60 minutes. Each minute of longitude at the Equator is approximately 6080 feet, and each foot contains 12 inches. The length of the nautical mile is also 1·8532 km (see page 13), so there are 185 320 cm in a nautical mile.

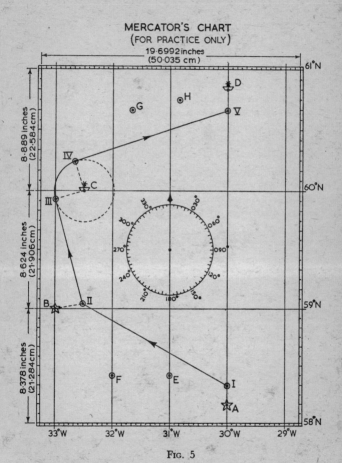

MERCATOR'S CHART
(FOR PRACTICE ONLY)

FIG. 5

28° 45′ W and 33° 15′ W. Draw in the parallels and meridians at degree intervals and subdivide the latitude and longitude scales on the borders of the chart into main divisions of 10 minutes and secondary divisions of 1 minute respectively. Insert a compass rose in the centre of the chart and graduate it from 0° to 360°.'

The appearance of the chart, when finished, is shown in Fig. 5, and some of the main features of construction are indicated. The points marked *ABCD*, etc., should be ignored at this stage, as they refer to work of a later chapter.

The first part of the job, of course, is to find the dimensions of the chart, i.e. how far apart we must space the meridians and the parallels of latitude.

The meridians are to be drawn 1° of longitude apart.

On the earth, they are spaced $60 \times 6080 \times 12$ inches apart along the Equator. Therefore, on the earth, along the parallel of 60° N, for which the natural scale is required, they are spaced $60 \times 6080 \times 12 \times \text{cosine } 60°$ inches apart.

Therefore, on the chart, they are spaced

$$\frac{60 \times 6080 \times 12 \times 0 \cdot 5}{500\ 000} \text{ inches apart}$$

$$= 4 \cdot 3776 \text{ inches apart.}$$

If the calculation is done in metric units the working is as follows:

On the earth the meridians of longitude in lat. 60° N are spaced $60 \times 185\ 320 \times \text{cosine } 60°$ cm apart. Therefore, on the chart they are spaced

$$\frac{60 \times 185\ 320 \times 0 \cdot 5}{500\ 000} \text{ cm apart}$$

$$= 11 \cdot 119 \text{ cm apart.}$$

Since $11 \cdot 119$ cm = $4 \cdot 3776$ inches, this is the same result as before.

The meridians of 28° 45' and 33° 15' are 4° 30' of longitude apart. Therefore the total width of the chart, in an East-West direction, is 4·3776 × 4·5 inches, and this equals 19·6992 inches. In metric units the figures are 11·119 × 4·5 cm = 50·035 cm.

Having ascertained this, lay your drawing-paper on the table, with its greater length up and down in front of you, like the page of this book, and draw a horizontal line across the paper about an inch above the lower edge. This line is to represent the parallel of 58° N. On this line mark off a distance of 19·6992 inches (50·035 cm) as accurately as you can, so as to leave an equal margin on either side.

The first meridian to draw in is that of 29° W. This is ¼° of longitude from the right-hand edge of the chart. Therefore it will be 4·3776 ÷ 4 = 1·0944 inches or 11·119 ÷ 4 = 2·78 cm from the right-hand edge. Similarly, the meridian of 33° W will be 1·0944 inches (2·78 cm) from the left-hand edge. The other three meridians will be spaced the full 4·3776 inches (11·119 cm) apart.

Now draw the meridians in pencil (they must be inked in later) and extend them right up the paper to the top margin. They must all be parallel to each other, and all exactly perpendicular to the parallel of 58° N. When you have drawn the meridians of 29° W, 30° W, 31° W, 32° W and 33° W all perfectly parallel to each other, and all exactly perpendicular to the parallel of 58° N, you may then draw in the East and West margins of the chart— the meridians of 28° 45' W and 33° 15' W.

Now we come to the next step, which is to draw in the parallels of latitude of 59° N, 60° N and 61° N. You will remember the formula:

Distance apart of parallels in lat. $x$° N or S equals distance apart of meridians multiplied by secant $x$°.

Therefore the distance in inches, in a North-South

direction, between the parallels of 58° N and 59° N on
the chart

$$= 4{\cdot}3776 \times \text{secant } 58° \ 30' \text{ inches}$$
$$= 4{\cdot}3776 \times 1{\cdot}9139 \text{ inches}$$
$$= 8{\cdot}378 \text{ inches} \qquad . \qquad . \qquad . \qquad . \qquad \text{(i)}$$

This distance in centimetres will be

$$11{\cdot}119 \times \text{secant } 58° \ 30'$$
$$= 11{\cdot}119 \times 1{\cdot}9139$$
$$= 21{\cdot}284 \text{ cm.}$$

Similarly, the distance between the parallels of 59° N
and 60° N on the chart

$$= 4{\cdot}3776 \times \text{secant } 59° \ 30' \text{ inches}$$
$$= 4{\cdot}3776 \times 1{\cdot}9703 \text{ inches}$$
$$= 8{\cdot}624 \text{ inches} \qquad . \qquad . \qquad . \qquad . \qquad \text{(ii)}$$

In centimetres this distance will be

$$11{\cdot}119 \times \text{secant } 59° \ 30'$$
$$= 11{\cdot}119 \times 1{\cdot}9703$$
$$= 21{\cdot}906 \text{ cm.}$$

And the distance between the parallels of 60° N and
61° N on the chart

$$= 4{\cdot}3776 \text{ secant } 60° \ 30' \text{ inches}$$
$$= 4{\cdot}3776 \times 2{\cdot}0308 \text{ inches}$$
$$= 8{\cdot}889 \text{ inches} \qquad . \qquad . \qquad . \qquad . \qquad \text{(iii)}$$

In centimetres this distance will be

$$11{\cdot}119 \times \text{secant } 60° \ 30'$$
$$= 11{\cdot}119 \times 2{\cdot}0308$$
$$= 22{\cdot}584 \text{ cm.}$$

Notice how the distance between the parallels gradually
increases as the secant of the latitude increases.

The sum of the distances (i), (ii) and (iii) gives us the dimensions of the chart in the North-South direction, and this equals a total of 25·89 inches (65·77 cm), which will fit nicely on to your drawing-paper, leaving a good margin at the top.

Now draw in the parallels of 59° N, 60° N and 61° N in their correct positions, making sure that they are exactly parallel to each other and exactly at right angles to the meridians. When you have done this, you can erase any parts of the meridians that extend above the parallel of 61° N.

Then divide *each separate* degree of latitude along the right- and left-hand margins into six equal parts, each of which will be 10 minutes of latitude. And also divide each degree of longitude, along the top and bottom margins, into six equal parts, each of which will be equal to 10 minutes of longitude. Then divide each of these smaller divisions, of both latitude and longitude, into ten equal parts, each of which will represent 1 minute of latitude and longitude respectively. In the book, the 10-minute divisions are only divided into two parts of 5 minutes each because of the smallness of the scale.

In the middle of the chart draw a compass rose and divide it into 360 degrees, with main divisions at 10-degree intervals and smaller divisions at 1-degree intervals. The compass rose in the book is only graduated at 5-degree intervals because of its very small size.

Finally, ink in the parallels, the meridians, the graduations and the compass rose, and rub out all your pencilled construction lines.

The chart is now ready for use when you come to work the chartwork problems in Chapter 3. Some of the lines belonging to the first of these problems are shown on the chart in Fig. 5. If you have done your construction properly, the chart you have made will be just as good for your purpose as one that you can buy, and you will have the satisfaction of knowing that you have made it yourself. It must be remembered, however, that the system of construction that has been used here assumes the earth to be a true sphere, and this is not strictly correct. For this reason, the resultant chart cannot be as accurate as one that has been constructed by a professional cartographer, who takes the oblate shape of the earth into account.

CHAPTER 2

# The Mariner's Compass

In the previous chapter some reference was made to direction on the earth's surface, and the reader will have drawn the compass rose on his chart similar to the one in Fig. 5, except that the larger rose that he has drawn will be graduated at intervals of 1°, from 000° to 360°.

This is the modern and, for many purposes, the most efficient method of indicating direction, and it is known as the 'Three Figure Notation' method. North is 000° (or 360°), East is 090°, South is 180° and West is 270°. Note that three figures are always used, e.g. 003° and 010° NOT just 3° and 10°. This is done to avoid confusion when giving helm orders and when signalling.

The older methods of expressing direction, however, are still used by some river and harbour pilots, and by navigators of small vessels. This is not entirely owing to nautical conservatism. A degree is a very small unit, and a compass divided into 32 'points' is more useful in pilotage waters, where large alterations of course have to be made, or to the man in charge of a lifeboat.

The 32 points, taken round the compass in a clockwise direction, are as follows:

N, N by E, NNE, NE by N, NE, NE by E, ENE, E by N, E, E by S, ESE, SE by E, SE, SE by S, SSE, S by E, S, S by W, SSW, SW by S, SW, SW by W, WSW, W by S, W, W by N, WNW, NW by W, NW, NW by N, NNW, N by W, N.

Reciting the above list of points is known as 'boxing the compass in points', and seamen have to be familiar with the half points and quarter points (such as E by N $\frac{1}{4}$ N) in addition to the above. If you say 'ENE $\frac{3}{4}$ E', however, you will be wrong, because the half and quarter points are always named by reference to Cardinal and Inter-cardinal points only.

If there are 32 points round the compass, it is not difficult to deduce that the spacing between any two adjacent points equals $11\frac{1}{4}°$. Now $11\frac{1}{4}° \times 2 = 22\frac{1}{2}°$ and $11\frac{1}{4}° \times 4 = 45°$. Thus, NNE in points equals $022\frac{1}{2}°$ in Three Figure Notation. Similarly, NE $= 045°$, E by N $= 078\frac{3}{4}°$, SE $= 135°$, SW by W $= 236\frac{1}{4}°$, and so on.

When degrees were first used to graduate ships' compasses, seamen were loth to give up the use of points entirely, so they devised a system wherein points and degrees are combined. This is known as the 'Quadrantal' system of notation, and it is still widely used because it is useful for the working of certain navigation problems.

In this system, the compass is divided into four quadrants by the cardinal points N, E, S and W. Directions are given as so many degrees to the East of North (up to 89°), to the East of South (up to 89°), to the West of South (up to 89°) and to the West of North (up to 89°).

Thus NE $= 045° =$ N 45° E in points, Three Figure Notation and Quadrantal Notation respectively. Similarly,

$$
\begin{aligned}
\text{ENE} &= 067\tfrac{1}{2}° = \text{N } 67\tfrac{1}{2}° \text{ E} \\
\text{SE} &= 135° \phantom{0} = \text{S } 45° \phantom{0} \text{ E} \\
\text{SSW} &= 202\tfrac{1}{2}° = \text{S } 22\tfrac{1}{2}° \text{ W} \\
\text{W by S} &= 258\tfrac{3}{4}° = \text{S } 78\tfrac{3}{4}° \text{ W} \\
\text{NW} &= 315° \phantom{0} = \text{N } 45° \phantom{0} \text{ W, and so on.}
\end{aligned}
$$

The modern navigator should be proficient in the use of all three systems. An exercise in conversion from one system to the other is set at the end of this chapter.

So far we have only been discussing direction in a general sense. In addition, however, to there being the above three different methods of expressing direction, there are also three different *kinds* of direction, which we will now investigate.

The compass rose in Fig. 5 gives True directions; i.e. directions measured relative to the True meridians, which all lie in a North-South direction and meet at the North and South Poles of the earth. Therefore, if one wishes to lay off a course of 045° True on the chart, one draws a line at an angle of 45° to any meridian in a north-easterly direction. One can also draw lines at 45° inclination to the meridians in south-easterly, south-westerly and north-westerly directions if one wishes to lay off courses of 135° T, 225° T and 315° T respectively.

If you were in a ship equipped with a gyroscopic compass, when you had 'laid off' the course of 045° T on the chart you could then tell the helmsman to steer 045°, and if there were no current, tide or wind your ship would proceed along the line that you had drawn on the chart.

But this would only happen if you steered by gyro compass, because this type of compass indicates directions relative to the True meridian. Most big ships are fitted with gyro compasses nowadays, but they are very complicated instruments, and they have been known to break down at the most inconvenient times.

For this reason, every British merchant ship is required by law to be equipped with a magnetic compass, whether she has a gyro compass or not. And most small vessels, including boats and yachts, are navigated by means of magnetic compasses, because these are relatively cheap and are entirely reliable when intelligently used.

The magnetic compass is not so *easy* to use as the gyro compass, however, because it does not show directions relative to the True meridian.

The first magnetic compass to be used at sea probably consisted of a long sliver of magnetite or lodestone (O.E. *lædan* = to lead), suspended by a thin cord tied round its middle. It was found that this piece of stone always aligned itself in approximately the same direction—North and South. It was also found that it did not always lie horizontal. If one sailed far enough North, the North end began to dip down; and if one sailed far enough South, then the South end began to dip down. Also, it was found that the North end of the piece of stone only pointed approximately North. One could observe, by comparison with the well-known Pole Star, that the North end of the 'needle' pointed to the East of North in some localities and to the West of North in others.

It was a long time before the reasons for this peculiar behaviour of the magnetic needle were fully appreciated. These reasons are simple enough to understand once they have been explained; but one thousand years ago there was no one to explain, and we owe a debt of gratitude to the many known and unknown men whose brilliant discoveries have contributed to our present understanding of magnetic phenomena.

The earth, we now know, behaves as if it were itself a huge magnet, with a 'Blue' pole in the Northern Hemisphere, and a 'Red' pole in the Southern Hemisphere. The North Magnetic Pole (blue) is not in the same position as the North Geographical Pole. It is approximately in lat. 71° N long. 97° W, i.e. near Baffin Land, in northern Canada. The South Magnetic Pole (red) is approximately in lat. 72° S long. 154° E—quite a long way from the South Geographical Pole.

In common with every other magnet, the earth magnet is surrounded by a 'magnetic field'. This is the space around the magnet which is occupied by its 'lines of force', and these flow out of the red pole and in at the blue pole. Any freely suspended magnetic needle, placed in the field of any magnet, will align itself with the lines of force of the field. It follows, therefore, that the early navigator's piece of lodestone was merely aligning itself with the lines of force of the earth's field. The direction of this field is horizontal at the Magnetic Equator, but as one travels northwards the lines of force begin to dip downwards, until, in Britain, they are inclined at an angle of about 60° to the horizontal. As one travels southwards from the Equator, the lines of force again tend towards the vertical, but the other end of the needle dips downwards.

At the North and South Magnetic Poles, the direction of the earth's field is entirely vertical, and, as we shall see, this makes the magnetic compass quite useless in those regions. In intermediate latitudes, however, between the Magnetic Equator and the Magnetic Poles, the earth's lines of force have both horizontal and vertical components.

That end of a freely suspended magnetic needle which dips downwards in the Northern Hemisphere is called the 'North' end of the needle. This is short for 'North-seeking' end. By a well-established convention this end of the needle is also called 'red', whilst the other end is called 'blue'. It is a useful point to remember that the earth is the only magnet which has a 'blue' North pole. Every other magnet or magnetic needle in existence has, by convention, a 'red' North pole, which, by the first law of magnetism, is attracted to the 'unlike' (blue) pole of the earth.

So far, we have been speaking of a 'freely suspended' magnetic needle. Such a needle today is made of hard steel and it is artificially magnetized by electricity; but if it is suspended like the old-time piece of lodestone, so that it can dip downwards in the Northern Hemisphere, it is called a 'Dip' needle. It is not a compass needle.

A compass needle, as we understand it today, is a suspended magnetic needle, which is constrained, by mechanical means, to always lie in the horizontal plane and is not permitted to dip downwards.

In the modern magnetic compass this is achieved by having more than one needle (there are usually four to eight) so arranged that their common centre of gravity is below the point of suspension of the compass card, the North and South points of which are aligned with the needles. It stands to reason that such an arrangement is necessary. A navigator wants to know his direction in the horizontal plane—not in the oblique plane of the earth's lines of force, which, except at the Magnetic Equator, are partly horizontal and partly vertical.

It follows, therefore, that a compass card, the North and South points of which are aligned with the North-seeking *horizontal* magnetic needles, will set its North and South points in line with the horizontal component of the earth's field.

At the Magnetic Equator, where the 'dip' is NIL, this horizontal component is maximum, and therefore the compass needle's directive force is maximum.

But, at the Magnetic Poles, the earth's field is vertical. There is no horizontal component of the lines of force to direct the horizontal compass needles, so their directive force is NIL and the compass is useless.

The above describes the basic construction of the magnetic compass and its inherent limitations. Let us now turn to another interesting point.

The lines of force surrounding the earth magnet, even when they are horizontal at the Equator, are not parallel to the geographical meridians. This also stands to reason, since the Magnetic Poles are in different positions from the Geographical Poles. But the lines of force do not flow in a constant direction from South Magnetic Pole to North Magnetic Pole. Their direction fluctuates considerably, and for this reason we cannot define the Magnetic meridian as 'the arc of a great circle joining the North and South Magnetic Poles', which, if we substitute 'Geographical Poles' for 'Magnetic Poles', is the definition of a Geographical meridian. We therefore define the Magnetic meridian as follows:

'The Magnetic meridian, at any place, is the direction that a compass needle will take up when under the influence of the earth's magnetic field only.'

If we take a magnetic compass on shore, and make sure that there is no iron or other magnetic material anywhere near it (nor any cables carrying electric current), then the compass needle will lie in the Magnetic meridian. The same will happen if we take a compass out to sea in an entirely wooden boat, or in any kind of vessel that has nothing magnetic in its structure or equipment.

The angle between the Magnetic meridian and the True meridian at any place is called the 'Magnetic Variation', or, briefly, the 'Variation'. It may be thought of as the angle, in degrees, by which the Magnetic meridian 'varies' from the True meridian. If the Magnetic meridian is to the left of the True meridian, then the Variation is West; if to the right, it is East.

If you consider the relative positions of the North Magnetic Pole and the North Geographical Pole, you will not find it difficult to understand that in some parts of the world, as in the British Isles, the Variation is West, whilst in other parts of the world it is East. That is to say, the value of the Variation differs from place to place, and there is also an annual or 'secular' change of a few minutes in any one place. In Britain, the westerly Variation is decreasing by about 10 minutes of arc annually. Thus, in six years, it changes about one degree. The reason for this phenomenon is that the North Magnetic Pole is moving slowly all the time; it makes a circle round the North Geographical Pole once in about one thousand years.

The value of the Variation in any given locality is given on the Admiralty chart of the area, either as a statement printed on the compass rose or by means of dotted lines called 'Isogonals', which are drawn on the chart so that they join all places that have the same Variation. The value of the secular change in the locality is also given.

Let us now derive a simple rule for converting True directions into Magnetic directions, and vice versa.

In Fig. 6 (*a*), *OA* is a direction (a course or bearing) which is 60° from the True meridian and 50° from the Magnetic meridian, the Variation being 10° East.

In Fig. 6 (*b*), *OA* is again 60° from the True meridian,

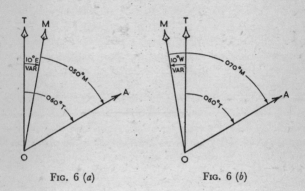

Fig. 6 (*a*)　　　　　　　Fig. 6 (*b*)

but it is 70° from the Magnetic meridian, because the Variation is 10° West.

We therefore derive our rule as follows:

'Variation West, Magnetic Best
Variation East, Magnetic Least.'

It is important to note that, when using this rule, the directions must always be expressed in Three Figure Notation, or the rule will not work properly in every case, i.e. for Fig. 6 (*b*), 060° T, Var. 10° W = 070° M, and for Fig. 6 (*a*), 050° M, Var. 10° E = 060° T.

So much, then, for Variation. But there is also another deflecting force that affects the compass needle.

Most ships today are built of steel, and even quite small boats have a certain amount of iron or steel in their structures. Iron and steel are magnetic materials and they cause a compass needle to *deviate* from the Magnetic meridian. Moreover, it must be remembered that a compass needle in a ship's binnacle always points approximately North and South, and when a ship changes her heading (or 'alters course' as seamen say) the iron or steel in the ship moves round the compass needle in such a way as to cause *a different Deviation on such heading*.

The iron of the ship is always magnetized, partly as a result of the hammering and vibration that the vessel receives when she is being built, and partly from other causes. The ship, in fact, is a big magnet, and, like any other magnet, it has a magnetic field. It is the lines of force of this field, which strike the needle at different angles for each course steered, that cause the compass needle to deviate from the Magnetic meridian, sometimes to the right (Easterly Deviation) and sometimes to the left (Westerly Deviation), but always changing its value with change of heading.

In the chart room of every ship will be found a Deviation card, which often takes the form of a graph, like the one in Fig. 7, and which gives the Deviation on every heading. The ship's compass is adjusted periodically by a compass adjustor, or by the ship's officers, so as to ensure that the deviations are kept small, but it is never possible to eliminate them entirely. The Deviation card shows the residual deviations, after these have been made as small as possible by the adjustor. These deviations have to be applied in order to convert a Magnetic course or bearing into a Compass course or bearing, or vice versa.

In Fig. 8 (*a*), *OA* is the direction of a Compass bearing that was observed when the ship was on a course of 135° by compass. For this heading the Deviation, from the Deviation card (Fig. 7), is 3° W. The bearing is 050°

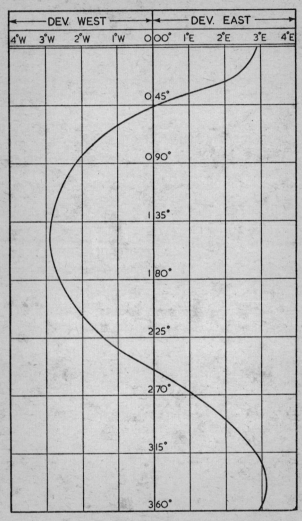

Fig. 7

Magnetic, but, since the compass needle is deviated 3° West of the Magnetic meridian, the bearing is 053° by compass.

In Fig. 8 (b), OA is the direction of a bearing that was observed when the ship was heading 330°. For this heading, the Deviation from the card is 3° E. Therefore, the Compass bearing of 067° becomes a Magnetic bearing of 070°.

It follows, therefore, that the method of applying Deviation is given by the following rule:

'Deviation West, Compass Best
Deviation East, Compass Least.'

Three Figure Notation must always be used.

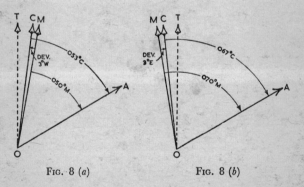

FIG. 8 (a)                    FIG. 8 (b)

So far we have seen how to convert a True direction into a Magnetic direction, or vice versa, and also how to convert a Magnetic direction into a Compass direction, or vice versa. In the first instance we applied Variation and in the second instance we applied Deviation, according to the above rules.

But by far the most common requirement in practice is the need to convert a True course or bearing into a Compass course or bearing, or vice versa.

For instance, a navigator lays off a course on the chart, and this course is True because it is drawn relative to the True meridian. He must convert this course to Compass before he can tell the helmsman what course to steer. Alternatively, he takes a bearing of a distant landmark by compass, and he must convert this bearing to True before he can plot it correctly on the chart.

In the first case he can, if he wishes, first apply Variation to the True course to obtain the Magnetic course, and then apply Deviation to obtain the Compass course. In the second case he can first apply Deviation to the Compass bearing to obtain the Magnetic bearing, and then apply Variation to obtain the True bearing for plotting on the chart. If he does the job in this manner, he must always do it in the correct order, i.e. True-Var.-Mag.-Dev.-Comp. and Comp.-Dev.-Mag.-Var.-True.

It is often far easier, however, to combine the Variation and Deviation together into one value, which is known as the 'Compass Error'.

Variation and Deviation are combined algebraically by using East and West instead of plus and minus. Thus Var. 10° E and Dev. 3° W gives an error of 7° E. Similarly, Var. 10° W and Dev. 3° E gives an error of 7° W.

Compass error may be defined as the amount that the compass needle is in error from the True meridian, and it is applied as follows:

From Fig. 9 (a) we see that, with an error of 7° E, 060° True = 053° Comp.; and in Fig. 9 (b), with an error of 7° W, 067° Comp. = 060° True. You should compare these results with those obtained by using the separate values for Variation and Deviation given in Figs. 6 and 8.

The appropriate rule, therefore, for applying compass error, again using Three Figure Notation, is:

'Error West, Compass Best
Error East, Compass Least.'

It is important to note that, in calculating the error, the Deviation used must be the Deviation for the direction of the ship's head. If it is a Compass bearing that is being corrected, however, the direction of the bearing does not affect the Deviation in any way. It is the heading of the ship at the time of taking the bearing that matters. The navigator has yet to be born with such a magnetic

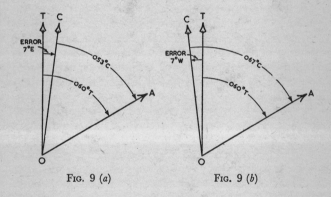

FIG. 9 (a)                    FIG. 9 (b)

personality that the act of placing his head over the compass to take a bearing will cause the compass needle to deviate. In this connection, it is the ship's head that is important, not the navigator's head!

In discussing Deviation we have said that its value is usually obtained from the Deviation card in the chart room. Strictly speaking, there should be two Deviation cards, one for converting Compass to Magnetic and another for converting Magnetic to Compass. But when the residual deviations are small, as they should be, one Deviation card, similar to the one in Fig. 7, is good enough for all practical purposes.

It should always be remembered, however, that the Deviation must be taken off the card for either the *Compass* heading or the *Magnetic* heading, and *never* for the True heading, as this would be quite wrong in principle and would cause serious inaccuracies, particularly if the Variation were large.

Finally, it should be noted that Deviation is often subject to quite unpredictable changes. Fortunately, these changes are usually small, but in any well-run ship the Deviation for the direction of the ship's head is checked at regular intervals by the officer of the watch, and is always checked as soon as possible after altering on to a new course. This practice is also followed in aircraft, in which magnetic compasses behave in very much the same way as they do in ships.

The detailed process of checking the Deviation will be described in later chapters, but the principle is quite simple, as it merely consists of comparing the Compass bearing of a distant object with a Magnetic bearing of the same object. The difference between the two bearings is the Deviation, which is named in accordance with the rule given above for naming Deviation.

Some practice in this will be given in the following Exercises.

## EXAMPLES FOR EXERCISES

### Exercise 1

Convert the following directions, given in Points, into (a) Three Figure Notation, (b) Quadrantal Notation:

   (1) N by E    (2) ENE   (3) SE by E    (4) SSW
   (5) NW by N

### Exercise 2

Convert the following directions, given in Three Figure Notation, into (a) Quadrantal Notation, (b) Points:

   (1) $067\frac{1}{2}°$ (2) $168\frac{3}{4}°$ (3) $202\frac{1}{2}°$ (4) $281\frac{1}{4}°$ (5) $337\frac{1}{2}°$

**Exercise 3**

Convert the following directions, given in Quadrantal Notation, into (*a*) Three Figure Notation, (*b*) Points:

(1) N $33\frac{3}{4}°$ E   (2) S $67\frac{1}{2}°$ E   (3) S $11\frac{1}{4}°$ W   (4) S $67\frac{1}{2}°$ W
(5) N $33\frac{3}{4}°$ W

**Exercise 4**

(*a*) Given Variation 10° W, convert the following Magnetic courses into True courses expressed in Three Figure Notation:

(1) NNE    (2) SE by S    (3) WSW    (4) N 60° W
(5) S 30° E

(*b*) Given Deviation for ship's head = 5° E, convert the following Compass bearings into Magnetic bearings expressed in Quadrantal Notation:

(1) 036°    (2) 124°    (3) SW    (4) N 20° W
(5) S 40° E

**Exercise 5**

(*a*) Given that the Variation is 1° E, use the Deviation given in Fig. 7 to determine the error of the compass on the following Compass headings:

(1) NNE    (2) 080°    (3) 175°    (4) WSW
(5) N 60° W

(*b*) Apply the errors just found to convert the above Compass headings to True headings, expressed in Quadrantal Notation.

## Exercise 6

Fill in the blanks in the following table, using Three Figure Notation:

|   | True Direction | Var. | Mag. Direction | Dev. | Comp. Error | Comp. Direction |
|---|---|---|---|---|---|---|
| 1 | 060° | 10 W | | 5° E | | |
| 2 | | | | 5° W | 15° W | N 20° W |
| 3 | | 10° E | 300° | | 10° W | |
| 4 | 240° | | 250° | | 20° E | |
| 5 | | 5° E | 310° | | | 305° |

# CHAPTER 3

# Chart Navigation

This chapter deals with the principal chartwork problems with which a navigator should be familiar.

In order to work these problems it is necessary to have a chart, so it is hoped that the reader will now have finished constructing the Mercator's chart described in Chapter 1. If the chart is not quite finished it should be completed now, because you cannot proceed further without it.

Before you start to use the chart, however, we must discuss the methods of measuring distances and speeds in navigation.

*Distances:* distances are measured in nautical miles, and, since one nautical mile equals one minute of latitude, the latitude scale of the Mercator's chart is used to measure distances. Because the latitude scale, on the chart, varies as one goes North or South from the Equator, you must always use that part of the chart scale of latitude which is abreast of the distance that is to be measured.

*Speeds:* 'one knot' means 'one nautical mile per hour', and 'ten knots' means 'ten nautical miles per hour'. Thus, a knot is a speed, and *not* a distance.

*The Log:* the log is an instrument used at sea to measure the distance a ship has run since the log was set. Nowadays it is a 'patent log', and it is something like a motor-car's speedometer, except that the hands can be easily moved for re-setting as required. They are usually re-set to zero each day at noon, so that by glancing at the face of the log the navigator can see how many nautical miles the ship has steamed through the water since noon. If he looks at the log at 6 p.m. and it reads 90 n. miles, then the ship has steamed at an average speed of 15 knots since noon. The patent log consists of a 'rotator' with fins on it, and this is towed astern of the ship by a special non-twisting 'log line'. As the log rotates, it actuates a clock-like instrument secured to the taffrail on the poop, and it is this clock that registers the distance run. There is usually an electrical connection to the bridge so that the log can be read in the chart room.

This log takes its name from the original 'Dutchman's log', which was literally a log. That is to say, it was a piece of wood, which was thrown overboard at the bow and allowed to float astern as the ship went ahead through the water. The time it took to travel from bow to stern gave the speed of the ship, depending on the ship's length. Thus, if the ship were 180 feet (54·86 metres) long, and the 'log' took 20 seconds to float from bow to stern, then the ship was making a speed of 5 knots through the water. This was calculated as follows:

$$\frac{180}{20} = 9 \text{ ft/s} = 9 \times 60 \times 60 = 32\ 400 \text{ ft/h.}$$

But there are 6080 feet in a nautical mile. Therefore, the speed of the ship through the water

$$= \frac{32\ 400}{6080} = 5\cdot33 \text{ knots.}$$

If this calculation is done in metric units, the working is as follows:

$$\frac{54\cdot86}{20} = 2\cdot743 \text{ m/s} = 2\cdot743 \times 60 \times 60 = 9\cdot875 \text{ km/h.}$$

$$\frac{9\cdot875}{1\cdot853} = 5\cdot33 \text{ knots, as before.}$$

This was rather a cumbersome method of determining the speed and it was wasteful of wooden logs. Also, without a good stop-watch—they had not then been invented—it was not very accurate.

So the next step was to secure the log to a log line, marked off by knots tied in the line and spaced at a certain distance apart. This line, with the log of wood attached, was allowed to run out over the stern, and when the operation was over it could be hauled back again.

The spacing of the knots that were tied in the line depended on the number of seconds taken for the sand of an hour-glass to run. The hour-glass most commonly used was one that took 28 seconds to run. If the ship were moving forward through the water at 1 nautical mile per hour, the line would be running out over the stern at a rate of 6080 feet (1853·2 metres) in 3600 seconds. The length of line that would run out in 28 seconds is given by the following formula, based on simple proportion:

$$\frac{x}{6080} = \frac{28}{3600} \therefore x = \frac{28 \times 6080}{3600} = 47 \cdot 3 \text{ ft.}$$

If this calculation is done in metric units, the working is as follows:

$$\frac{x}{1853 \cdot 2} = \frac{28}{3600} \therefore x = \frac{28 \times 1853 \cdot 2}{3600} = 14 \cdot 4 \text{ metres.}$$

(14·4 metres = 47·3 feet.)

The knots in the line were therefore spaced 47·3 feet or 14·4 metres apart. If five knots ran out in the 28 seconds measured by the hour-glass, then the ship was making a speed of 5 nautical miles per hour, i.e. '5 knots' through the water; if six knots ran out, she was making a speed of 6 knots, and so on.

The above explains the derivation of the terms 'log' and 'knot'; but it must be remembered that the modern 'patent' log measures distances run, and not speeds. In order to obtain the speed in knots, one must divide the time in hours that has elapsed since the log was set into the distance in nautical miles that the instrument shows on its face.

It should be noted, however, that in aircraft the speed at which the aeroplane is flying through the air is measured by the air-speed indicator. This depends for its action on the air pressure built up on a diaphragm in the instrument as a result of the aircraft's forward motion. The air navigator, therefore, is given the *speed* by his instrument; in order to find the distance he has flown from his departure point, he must multiply the speed by the time in hours that has elapsed since departure.

You are now in a position to proceed with your chart-work, as follows:

First of all you should plot on your chart the following imaginary objects in their respective positions:

Lighthouse *A* in lat. 58° 10′ N long. 30° 00′ W
Lighthouse *B* in lat. 59° 00′ N long. 33° 00′ W
Lightvessel *C* in lat. 60° 00′ N long. 32° 30′ W
Lightvessel *D* in lat. 60° 50′ N long. 30° 00′ W

These positions must be plotted very carefully and accurately. The safest method is to use a long straight-edge from margin to margin of the chart to mark in, first, the latitude of the given point, keeping the straight-edge horizontal, and then the longitude, keeping the straight-edge vertical. The straight-edge must, in each case, pass through the appropriate latitude or longitude gradua-tions on both margins.

The points *A*, *B*, *C* and *D* are shown on the copy of the chart in Fig. 5. Note that, whereas the position of a light-house is indicated on the chart by the centre of the light, that of a lightvessel is indicated by a small circle on the waterline.

## Plotting the Course

One of the simplest problems in chartwork is to plot the course from one place to another round a coastline, and an example of this procedure is now given relative to the above imaginary coastal objects.

The requirements for the particular voyage are as follows:

'From a position with Lighthouse $A$, bearing 180° T dist. 10 n. miles, find the Compass course to steer and the distance in n. miles to a position with Lighthouse $B$, bearing 260° T dist. 15 n. miles. Thence find the two Compass courses to steer to reach a position 10 n. miles 180° T from Lightvessel $D$, passing Lightvessel $C$ on the starboard hand and maintaining a distance of 15 n. miles from it whilst rounding. Give the distance on each course, and the distance rounding $C$. If the ship steams at 12 knots and there is no wind or current, give also the total steaming time. Use Variation 30° W throughout, and the Deviations taken from the card in Fig. 7.'

In order to carry out these requirements, proceed in the following manner and refer to Fig. 5, on which this first chartwork problem is plotted:

(1) First plot position I, the departure point. Note that this is 10 n. miles due North of Lighthouse $A$, because $A$ bears 180° *from* the ship.

(2) Plot position II, the first turning point, with Lighthouse $B$, bearing 260° T dist. 15 n. miles. Note that position II is 15 n. miles in a direction 080° T *from B*. To lay off this bearing, draw a line through the compass rose in a direction 080°-260°, and then draw a line through $B$ parallel to this direction. Use parallel rules if you have them: otherwise, use your set-square and ruler to draw parallel lines. Alternatively, you can draw a meridian through $B$ and use an ordinary protractor to lay off the direction 080° that is required.

(3) Join position I to position II with a straight line and measure its direction, either by reference to a parallel line drawn through the compass rose or by means of a protractor placed against any one of the

meridians that the line crosses. It will be found that the direction from I to II is 298° T in Three Figure Notation. This is the True course required.

Apply 30° W Variation, and 298° T = 328° M.
Enter Deviation card against 328° and find Dev. = 3°E.
Apply this deviation, and 328° M = 325° Comp.
Check your figures by using the Compass error.
i.e. Var. 30° W and Dev. 3° E = error 27° W
     298° T, error 27° W = 325° Comp.

Therefore 325° is the first Compass course required.

Now measure the distance from I to II using, of course, the minutes of the latitude scale, because each minute of latitude equals one nautical mile.

But be careful to use that part of the latitude scale that is abreast of the course line, i.e. *abreast of the distance that you wish to measure.* The best practical way to measure this distance, therefore, is to take, say, 50 n. miles in the dividers (between 58° 10′ N and 59° 00′ N), place one leg on position I and mark how far the other leg reaches along the course line. Then measure the remaining distance to position II, using the same part of the latitude scale, and you will find that it equals 40 n. miles. Hence the total distance from position I to position II is 90 n. miles.

*Caution:* never use the longitude scale to measure distances, because one minute of longitude is *not* a nautical mile, except at the Equator.

(4) Now draw a circle of 15 n. miles radius, round Lightvessel *C*, and also plot the final position V, 10 n. miles due South of Lightvessel *D*. From position II draw a line tangent to the circle round *C* (with *C* to starboard) and mark the tangential point. This is position III. Then draw a line *back* from position V also tangent to the circle round *C* and mark this tangential point, which is position IV. The ship is to

proceed from II to III, round $C$, along the arc of the circle, to IV, and thence to V.

(5) Having marked the turning-points and drawn in the course lines, now determine the following:

(a) The course and distance from II to III.

Course = $345\frac{1}{2}°$ T, Var. 30° W = $015\frac{1}{2}°$ M, Dev. $2\frac{1}{2}°$ E = 013° Comp.

Distance 55 n. miles (measured on latitude scale abreast of course line).

(b) The course and distance from IV to V.

Course = 072° T, Var. 30° W = 102° M, Dev. $2\frac{1}{2}°$ W = $104\frac{1}{2}°$ Comp.

Distance = 83 n. miles (measured as above).

(c) Distance rounding $C$.

To find this, the most accurate method is to measure the angle at $C$ between the bearings of the two tangential points. This angle is 87°.

The whole circumference of the circle round $C$

$$= 2 \times \frac{22}{7} \times 15 \text{ n. miles.}$$

∴ Part of circumference between the tangential points

$$= 2 \times \frac{22}{7} \times 15 \times \frac{87}{360} = 22 \cdot 8 \text{ n. miles.}$$

Finally, determine the total steaming time.

Total distance = $90 + 55 + 83 + 22 \cdot 8 = 250 \cdot 8$ n. miles.

Speed 12 knots ∴ Steaming time
$$= \frac{250 \cdot 8}{12} \text{ h}$$
$$= 20 \cdot 9 \text{ h}$$
$$= \underline{20 \text{ h } 54 \text{ min.}}$$

The courses have now been plotted, and the measurements on your own chart should agree with those given here within a reasonable degree of accuracy. You should ink in positions $A, B, C$ and $D$ and leave positions I, II, III, IV and V on the chart in pencil, as they will be required later.

## Finding the Current and the Course and Distance Made Good

Up to the present we have only discussed the simple case of plotting courses when there is no wind or current. If there is a current, it means that the water through which the ship is steaming is being moved bodily in a given direction. This, of course, complicates matters, and we must see what happens in these circumstances.

Let us suppose that our ship sets course from position I at 1000 hours, intending to reach position II. The True course is 298°, and the ship is steaming through the water at 12 knots.

Plot on your chart Landmark $E$ in 58° 25′ N 31° 00′ W, and Landmark $F$ in 58° 25′ N 32° 00′ W. Ink these points in, as they will be used again later. Refer now to Fig. 10, which represents that part of your chart that we are now using, but to a much smaller scale.

At 1400 hours $E$ bears 148° Comp. and $F$ bears 250° Comp. Plot these bearings and find the ship's position at 1400 hours. To do this, proceed as follows:

The bearings are taken by compass, and they must therefore be converted to True before they can be plotted on the chart. Remember that the Deviation to apply is that which is appropriate to the direction of the ship's head by compass, which we know to be 325° Comp.

The Deviation on this course is 3° E, Variation is 30° W and therefore the error is 27° W.

Apply this to each bearing, and we have:

$E$ bears 148° Comp., error 27° W = 121° T.
$F$ bears 250° Comp., error 27° W = 223° T.

Now draw in these lines of bearing on the chart and it

will be seen that they intersect at *H*, which is the position of the ship 'by observation' at 1400 hours. We find this position to be 58° 37′ N 31° 39′ W.

But the ship has been steering 298° T for 4 hours at 12 knots, and therefore she *should* be in position *G*, 48 n. miles along the course line from position I towards position II. Position *G* is called the 'Dead Reckoning' position at 1400 hours, and is indicated on the chart by a small triangle to distinguish it from the position by observation, or 'Fix', at *H*.

But why is the ship not at *G*? The answer, of course, is because of the current, which has set the ship from *G* to *H* in 4 hours. The direction *from G to H* (239° T) is called the 'Set' of the current, and the distance from *G* to *H* (11 n. miles) is called the 'Drift' of the current. Note the three arrows used to indicate a current.

Since the drift has acted over a period of 4 hours, it follows that the 'Rate' of the current is $\frac{11}{4} = 2\frac{3}{4}$ knots.

Also note the important point that the current always sets *from* the Dead Reckoning position *to* the Observed position.

The ship, then, instead of proceeding in a direction 298° T, has actually proceeded in quite a different direction, owing to the effect of the current. This actual direction is called the 'course made good over the ground', or, more briefly, the 'course made good'. This is the direction from position I to *H* in Fig. 10, and you should now draw this line on your chart. The distance from position I to *H* is called the 'distance made good over the ground', or, briefly, the 'distance made good'. If you divide this distance by the time taken in hours, you obtain the 'speed made good over the ground', known briefly as the 'ground speed'. Note the two arrows that are used on the chart to indicate a course made good, so that it cannot be confused with a course steered, which is indicated by one arrow.

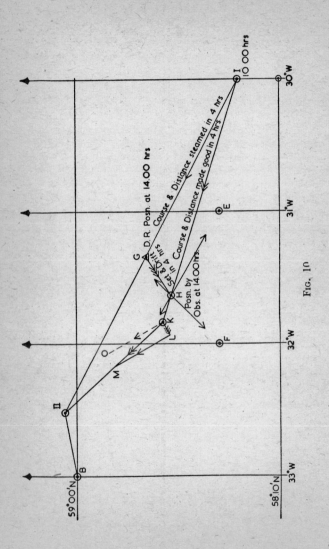

Fig. 10

If you have plotted everything carefully, you should obtain the following results:

$$\text{Course made good} = 288° \text{ T}$$
$$\text{Distance made good} = 54 \text{ n. miles}$$
$$\text{Ground speed} = \frac{54}{4} = 13\tfrac{1}{2} \text{ knots.}$$

## Setting Course to Counteract Current and finding the E.T.A.

After finding the position at 1400 hours in the last example, it should be obvious to the navigator that he is badly 'off track', owing to the effect of the current. If he doesn't do something about it, he will not reach position II, as he intends.

He therefore decides to plot his expected position at 1430 hours, making allowance for the current, and when he reaches the 1430 position to alter course for position II in such a manner as to counteract the effect of the current. This is done as follows:

First produce the course made good (from position I to $H$) for a distance equal to that covered in half an hour at the ship's ground speed, i.e. for 6·75 n. miles. This is the line $HK$ in Fig. 10. $K$ is the position that the ship will be in at 1430 hours.

Now join $K$ to position II with the line $K$ II. This is the course and distance that is required to be made good over the ground from $K$ to position II, and it is often called briefly the 'required track'.

Now choose a suitable 'Vector' scale. A vector is a line which represents a velocity. It therefore represents two things: (i) a direction and (ii) a speed. The vector scale has to be chosen so that it will fit easily on to the chart. The scale used in Fig. 10 is about $\frac{1}{20}$ inch to 1 knot. For your chart, which is about six times larger than Fig. 10, use a scale that is about six times larger, e.g. a scale of $\frac{1}{4}$

inch to 1 knot. If metric measurements are preferred, a scale of 1 cm to 1 knot would be suitable.

Then proceed as follows: From $K$, draw the vector $KL$ to represent the set and rate of the current, i.e. draw $KL$ in a direction 239°, and make it $\frac{11}{16}$ inches long. $\frac{11}{16}$ inches represents the current's rate of speed or $2\frac{3}{4}$ knots to the chosen scale. If the chosen scale is 1 cm to 1 knot, then $KL$ will be 2·75 cm long. Note that the current must be drawn *downstream*, i.e. in the direction in which the water is moving.

Now take a length of 3 inches in the dividers. This will be 12 cm if the scale used is 1 cm = 1 knot. This represents the ship's steaming speed of 12 knots to the chosen vector scale. With centre $L$, and this vector in the dividers, cut the required track in $M$. Join $LM$.

The 'triangle of velocities' $KLM$ is now complete, and from it we obtain the following information:

The direction $LM$ gives the direction of the True course to steer to counteract the current. You will find that it is 330° T. This does not mean that the ship steams along the line $LM$. As we know, she starts from $K$, and she steers from there in the direction 330° T, which is shown as the dotted line $KO$ in Fig. 10. But she is, of course, being affected by the current all the time, and she will actually proceed 'over the ground' along the required track from $K$ towards position II. This completes the operation of 'setting course to counteract current'. You will realize that we should get the same result whatever vector scale we might decide to use. If we had chosen $\frac{1}{2}$ inch to 1 knot (or 2 cm to 1 knot instead of 1 cm to 1 knot), it would simply mean that the triangle of velocities would be twice as large, but the *direction* of $LM$ would be just the same. Always use as large a vector scale as possible because, by making the vector triangle large, you obtain more accurate results.

But we do not only want to know in what direction to

steer in order to reach position II. We also want to know the 'Expected Time of Arrival', or E.T.A.

In order to find this, first measure the distance in nautical miles from $K$ to position II, using, of course, the distance scale of the chart (1 minute of lat. to 1 n. mile). This distance is found to be $31\frac{1}{2}$ n. miles.

Now, return to the triangle of velocities (the 'vector triangle') and measure the side $KM$ to the vector scale. It will be found to be $3\frac{1}{8}$ inches, and this equals $12\frac{1}{2}$ knots. If a scale of 1 cm to 1 knot has been used, then $KM$ will be $12\frac{1}{2}$ cm, which equals $12\frac{1}{2}$ knots. This means that the vessel's speed over the ground, along the required track from $K$ to position II, will be $12\frac{1}{2}$ knots. The time taken will therefore be $\dfrac{31\cdot5}{12\cdot5} = 2\cdot6$ h, or 2 h 36 min.

Therefore the E.T.A. at position II is $1430 + 2$ h 36 min, and this is 1706 hours.

All that now remains to be done is to alter course at 1430 hours. The required True course to counteract current is 330° T, Variation 30° W, and therefore the Magnetic course is 360° M. The Deviation for this course (from Fig. 7) is 3° E. Therefore the Compass course to steer at 1430 hours is 357° Comp. If, at exactly 1430 hours, the helmsman alters course accordingly, the ship should be in position II at 1706 hours.

## Allowing for Current to find an Estimated Position

We have seen how to find the current and how to counteract it. It frequently happens, however, that the set and rate of the current in a particular locality is known from previous experience, or can be ascertained by consulting a current chart, or a Table of Tidal Streams, which all ships carry.

If we have this advance information, we can use it to find an estimated position at any time during the passage.

For instance, if, in Fig. 10, we start from position I at 1000 hours steering 298° T at 12 knots, and if we know that the current in the locality sets 239° T at $2\frac{3}{4}$ knots, we can find the ship's estimated position at any time—say at 1400 hours.

All we do in these circumstances is to lay off the True course steered and plot on it the D.R. position at 1400 hours. From the D.R. position, lay off the set and drift of the current in 4 hours, i.e. 239° T for 11 n. miles. This will give position $H$, which is, in this case, the Estimated position of the ship at 1400 hours. The fact that it agrees with the Observed position, obtained by the cross bearings of E and $F$, merely indicates that the estimated current used was the correct one.

## Effect of Wind; Leeway

Wind power, as we know, drives sailing ships and yachts. But wind also affects the navigation of any type of craft. In the navigation of aircraft, one has to remember that the direction of the wind is given as the direction *from* which it blows. If we are told, therefore, that the wind velocity is North at 30 knots, we must realize that the air in which the aircraft is flying is moving South at 30 knots. We can then treat the wind velocity in air navigation exactly as we treat the set and rate of the current in sea navigation.

But wind also affects the navigation of powered surface vessels, such as steam or motor ships. If the wind is dead ahead, it reduces a vessel's speed through the water. If it is dead astern, it increases the speed through the water. But if it is on either side, i.e. 'on the bow', 'on the beam' or 'on the quarter', then it causes Leeway.

Leeway is the angle between a vessel's True heading and the direction of her bodily movement through the water.

Fig. 11 shows a ship heading East True with a strong

wind on the port beam. As you would expect, although she is *heading* East all the time, she is moving bodily in the direction *AB*. If the direction *AB* is 100° T and her heading is 090° T, then we say that the ship is making 10° of leeway to starboard.

Leeway must be allowed for in Dead Reckoning navigation, but its magnitude can only be estimated from experience. An experienced master of a fast liner will look astern at the wake of the ship as she steams along in a fresh beam wind, and will ask the officer of the watch, 'How much leeway are you allowing?' If he does not agree with the officer's estimate, he may order the course to be altered slightly.

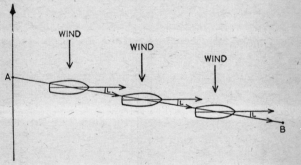

Fig. 11

Once the leeway has been estimated, it may be used in either of two ways:

(i) It may be 'counteracted'.

If, in Fig. 11, one wishes the vessel to move bodily through the water in a direct 100° T, then the course to steer, so as to counteract leeway, must be 090° T.

(ii) It may be 'allowed for'.

If a vessel is actually steering 090° T, as in Fig. 11, and the navigator wishes to lay off on his chart the direction in which the vessel is moving bodily through the water, then he 'allows' the leeway (in this case 10°), and he lays off the 'True course with leeway allowed' of 100° T.

It must be noted, however, that leeway, whether it is being counteracted or allowed for, must always be applied to the *True* course. Never apply it to a Compass course or to a Magnetic course, since leeway concerns True directions only.

It should also be noted that leeway does not affect the recording of a vessel's speed through the water. The rotator of the patent log, which is towed astern, will lie in the direction of the vessel's bodily movement through the water—in the direction *AB* in Fig. 11—and it will record the distance that the vessel travels in that direction.

In chartwork problems, where both leeway and current are involved, you should adopt the following procedure, strictly in the order given:

(i) When setting course to counteract current, apply current first, in the vector triangle, to find the True course to steer. Then counteract the leeway. Then apply the compass error.

(ii) When finding an estimated position, first lay off the True course with leeway allowed, and on it plot the dead reckoning position. Then apply the current.

Finally, if you are told that a lighthouse or other landmark is 'abeam' at a certain time, remember that 'abeam' means at 90° to the direction of the ship's head. It does *not* mean at 90° to the course made good over the ground, or at 90° to the True course with leeway allowed. The same applies to bearings at other angles on the bow or quarter. Thus, in Fig. 11, if you are told that a lighthouse is observed 30° on the port bow, then you will know that the True bearing of the lighthouse is 060° T, *not* 070° T, because all bearings given as angles on the bow, beam or quarter are always measured relative to the ship's head.

Some practice in the application of the above principles will be given in the examples for exercise at the end of this chapter.

## The 'Running Fix'

In the example of finding the current that we have just described, the ship's position by observation was obtained by the method of simultaneous cross-bearings.

When a ship is steaming along a coastline, however, it frequently happens that only one shore object is visible at a time. When this happens, only one bearing can be obtained at any given instant, and this only gives a single line of position (or 'position line', as it is usually called), somewhere on which the ship is situated.

If, however, another bearing of the same object, or of a different object, can be obtained after an interval of time, and if the ship's course and speed over the ground in the interval is known, then the position of the ship at the time of the second bearing can be plotted. The only essential condition is that there must be a reasonable 'angle of cut', of 30° or more, between the directions of the first and second bearings.

As an example of this method, let us suppose that our ship is proceeding from position IV to position V, and is steering the course that we have already plotted for this leg of the passage, i.e. she is steering $104\frac{1}{2}$° Comp. = 072° T at 12 knots. From the current chart we ascertain that the current on this part of the coast sets in a direction 210° T at 2 knots. At 0130 hours a lighthouse $G$, in position 60° 40′ N 31° 40′ W, bears 075° by compass, and the log reads 15. The lighthouse is then obscured by haze, but at 0310 hours the haze lifts, and the lighthouse is observed again bearing 015° by compass. The log now reads 35. From this information, find the ship's position at 0310 hours and also estimate her position at 0130 hours, when the first bearing was taken. Use the Deviation card of Fig. 7.

The method is illustrated in Fig. 12, which is a reproduction of that part of your chart which lies between positions IV and V, to a scale $\frac{1}{10}$ inch (0·254 cm) to 1 n. mile.

We must first correct the Compass bearings, i.e. they must be changed into True bearings, before we can plot them on the chart. The Deviation for the Compass course

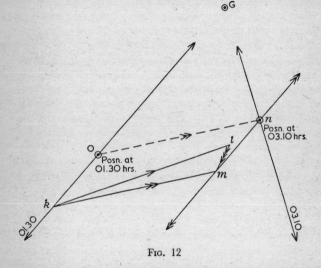

FIG. 12

of $104\frac{1}{2}°$ is $2\frac{1}{2}°$ W, and the Variation is 30° W. Therefore the compass error is $32\frac{1}{2}°$ W.

0130 bearing = 075° Comp., error $32\frac{1}{2}°$ W = $042\frac{1}{2}°$ T.
0310 bearing = 015° Comp., error $32\frac{1}{2}°$ W = $342\frac{1}{2}°$ T.

Now plot these two lines of bearing, as shown in Fig. 12, labelling them 0130 and 0310 respectively. Note the single arrow at each end of the line of bearing, which is the symbol used to indicate an observed position line.

At 0130 hours the ship is *somewhere* on the 0130 position line, and at 0310 hours she is *somewhere* on the 0310 position line. In order to find out exactly *where* she is on these position lines, we proceed as follows:

Take *any* point $k$ on the 0130 position line, and from it lay off the True course and distance steamed through the water from 0130 to 0310, i.e. 072° T, 20 n. miles. This line reaches to point $l$. From $l$ lay off the set and drift of the current during the same interval of time, i.e. 210° T, 3·3 n. miles (1 h 40 min at 2 knots). This reaches point $m$. Now, through $m$ draw a line parallel to the 0130 position line and mark it with two arrows at each end to indicate that it is a transferred position line. At 0310 the ship is somewhere on the other position line. Therefore, she can only be in position $n$, where the two lines intersect.

You should verify that you will get the same result whatever point you choose on the 0130 position line from which to start your construction, i.e. $k$ can be anywhere on the line. Try it and see, because there is nothing like proving things for yourself.

You should now take off, from your chart, the position of $n$ in latitude and longitude, and you will find that it is in 60° 29' N 31° 32½° W.

If you now go back to your construction and join $k$ to $m$, you will realize that the line $km$ is in the direction of the course made good, since it is the resultant of the course and distance steamed and the current. If you now draw a line, parallel to $km$, backward from $n$, it will meet the 0130 position line in $o$. This is where the ship actually was at 0130 hours in lat. 60° 26' N long. 32° 07' W. And the line from $o$ to $n$ is the actual course and distance made good between 0130 and 0310 hours. Note the single arrow to indicate the True course steered, and a double arrow to indicate a course made good over the ground.

The positions $n$ and $o$ may also be given in another form, as bearings and distances from Lighthouse $G$. Thus, we may say that $n$ is '162½° $G$ dist. 12 n. miles'. This is nautical shorthand for '$n$ is in a position which bears 162½° T from $G$ at a distance of 12 n miles'. Note that

$162\frac{1}{2}°$ T is the reverse of the bearing of $G$ from the ship. Similarly, we may say that $o$ is '$222\frac{1}{2}°$ $G$ dist. 20 n. miles'.

In the above problem you should appreciate the point that there is no need at all for the two bearings to be taken of the *same* object. The second bearing could just as well be taken of some other object, which happened to bear $342\frac{1}{2}°$ T at 0310 hours. The simple principle of the construction is that one position line is transferred up to the time of the other; and it doesn't matter how the position lines are obtained so long as they are accurate and cut at a reasonable angle.

Finally, you should note that, if there is no current, the construction is simplified. The transferred position line is then drawn straight through point $l$ in Fig. 12, since, with no current, the True course steered and the course made good are the same.

## 'Doubling the Angle on the Bow', and the 'Four Point Bearing'

When there is no current, there is a simple practical method of finding a vessel's distance off a single landmark, which is called 'doubling the angle on the bow'. This is illustrated in Fig. 13.

A ship is steaming along a coastline, steering 080° T at 12 knots. At 1000 hours Lighthouse $L$ is observed bearing 050° T, which means that it is 30° on the port bow. The ship is then somewhere on the position line $PL$. At 1030 hours $L$ is observed bearing 020° T, which means that it is now 60° on the port bow and the ship is somewhere on the position line $DL$. If, in between the two position lines, we now fit in the line $AB$, which represents the True course and distance made good between the two bearings (080° T, 6 n. miles), then $B$ is the position of the ship at 1030 hours. This is just a quick method of doing the running-fix problem, when there is no current.

But consider the triangle *ABL*. The exterior angle $L\hat{B}X = 60°$, and one of the opposite interior angles, $L\hat{A}B = 30°$. Therefore, the other opposite interior angle $A\hat{L}B$ must also equal 30°. Therefore, *ABL* is an isosceles triangle and, if this is so, *BL* must be equal to *AB*. In words, therefore, we can say: 'When, if there is no current or tidal stream, the angle on the bow is doubled, the distance off the observed object at the time of the second bearing is equal to the distance run between the two bearings.'

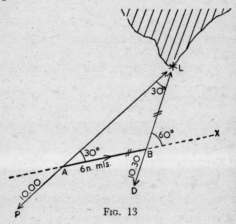

Fig. 13

Thus, in the above example, we know that when the lighthouse bears 60° on the bow, the ship is at *B*, 6 n. miles off the lighthouse.

This principle, of course, applies to any angle on the bow that is doubled. In practice, however, seamen usually prefer to know how far they are off a landmark when it is abeam, i.e. when it is 90° on the bow. This preference has given rise to the practice of observing what is known as a 'four point bearing'.

This means that the officer of the watch stands beside the standard compass and watches a certain shore light until it bears four points, or 45°, on the bow. He then goes quickly down to the chart room and reads the log. Let us suppose that it reads 80 n. miles. He makes an entry in the log book as follows: '2210 hours. Light $L$ bears 4 points on the port bow. Log. 80 n. miles', and he then resumes his watch on the bridge, but keeps noticing the position of the light. As it approaches the beam, he again goes to the standard compass and notes when the light is exactly abeam, i.e. when it is 90°, or 8 points, on the bow. He also takes the log reading again, and finds that it now reads, say, 92 n. miles. He then makes another entry in the log book '2310 hours. Light $L$ abeam to port, distance 12 n. miles. Log 92 n. miles.'

Finding the distance off a light by the above method is obviously a very simple procedure, provided, of course, that the light is not obscured by mist or rain when it is on either the four point or eight point bearing. If this should happen, the light is observed whenever it is visible, and an ordinary 'running fix' is plotted on the chart.

## Fix by Horizontal Angles

In a later chapter in this book we shall discuss the marine sextant. This instrument is principally used for measuring angles in the vertical plane, but it may also be used to measure angles in the horizontal plane between shore objects, and when used in this manner it provides a very accurate means of determining the ship's position.

Three landmarks must be visible to use this method, which is illustrated in Fig. 14. The figure represents a portion of your chart between positions IV and V, but farther to the eastward than the part of the chart represented in Fig. 12. The scale of Fig. 14 is $\frac{1}{20}$ inch (0·127 cm) to 1 n. mile.

After finding the ship's position at 0310, it was decided that the estimated current was incorrect, so the course was altered to 109° Comp. Some time later it was decided to check the ship's position to ascertain if she was making good the required track towards position V.

To find the position, it is decided to use landmarks *G* and *D*, which are already plotted on your chart, and an additional landmark *H*, which is in 60° 45′ N 30° 50′ W. In order to check that you have the three landmarks correctly plotted, you should verify that *H* is 080° *G* dist. 25 n. miles, and that *D* is 079° *H* dist. 25¼ n. miles.

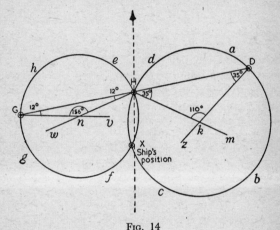

Fig. 14

When you are ready to find the ship's position, take the sextant and with it measure the horizontal angle between *D* and *H*. This is found to be 55°. Then measure the horizontal angle between *H* and *G*, and this is found to be 78°. The two angles should be taken simultaneously, but if one is taken immediately after the other no harm will result, unless the ship is moving very fast or is very close to the observed landmarks. Five minutes' tuition from anyone who knows how to use a sextant will enable a beginner to measure these angles.

Having entered these observed horizontal angles in the log book as '*G* 78° *H* 55° *D*' (this is more nautical shorthand, the meaning of which should be fairly obvious), we must now plot the ship's position.

This may be done by means of a 'station pointer', which is another instrument that is very easy to use; but the beginner should use an ordinary protractor and a pair of compasses. These will give just as good results as a station pointer and will illustrate much better the principles that are used.

The method of plotting is as follows:

Join $D$ to $H$. At $D$ and $H$ draw $Dz$ and $Hm$, each making an angle of 35° with $DH$. (Note that 35° is the complement of 55°.) $Dz$ and $Hm$ intersect at $k$. With $k$ as centre, describe the circle $abcd$ passing through $D$ and $H$. The ship's position is somewhere on the circumference of this circle. Now repeat the procedure for $G$ and $H$, i.e. join the two points, and at $G$ and $H$ draw $Gv$ and $Hw$, each making an angle of 12° with $GH$ (12° is the complement of 78°). $Gv$ and $Hw$ intersect at $n$. With $n$ as centre, describe the circle $efgh$, passing through $G$ and $H$. The ship is somewhere on the circumference of this circle. Therefore, she can only be at $X$, where the two circles intersect. The position of $X$ will be entered in the log book in latitude and longitude, or more probably as a bearing and distance from $H$, i.e. '183° $H$ dist 11 n. miles'. This is the result that you should obtain if you have plotted accurately, and you will observe that the ship is, in fact, on the required track.

The reader with a liking for geometry will realize that this method is based on the theorem that the angle at the centre of a circle, subtended by a given chord, is twice the angle at the circumference subtended by the same chord.

There is only one variant of the above construction, and that arises when the observed angle is more than 90°. When this happens, the complement of the observed angle (the difference between the angle and 90°) is still laid off relative to the chord joining the two landmarks, but it is laid off on the *opposite side* of the chord to the side on which the ship is situated. Thus, if the observed angle between $D$ and $H$ were 110°, angles of 20° would be laid off on the northern side of $DH$, so that the centre of the circle would be on that side also. Mathematically minded readers will realize that, in these circumstances, we are applying the same geometrical theorem as before, but in this case we are concerned with the 'reflex angle' at the centre of the circle.

## Checking the Deviation

The above method of fixing the ship's position has one very important advantage, i.e. it is a method which is independent of compass Deviation. You will remember that in all previous examples when we have taken Compass bearings they have had to be converted into True bearings before they could be plotted on the chart. And in order to do this the Deviation for the direction of the ship's head had to be found from the Deviation card.

The 'horizontal angle' method of fixing position, however, gives the ship's position accurately, without using Deviation.

Now, if we have the ship's accurate position plotted on the chart, we can take off from the chart the True bearing of any landmark that is marked on it.

Thus, in our previous example, we can measure off the chart that landmark $H$ bears 003° True from the ship's position at $X$. If we now apply the local Variation of 30° W to this True bearing, we obtain the Magnetic bearing of $H$ from $X$, which is 033° Magnetic.

So, if we *observe* a Compass bearing of $H$ when the ship is at $X$, we can compare the Compass bearing with the Magnetic bearing and thus obtain the Deviation of the compass for the direction of the ship's head.

Let us suppose, then, that when the ship is at $X$, $H$ is observed to bear $035\frac{1}{2}$° by compass. But we have just found out that it also bears 033° Magnetic. So, by using the rule 'Deviation West, Compass Best', we conclude that the Deviation for the Compass heading of 109° is $2\frac{1}{2}°$ W. You will see that this agrees quite well with the Deviation for a heading of 109° Comp. given on the Deviation card (Fig. 7).

Oddly enough, the compass itself may be used, instead of the sextant, to obtain horizontal angles. Thus, if when our ship is at $X$ we take Compass bearings of $D$, $H$ and $G$, we shall obtain the following results: $D$ bears $090\frac{1}{2}°$ Comp., $H$ bears $035\frac{1}{2}°$ Comp. and $G$ bears $317\frac{1}{2}°$ Comp.

Now, the probability that the North point of the compass card is deviated from the Magnetic meridian does not alter the fact that the card's graduations are equally spaced around its circumference. So, if we take the difference between the above Compass bearings, we obtain 55° as the angle between $D$ and $H$, and 78° as the angle between $G$ and $H$—exactly the same result as we obtained with the sextant. In fact, the only advantage in using the sextant to obtain horizontal angles is that it measures the angles more accurately than the compass.

As a final check on the above reasoning, you should apply the compass error of $32\frac{1}{2}°$ W to each of the above three Compass bearings. This will give True bearings as follows: $D$ bears 058° T, $H$ bears 003° T and $G$ bears 285° T. If you now plot these True bearings, you will find that they intersect at $X$, which is exactly the same result as that obtained by horizontal angles. But it must be noted that this is only so because we have used an error of $32\frac{1}{2}°$ W, which incorporates the *correct Deviation* for the direction of the ship's head at the time the bearings were taken.

It follows, therefore, that, when the Deviation of the compass is not known accurately, the 'horizontal angle' method of plotting position is the better method to use, because Deviation is not involved in the construction.

This is the method that is adopted by careful navigators when entering a strange anchorage, where the Deviation may change unexpectedly, owing to the vessel passing close to other ships, sunken wrecks, power cables or magnetic deposits on the sea-bed or on the surrounding coastline.

## Checking Deviation by Transit Bearing

The navigator of a ship steaming along a coastline may check the Deviation for the direction of his ship's head by the following method.

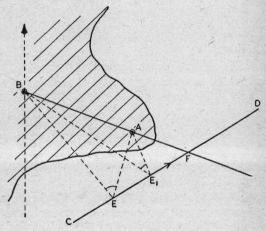

FIG. 15

In Fig. 15, *CD* is the direction of the True course, which is plotted on the chart. Let this be 060° T. Let the Variation be 30° W. Then the Magnetic heading of the ship is 090° M. The navigator wishes to find the Deviation appropriate to this Magnetic heading.

*A* and *B* are two shore objects. When the ship reaches the point *E*, the two objects subtend the angle $A\hat{E}B$ at the ship. A little later they will subtend the angle $A\hat{E}_1B$. As the ship proceeds, the angle gradually gets less, until at the instant that the ship reaches point $F$ the two objects appear to be in line (or 'in transit', as seamen say). The ship is then somewhere on the line $AB$ produced, and the True direction of this line can be taken off the chart. Let this direction be 290° T, as in Fig. 15. The Variation is 30° W. Therefore, the Magnetic direction of $A$ transit $B$ is 320° M.

But if at the instant that the navigator sees $A$ and $B$ in transit he observes their Compass bearing to be 322° Comp., then he can find the Deviation by comparing the Compass bearing with the Magnetic bearing. The Compass bearing is 'best'. Therefore, the Deviation for ship's head 090° M is 2° W, and this agrees with that given on the Deviation card.

If the navigator wishes to check the Deviation on any other heading he could alter course so as to re-cross the line of $A$ and $B$ in transit with his ship on the new heading and carry out the same procedure as before.

## Distance Off by Vertical Sextant Angle

We have seen how horizontal angles, measured with a sextant or compass, may be used to determine a ship's position relative to shore objects.

If the height of an object above sea-level is known, however, the sextant may be used in the vertical plane to measure the vertical angle subtended by the object, and from this the distance off the object can be obtained.

It is for this purpose that the heights of lighthouse lanterns above sea-level at Mean High Water Spring Tides are always given on Admiralty charts.

Let us suppose, then, that a ship is passing close to a lighthouse and the chart says that the lantern of the lighthouse is 95 feet (28·96 metres) above M.H.W.S.

The navigator will ascertain from his Tide Tables that the sea-level at the time of observation is 5 feet (1·52 metres) below the level of M.H.W.S. Therefore, the effective height of the lighthouse lantern above the level of the sea at the time of observation is 100 feet (30·48 metres).

Wishing to know his distance from the lighthouse, the navigator will observe the vertical sextant angle that it subtends. Let us suppose that he finds it to be 0° 54′. This is illustrated in Fig. 16.

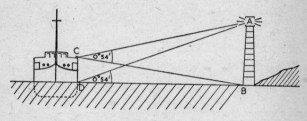

FIG. 16

The diagram, which is not drawn to scale, shows that no appreciable error is involved by assuming that the navigator will obtain the same vertical angle if he were situated at $D$, on the waterline, instead of at $C$, on the bridge. But $ABD$ is a right-angled triangle, so that $BD$, the distance from the ship to the lighthouse, equals $AB \times \cot A\hat{D}B$.

Therefore $BD$ in feet $= 100 \times \cot 0° 54′$.

From the Table of Natural Cotangents at the back of this book we find that $\cot 0° 54′ = 63·657$.

Therefore $BD = 100 \times 63·657 = 6365·7$ feet.

There are 6080 feet in 1 nautical mile, and therefore the distance of the ship from the lighthouse equals $6365·7 \div 6080 = 1·047$ nautical miles.

If this calculation is done in metric units, the figures are as follows:

$$BD = 30·48 \times 63·657 = 1940·3 \text{ m} = 1·9403 \text{ km.}$$
$$\therefore BD = \frac{1·9403}{1·8532} = 1·047 \text{ n. miles, as before.}$$

The professional navigator uses a special table, which gives him the distance off directly, instead of having to work it out. Or he may use this formula, which is based on radian measure:

Distance off in n. miles

$$= \frac{\text{Ht. of lighthouse in feet} \times 0.565}{\text{Vertical angle in minutes}}$$

∴ Distance off in n. miles

$$= \frac{100 \times 0.565}{54} = \frac{56.5}{54} = 1.047 \text{ n. miles}$$

which is the same result as before.

If you should wish to use this formula when the height of the lighthouse is given in metres, it is best first to convert the given height into feet, e.g. 30.48 metres equals 100 feet.

When a navigator wishes to maintain a certain distance off a lighthouse whilst he is rounding it, he will often use a vertical sextant angle to do so. If, as in the above example, he wished to maintain a distance of 1.05 n. miles off the lighthouse, he would set an angle of 0° 54′ on his sextant. If, as he rounded the lighthouse, he saw that the angle was increasing, he would know that he was getting too close, and he would alter course away from the lighthouse until the angle was again 0° 54′.

## Distance Off Lights when they are 'Rising' or 'Dipping' on the Horizon

Fig. 17 shows a portion of the curved surface of the earth. $LX$ is a lighthouse, $H_1$ feet high, and $XY$ is a ray of light from the lighthouse.

Professor Einstein has shown that rays of light do, in fact, bend slightly under certain circumstances, but it is safe enough for ordinary folk to assume that light travels in a straight line.

Therefore $XY$ is a straight line tangent to the earth's surface at $Z$. A navigator on the bridge of a ship at $A$ cannot see the light, as the ray is passing over his head, and he cannot see through the bulge of the earth at $Z$. Similarly, he cannot see the light at $B$.

The ship continues to steam towards the light, however, and suddenly, when she reaches position $C$, the light 'rises' above the horizon. In point of fact, the ray of light has been there all the time, but the navigator on the bridge of his ship at $C$ has just arrived at a point where he can see it, i.e. his eye has reached the straight line $XY$.

Now, as soon as he sees the light, he will take a Compass bearing of it. He will convert the bearing to True and plot the line of position on the chart.

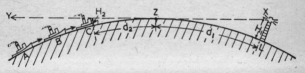

Fig. 17

Such a position line is very useful in itself. But it is also desirable to know the distance off the light at the instant that it rose above the horizon. The distance off the light, in Fig. 17, is distance $d_1$ plus distance $d_2$.

If $H_1$ is the height of the light above sea-level obtained as in the last example, and if $H_2$ is the height of the navigator's eye above sea-level (which he knows), then he can enter a table called 'The Distance of the Sea Horizon' table and extract from it the distances $d_1$ and $d_2$.

Alternatively, he may use the formula:

$$d_1 \text{ in n. miles} = 1 \cdot 15 \times \sqrt{\text{Ht. of light in feet}}$$

$$\text{and} \quad d_2 \text{ in n. miles} = 1 \cdot 15 \times \sqrt{\text{Ht. of eye in feet}}.$$

Thus, if $H_1 = 400$ feet and $H_2 = 36$ feet, then:

$$d_1 = 1 \cdot 15 \times \sqrt{400} \text{ n. miles}$$
$$= 1 \cdot 15 \times 20 \text{ n. miles} = 23 \text{ n. miles}$$
and $\quad d_2 = 1 \cdot 15 \times \sqrt{36} \text{ n. miles}$
$$= 1 \cdot 15 \times 6 \text{ n. miles} = 6 \cdot 9 \text{ n. miles}.$$

Therefore, the distance of the ship from the lighthouse at the instant that the light rose above the horizon was $d_1 + d_2$, which equals $29 \cdot 9$ n. miles.

If this formula is to be used when the height of the light and the height of the observer are given in metres, the formula must be amended to read:

$$d_1 = 1 \cdot 15 \times \sqrt{\text{Ht. of light in metres} \times 3 \cdot 28}$$
$$d_2 = 1 \cdot 15 \times \sqrt{\text{Ht. of eye in metres} \times 3 \cdot 28}.$$

If the ship is steaming away from the light, then the navigator waits on the bridge, at a height of eye less than that of the standard compass, until he sees the light disappear or 'dip' below the horizon. He then climbs smartly up to the standard compass, whence he can still see the light, and takes a Compass bearing of it before it finally disappears. The distance off is then ascertained as before.

Finally, if you study an Admiralty chart, you will see that the range or 'visibility' of a light is often given on the chart, against the light, in nautical miles.

The range of a light depends, of course, on the height of eye of the observer, but it also depends on the luminosity of the light.

### EXAMPLES FOR EXERCISE IN CHARTWORK

*(Use Variation 30° W and the Deviation from Fig. 7)*

### Exercise 7

(a) From a position with Lightvessel *D*, bearing North True, dist. 15 n. miles, find the two Compass courses to steer to reach a position with Lighthouse $B$, bearing 330° T, dist. 20 n. miles, passing Lightvessel $C$ on the port hand, and maintaining a distance of 10 n. miles whilst rounding. Give the distance on each course, and the distance rounding $C$.

(b) Thence find the Compass course and distance to a position with Lighthouse $A$, bearing South True, distance 30 n. miles.

(c) If the ship steams at 10 knots, and there is no wind or current, find the total steaming time for the passage.

## Exercise 8

Your ship left the first position (Lightvessel $D$, bearing North True, dist. 15 n. miles) at 2000 hours, steering 280° by compass. Log was set at zero. At 2330 hours, when the log read 35, Lightvessel $H$ bore 060° Comp. and at the same time Lightvessel $G$ bore 330° Comp. Find:

(a) The observed position of the ship at 2330 hours expressed as a True bearing and distance from $G$.

(b) The set and drift of the current experienced since 2000 hours.

(c) The rate of the current.

(d) The course and distance made good over the ground between 2000 hours and 2330 hours, and the ground speed.

## Exercise 9

(a) From the above information, plot the vessel's estimated position at midnight, assuming the ship's speed to remain unaltered at 10 knots. Give this position as a True bearing and distance from $G$.

(b) From this estimated position, set course to reach a position with $C$ bearing 162° T, dist. 10 n. miles, so as to counteract the effect of a current which sets 355° T at a rate of 1·8 knots. Give the True course and also the Compass course to steer.

(c) Give also the ground speed on the new course and the E.T.A. at the position off C.

(d) If a fresh southerly wind arose at 0100 hours and you estimated that it would cause 5° of leeway, what alteration of course would you make to counteract the effect of leeway? Give the new course, True and Compass.

## Exercise 10

At 0600 hours a Compass course of 220° Comp. was set from a position with C bearing 087° T dist. 10 n. miles. The log read 106. From the current chart it was estimated that the current would set 090° T at 2 knots in this area. The wind had now veered to the westward, and it was estimated that the ship would make 5° of leeway. Find the estimated position of the ship at 0900 hours, when the log reads 136, allowing for the effect of current and leeway.

(a) Give the estimated position as a True bearing and distance from C.

(b) Give the 'True course with leeway allowed'.

(c) Give the True course and distance made good between 0600 hours and 0900 hours.

## Exercise 11

The vessel continued on the course that you have just worked out in the last question, with leeway and current unchanged. At 1000 hours, log 146, Lighthouse B was observed 30° on the starboard bow. At 1200 hours, log 166, B was observed abeam to starboard. Give:

(a) The True bearing of B at 1000 hours and at 1200 hours.

(*b*) The position of the ship at 1200 hours as a True bearing and distance from *B*.

(This problem is a 'running fix, with current and leeway'.)

## Exercise 12

Later, the course was altered to 125° Comp., but owing to overcast conditions it was impossible to check the Deviation of the compass by astronomical observation. At 1800 hours, however, the haze lifted, and landmarks *E*, *F* and *A* became visible. The following Compass bearings were observed: *F* = 283° Comp.; *E* = 247° Comp.; *A* = 179° Comp. Find:

(*a*) The ship's position by the 'horizontal angle' method. Give this position as a True bearing and distance from *E*.
(*b*) The Deviation and error of the compass for the course of 125° Comp.

## Exercise 13

(*a*) The navigator of a ship steaming along a coastline is uncertain of the compass Deviation on the course that he is steering. He notices two landmarks coming into transit. At the instant that they are in transit, he observes their Compass bearing to be 040° Comp. From the chart he finds that their True bearing when in transit is 065° T. If the local Variation is 20° E, what is the Deviation of the compass for the direction of the ship's head?
(*b*) Wishing to check the Deviation again when on the return passage, the navigator then steers his ship so as to re-cross the transit line on the reverse course. On this occasion, the Compass bearing of the landmarks in transit is observed to be 050° Comp. What is the Deviation on this course?

## Exercise 14

(a) The navigator of a ship passing close to a lighthouse 200 feet (60·96 metres) high takes a vertical sextant angle of the lighthouse and observes it to be 1° 53′. What is the distance of the ship from the lighthouse?

(b) If, on the return passage, the navigator wishes to maintain a distance of 2 n. miles off the lighthouse, what angle must be set on his sextant?

## Exercise 15

The navigator of a ship is on the bridge, with his eye 49 feet (14·93 metres) above sea-level. A shore light which is known to be 100 feet (30·48 metres) above sea-level is observed to 'dip' below the horizon. How far is the ship from the light?

# CHAPTER 4

# Simple Calculations

So far we have learnt how to plot a vessel's course and distance from one point to another on a Mercator's chart, and, as we have seen, this is not a difficult matter.

A competent navigator, however, must be able to find the course and distance by calculation as well as by plotting on a chart, and the different methods of doing this will now be described.

Because these methods were evolved when ships literally sailed the seas, they are called 'Sailings', i.e. Parallel Sailing, Plane Sailing, Mercator's Sailing and Great Circle Sailing respectively. If they had been evolved more recently, they would no doubt have been called 'Steamings' or 'Flyings', but their principles would have been just the same as those of the 'Sailings'.

## Parallel Sailing

This simply means 'sailing along a parallel of latitude' and from the earliest times it has been one of the most popular ways of navigating across the oceans in an easterly or westerly direction.

As we shall see in a later chapter, it is very easy indeed to find the latitude by astronomical observation; and it no doubt gave early navigators a certain degree of confidence to feel that they were at least sure of the parallel of latitude on which their ship was situated.

Finding longitude, however, has always been more difficult than finding latitude, and it could never be found very accurately at sea until the invention of the temperature-compensated chronometer in the middle of the eighteenth century. Captain Cook was one of the first navigators to use this comparatively modern instrument.

Before Captain Cook's time, however, the longitude could be determined with some degree of accuracy by keeping a careful check, by means of the log, on the distance, in nautical miles, which the ship sailed along a given parallel of latitude. This distance was so important to the navigator that it was given a special name—'The Departure'.

You will recollect that in Chapter 1 of this book we established the fact that, on the surface of the earth, the distance apart of any two meridians in latitude $x°$ equals their distance apart at the Equator multiplied by cosine $x°$.

But the distance apart of two meridians in any given latitude is the distance in nautical miles between them measured along the given parallel of latitude, i.e. it is the Departure. And the distance in nautical miles between the same two meridians at the Equator is the Difference of Longitude in minutes between them. (Because, at the Equator, one minute of longitude equals one nautical mile.)

From this reasoning, therefore, we arrive at the basic 'Parallel Sailing' formula, viz.:

Departure, in n. miles = D. long. in minutes × cosine lat.

This basic formula enables us to work problems such as the following:

'A ship leaves a place in lat. 50° 00′ N long. 10° 00′ W and steams due West until she reaches long. 20° 00′ W. How far has she steamed? (Or, in nautical terminology, "What is the Departure made good?")'

In this problem, the D. Long. is 10° 00′, and this equals 600 minutes of longitude.

$$\therefore \text{ Departure (in n. miles)} = 600 \times \text{cosine } 50°$$
$$= 600 \times 0 \cdot 6428$$
$$= 385 \cdot 58 \text{ n. miles. } Ans.$$

But this does not tell us how the early navigators found their longitude. We can see how this was done, however, if we transpose our basic formula, as follows:

$$\text{Departure} = \text{D. long.} \times \text{cosine lat.}$$
$$\therefore \text{D. long.} = \frac{\text{Departure}}{\text{cosine lat.}}.$$

But we know that $\dfrac{1}{\cos A} = \text{secant } A$, or, in words, we may say: 'Dividing by the cosine is the same as multiplying by the secant'.

$$\therefore \text{D. long. in minutes} = \text{Departure in n. miles} \times \text{secant lat.}$$

Using the Parallel Sailing formula in this form, we can now solve the sort of problem that Columbus dealt with quite effectively, e.g.:

'A ship leaves a point of land in lat. 50° 00′ N long. 10° 00′ W and steers due West for a distance of 385·68 n. miles by her log. What longitude does she arrive at?'

From the above formula:

$$
\begin{aligned}
\text{D. long. in minutes} &= 385\cdot68 \times \text{secant } 50° \ 00' \\
&= 385\cdot68 \times 1\cdot5557 \\
&= 600 \text{ minutes of long.} \\
&= 10° \ 00' \text{ of long.}
\end{aligned}
$$

Therefore the ship arrives at long. 20° 00′ W.

You will realize, of course, that the second of the above two problems is the reverse of the first one.

If you wish to show that you understand the principles of Parallel Sailing, without, however, being very practical, you can transpose the basic formula, as follows:

$$\text{Departure} = \text{D. long.} \times \text{cosine lat.}$$
$$\therefore \frac{\text{Departure}}{\text{D. long.}} = \text{cosine lat.}$$

Thus, if you are given the departure in nautical miles

between two places in the same latitude, and also their difference of longitude, you can find on which parallel of latitude the two places are situated.

## Plane Sailing

'Plane' Sailing is so called because, when using this method of calculation, we assume the surface of the earth to be a plane, i.e. flat.

Now, we all know that the earth is not flat; so we therefore know that any method of calculation which assumes it to be flat cannot be very accurate.

Nevertheless, the Plane Sailing method is widely used in practice, because it gives reasonably accurate results, provided the distance involved is not too great—provided, in fact, that the distance is small enough for the curvature of the earth to be neglected. Some navigators will use Plane Sailing for distances up to 500 n. miles. The writer, personally, would only use it up to about 200 n. miles; but it all depends on what degree of accuracy is required.

The main reason for using the Plane Sailing method of calculation is that it is relatively easy. By assuming the earth's surface to be a plane over a short distance, we can solve our problem by plane trigonometry, which is very simple to use.

The method is best explained by means of an example.

You should first refer back to your chart, and make a note of the latitude and longitude of positions I and II, which are shown in Fig. 5. You will find that position I is in 58° 20′ N 30° 00′ W and that position II is in 59° 03′ N 32° 32′ W. These two positions are shown in Fig. 18, but in this figure position I is called A and position II is called B.

Our problem is to find, by calculation, the True course and distance from A to B, which we have already done by plotting on the chart, where A was called position I and B was called position II.

Since the distance is relatively small, we can ignore the curvature of the earth and use the Plane Sailing method of calculation, as follows:

Through the point of departure $A$ draw the meridian $AX$, and through the destination $B$ draw the parallel of latitude $BY$. $AX$ and $BY$ intersect at right angles in $C$. $ABC$ is thus a right-angled triangle, which can be solved by right-angled plane trigonometry if we know two of its parts.

We know one of its parts immediately, namely $AC$, the difference of latitude between $A$ and $B$, which is 43 minutes of lat., or 43 n. miles.

We do not know the side $BC$ immediately, but it can be found, because we do know the longitude of $A$ and the longitude of $B$. Their difference of longitude is

$$32° \ 32' - 30° \ 00' = 2° \ 32' = 152 \text{ minutes of long.}$$

This can be changed into Departure by using the formula:

Departure in n. miles
$$= \text{D. long. in minutes} \times \text{cosine } mean \text{ lat.}$$

Note that here we use the *mean* latitude, i.e. the latitude midway between $A$ and $B$, because $A$ and $B$ are not on the same parallel. This mean latitude is $58° \ 41\frac{1}{2}'$ N.

$$\therefore \text{ Departure} = 152 \times \text{cosine } 58° \ 41\frac{1}{2}'$$
$$= 152 \times 0 \cdot 5196$$
$$= 78 \cdot 98 \text{ n. miles}$$
$$\therefore \ BC \text{ in Fig. 18} = 78 \cdot 98 \text{ n. miles.}$$

We now have both $AC$ and $BC$ expressed in the same units of measurement, and therefore we can now find the 'Course Angle' $B\hat{A}C$, as follows:

$$\text{Tangent } B\hat{A}C = \frac{BC}{AC}$$

or, in the particular application to this problem:

$$\text{Tangent of course angle} = \frac{\text{Departure}}{\text{D. Lat.}}$$

$$= \frac{78 \cdot 98}{43} = 1 \cdot 8368.$$

$$\therefore \text{ Course angle} = 61° \ 26' \text{ (from Table of Tangents).}$$

This angle is to the West of North, and therefore the True course from $A$ to $B$ is N 61° 26′ W or 298° 34′. This agrees closely with the result obtained by plotting the True course from position I to position II on the chart. Needless to say, the calculation method is more accurate than plotting.

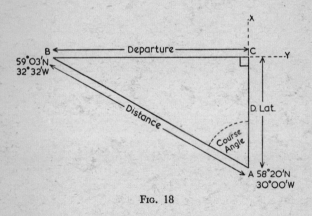

FIG. 18

Now, to find the distance, we must do some more trigonometry. From Fig. 18 we see that:

$$\frac{AB}{AC} = \text{secant } B\hat{A}C$$

$$\therefore AB = AC \times \text{secant } B\hat{A}C$$

or, in the particular application to this problem:

$$\text{Distance} = \text{D. lat.} \times \text{secant of course angle}$$
$$= 42 \times \text{secant } 61° \, 26''$$
$$= 43 \times 2 \cdot 0912$$
$$= 89 \cdot 9 \text{ n. miles}$$

which is very close to the 90 n. miles that we obtained by measurement on the chart. This method is, again, more accurate than plotting.

So far so good. But our discussion of Plane Sailing would not be complete if we did not consider the reverse of the above problem. We have seen how to find the True course and distance from one position to another, but the navigator often has to deal with another equally important calculation: namely, having set course from a given position, to find the latitude and longitude of the position arrived at after steaming for a given distance on the given course. The problem can be presented in this form:

'A ship leaves position $A$ in 58° 20′ N 30° 00′ W and steers N 61° 26′ W (True), for a distance of 90 n. miles. What is the latitude and longitude arrived at?'

Fig. 18 illustrates this problem quite well, but in this case different parts of the triangle are given from those given in the previous example, i.e. we are now given angle $B\hat{A}C$ and the side $AB$, which is in n. miles.

By right-angled trigonometry, therefore, we first find side $AC$ (the D. lat. between $A$ and $B$) and side $BC$ (the Departure between $A$ and $B$). We then change the Departure into D. long., and thus find the latitude and longitude of $B$, as required. The working is as follows:

$$\frac{AC}{AB} = \text{cosine } B\hat{A}C \quad \therefore \quad AC = AB \times \text{cosine } B\hat{A}C,$$

i.e. D. lat. = Distance × cosine course,

$$\text{D. lat.} = 90 \times \text{cosine } 61° \, 36′$$
$$= 90 \times 0 \cdot 4782$$
$$= 43 \text{ n. miles or minutes of lat.}$$

Therefore, lat. of $B$ = 58° 20′ N + 43′ N = 59° 03′ N.

$$\frac{BC}{AB} = \text{sine } B\hat{A}C \quad \therefore \quad BC = AB \times \text{sine } B\hat{A}C,$$

i.e. Departure = Distance × sine of course angle
= 90 × sine 61° 26′
= 90 × 0·8783
= 79 n. miles

But this is Departure, and it must be converted into D. long., using the formula:

D. long. in minutes
= Dep. in n. miles × secant mean lat.

The mean latitude between 58° 20′ N and 59° 03′ N is 58° 41½′ N,

$\therefore$ D. long. = 79 × secant 58° 41½′
= 79 × 1·9244
= 152 minutes of long.
= 2° 32′ of long.

Therefore, longitude $B$

= 30° 00′ W + 2° 32′ W = 32° 32′ W.

We have thus found the latitude and longitude of the position arrived at after steering a given True course and distance from a given position.

The professional navigator will use somewhat quicker methods than the above, because he wishes to work as fast as possible. He may, therefore, use logarithms or a slide rule to effect the above multiplications and divisions. But he is more likely to use a 'Traverse Table', which, like many other nautical tables, cannot be included in a book of this size.

The Traverse Table is merely a tabulated device for solving right-angled triangles, with particular application to Plane Sailing. By entering the table with course and distance, you can take out the corresponding D. lat. and

Departure. Or, by entering with D. lat. and Departure, you can take out the corresponding course and distance. The table may also be used to convert Departure into D. long., and vice versa.

## The 'Day's Work'

When a number of courses and distances, in succession, are steered from a given position, and it is required to find the D.R. or Estimated position at the end of the series of courses, the problem is called a 'Day's Work', because such a problem had to be worked by the navigator of a sailing ship at the end of each day's run. The 'day' began and ended at noon, and during the intervening 24 hours the ship would have steered several different courses in order to take advantage of the most favourable winds.

A modified form of this problem is still worked by the navigator of a modern steamship in order to find his D.R. position as accurately as possible. The Traverse Table is used for this purpose, but the principles involved are those of Plane Sailing, i.e. a Day's Work is a succession of Plane Sailings, one for each course that the ship has 'traversed' during the day.

## Mercator's Sailing

As we have explained above, Plane Sailing is accurate enough for all practical purposes when the distance to be covered is small. But if the navigator of a ship or aircraft requires to know the rhumb line course and distance from *A* to *B* when *A* and *B* are, perhaps, 2000 n. miles apart, then Plane Sailing methods cannot be used. You can't assume the earth to be flat for a distance of 2000 n. miles. If you do make such a supposition, you will get very inaccurate results.

How, then, may we calculate the rhumb line course

and distance from one place to another when the distance between the two places is great?

The answer is that we use a method of calculation based on the principle of the Mercator's chart.

It will be recollected that the principle of the Mercator's chart is such that the curved surface of the earth is 'projected' on to a flat piece of paper in such a way that a rhumb line on the earth is represented by a straight line on the flat paper.

Therefore, in order to find the rhumb line course and distance from one place to another on the earth, we transfer the two places, in theory, on to a flat Mercator's chart. And then, with a little ingenuity, we can still use plane trigonometry to solve our problem. This is done in the following manner:

First of all, refer back to Fig. 2. Suppose it is required to find the rhumb line course and distance from $A$ to $B$ in Fig. 2. $A$ is in 15° 00′ N 45° 00′ W and $B$ is in 60° 00′ N 60° 00′ E. Fig. 19 is an enlarged diagram of these two places as they appear on the Mercator's chart of Fig. 2 (b).

The method of drawing this figure is similar to that used in drawing the figure for the Plane Sailing problem. Through the point of departure $A$, draw the meridian $AX$, and through the point of arrival $B$, draw the parallel of latitude $BY$. $AX$ and $BY$ intersect at $C$, thus forming the right-angled $ABC$, in which angle $B\hat{A}C$ is the course angle and $AB$ is the distance.

You will realize that we have the same information given here as in the Plane Sailing problem, i.e. we know the D. lat. and D. long. between $A$ and $B$. But we cannot use the Plane Sailing method of calculation, because that method is only applicable to plane surfaces.

So we must introduce some new units of measurement, which are called 'Meridional Parts'.

'One meridional part' may be defined as 'the chart length of one minute of longitude on a Mercator's chart'. And the 'meridional parts for any given latitude' are 'the number of meridional parts contained between that latitude and the Equator'.

Thus, in Fig. 19, the meridional parts for latitude $A$ (15° 00′ N) is the distance from the Equator ($QQ$) to $A$, measured in minutes of longitude, taken from the longitude scale of the chart. Similarly, the meridional parts for latitude $B$ (60° 00′ N) is the distance from the Equator to $B$, also measured in minutes of longitude, taken from the longitude scale of the chart.

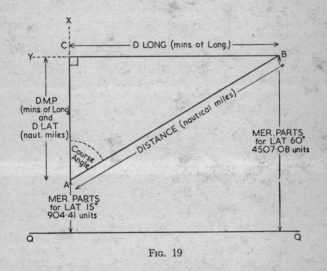

FIG. 19

The side $AC$ of our triangle, therefore, can now be expressed as the 'Difference of Meridional Parts' (abbreviated to 'D.M.P.') between the latitudes of $A$ and $B$.

Since one meridional part is equal to one minute of longitude on a Mercator's chart, the reader will now appreciate what all this is about. He will see, in fact, that we have now expressed the side $AC$ of the triangle in the *same units* (minutes of longitude) as the side $BC$. We have done this so that we can solve the triangle $ABC$

by plane trigonometry, and thus find the course angle $B\hat{A}C$.

'But where do these meridional parts come from in practice?' the reader may well ask. The answer, again, is 'From Nautical Tables'. These tables occupy too much space to be reproduced in this book, but the necessary extracts from them will be given as required. The tables are easy to use. One simply enters them with the latitude, in degrees and minutes, and then one takes out the corresponding meridional parts for that latitude. The modern tables are very accurate, and they take into account the fact that the earth is not an exact sphere but a slightly oblate spheroid. These 'Meridional Parts for the Terrestrial Spheroid', as they are called, are used by professional cartographers in constructing Mercator's charts. Consequently, the professionally constructed chart is just a little more accurate than the one we have constructed in this book, since we have assumed the earth to be a true sphere.

But to return to our problem. From the Meridional Parts Table we obtain the following information:

Mer. parts for lat. $A$ (15° 00′ N) =   904·41
Mer. parts for lat. $B$ (60° 00′ N) = 4507·08

$\therefore$ D.M.P. = $\overline{3602\cdot67}$.

Long. of $A$ 45° 00′ W
Long. of $B$ 60° 00′ E

$\therefore$ $\underline{\text{D. long. } 105° \ 00′}$   = $\underline{6300 \text{ minutes of long.}}$

Now, in the triangle $ABC$, $\tan B\hat{A}C = \dfrac{BC}{AC}$, or, in the

particular application to this problem:

$$\text{Tangent of course angle} = \frac{\text{D. long.}}{\text{D.M.P.}}$$

Therefore, inserting the appropriate figures in the formula, we have:

$$\text{Tangent of course angle} = \frac{6300}{3602 \cdot 67} = 1 \cdot 7487$$

∴ from Tangent Table, course angle = 60° 14'
i.e. True rhumb line course from $A$ to $B$

$$= \text{N } 60° \text{ 14}' \text{ E.}$$

But we still have to find the distance from $A$ to $B$ in nautical miles; and in order to do this we must change the units by which we measure the sides of our triangle from minutes of longitude to minutes of latitude, each one of which is a nautical mile.

Since $A$ is in 15° 00' N and $B$ is in 60° 00' N, their D. lat. is 45° 00', which equals 2700 minutes of lat. or nautical miles.

Now, in the triangle $ABC$,

$$\frac{AB}{AC} = \text{secant } B\hat{A}C$$

$$\therefore AB = AC \times \text{secant } B\hat{A}C$$

or, in the particular application to this problem:

Distance in n. miles = D. lat. in minutes (or n. miles) × secant of course angle,
i.e. Distance in n. miles = 2700 × secant 60° 14'
= 2700 × 2·0143
= 5438·6 n. miles.

We have thus determined that the rhumb line course and distance from $A$ to $B$ is N 60° 14' E (True) 5438·6 n. miles.

## Great Circle Sailing

As we have seen in Chapter 1, the shortest distance between two points on the earth's surface is along the arc of the great circle which passes through the two points.

When the distance between the points is large, the great circle distance is considerably less than the rhumb line distance. For this reason, transatlantic and transpacific sea and air liners often follow the great circle track across their respective oceans.

We have also seen that the great circle track between two points changes its direction all the time, so that the calculation of such a track is a tedious process.

Fig. 20 shows half the Northern Hemisphere of the earth, with the great circle track from $A$ in 15° 00′ N 45°

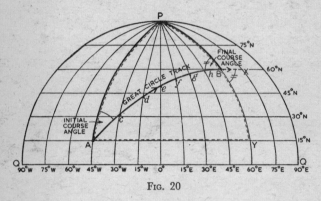

Fig. 20

00′ W to $B$ in 60° 00′ N 60° 00′ E drawn on it. $P$ is the North Geographical Pole.

Angle $P\hat{A}B$ at $A$ is called the Initial course, and angle $P\hat{B}A$ at $B$ enables us to find the Final course, which is in the direction $BX$. As can be seen from the figure, the track crosses each meridian at a different angle, and each of these angles must be determined.

Each one of these angles *could* be calculated by spherical trigonometry, but, in practice, the positions in latitude and longitude of the points $c$, $d$, $e$, $f$, etc., are often determined by plotting on a special chart, which will be described later. Having determined the latitude and longitude of each one of these points, they can be plotted on a Mercator's chart, and the rhumb line course and distance between each successive pair of points can be found. In practice, therefore, when a ship or aircraft follows a great circle track from $A$ to $B$, she really steers along a series of short rhumb line tracks, which together approximate very closely to the great circle track from $A$ to $B$.

The great circle distance from $A$ to $B$, and the Initial and Final courses, however, are usually calculated by spherical trigonometry, and the method of doing this will now be described.

The principal difference between plane and spherical trigonometry is simply that the latter is concerned with the solution of triangles on the surface of a sphere, i.e. spherical triangles.

Each side of a spherical triangle *must* be the arc of a great circle. Thus, in Fig. 20, $PAB$ is a spherical triangle, but $PAY$ (shown dotted) is *not* a spherical triangle, because $AY$ is a parallel of latitude and is therefore only the arc of a small circle.

Also, 1 nautical mile, measured along the arc of a great circle on the earth's surface, subtends an angle of 1 minute at the earth's centre, and it is for this reason that the *sides* of spherical triangles, as well as the angles, are measured in degrees and minutes. Each degree equals 60 n. miles along the arc, and each minute equals 1 n. mile.

In the same manner as plane triangles are solved by plane trigonometrical formulae, spherical triangles are solved by spherical trigonometrical formulae. The principal formula used by navigators is called the 'Spherical Haversine' formula.

Nautical tables, as used by professional navigators, contain tables of haversines, both in logarithms and in natural numbers. These tables occupy more than 100 pages, so they obviously cannot be included in this small book. But we can manage quite well without them. We can, in fact, make our own haversines, when we require them, as follows:

'Haversine' is an abbreviation of 'half versed sine' or 'half versine'. The versed sine or versine of angle $A$ equals $1 - \text{cosine } A$.

Therefore, haversine of angle $A = \dfrac{1 - \text{cosine } A}{2}$.

From this it follows that if we know the cosine of an angle—and we can find it from the table of cosines at the end of this book—we can calculate the haversine of the angle. Conversely, if we have the haversine of an angle in our calculations, we can find the corresponding cosine by simple transposition, as follows:

$$\text{hav } A = \frac{1 - \cos A}{2},$$
$$\therefore\ 2 \text{ hav } A = 1 - \cos A,$$
$$\therefore\ \quad \cos A = 1 - 2 \text{ hav } A.$$

As a numerical example, suppose we wish to find the haversine of 60°.

From the table of cosines, we find that the cosine of 60° is 0·5.

Therefore, haversine $60° = \dfrac{1 - 0\cdot5}{2} = \dfrac{0\cdot5}{2} = 0\cdot25$.

Conversely, if we are told that the haversine of an angle is 0·25 and we wish to find the value of the angle, we first find the value of its cosine, as follows:

$$\text{cosine } A = 1 - 2 \text{ haversine } A,$$
$$\therefore\ \text{cosine } A = 1 - 2 \times 0\cdot25 = 1 - 0\cdot5 = 0\cdot5.$$

Whence, from the Cosine Table, $A = 60°$.

It is not always quite as simple as this, however, because of the awkward fact, known to mathematicians, that the cosine of an angle which lies between 90° and 180° is negative. Because of this awkward fact, we must proceed in the following manner when the angle for which we require the haversine is more than 90°—it will never be more than 180°.

Suppose we wish to find the haversine of 120°. We must first find the cosine of 120°. In order to do this, we look up the cosine of its 'supplementary angle', 60° (180° −120° = 60°). Cosine 60° = 0·5, and this is also the numerical value of cosine 120°. But because 120° lies between 90° and 180°, its cosine is negative, i.e. cosine 120° = −0·5. By algebra, therefore,

$$\text{hav } 120° = \frac{1-(-0\cdot5)}{2} = \frac{1+0\cdot5}{2} = \frac{1\cdot5}{2} = 0\cdot75.$$

You will note that the haversine of any angle between 0° and 180° is always positive, and that is why haversine formulae are so frequently used in navigation, when Haversine Tables are available, so as to avoid the minus signs that apply to the cosine, secant, tangent and co-tangent for angles between 90° and 180°.

Conversely, if we are told that the haversine of a given angle is 0·75, and we require to find the value of the angle, we proceed as follows:

cosine $A = 1-2$ haversine $A$,
∴ cosine $A = 1-2\times0\cdot75 = 1-1\cdot5 = -0\cdot5$.

The fact that we get a negative result for the cosine tells us that the angle concerned lies between 90° and 180°. We therefore look up 0·5 in the Cosine Table, which gives us an angle of 60°. But because the given cosine is negative, we know that 60° is the 'supplementary angle', and, therefore, the angle that we require is 180° − 60° = 120°.

Having shown how to deal with haversines, we will now give the haversine formula in the form that it can be used for the solution of triangle *PAB*, in Fig. 20.

Let us suppose, in the first instance, that we are given the three sides of the triangle, *PA*, *PB* and *AB*, and we are required to find angle $P$. The formula then takes this form (the symbol $\sim$ means 'difference between'):

$$\text{hav } P = \frac{\text{hav } AB - \text{hav } (PA \sim PB)}{\text{sine } PA . \text{sine } PB} \qquad . \qquad \text{(i)}$$

To find angle $A$, the formula takes the form:

$$\text{hav } A = \frac{\text{hav } PB - \text{hav } (PA \sim AB)}{\text{sine } PA . \text{sine } AB} \qquad . \qquad \text{(ii)}$$

To find angle $B$, the formula takes the form:

$$\text{hav } B = \frac{\text{hav } PA - \text{hav } (PB \sim AB)}{\text{sine } PB . \text{sine } AB} \qquad . \qquad \text{(iii)}$$

Note the 'symmetry' of these formulae. They can be expressed in words as:

'The haversine of a required angle equals the haversine of the opposite side, minus the haversine of the difference between the two including sides, all divided by the product of the sines of the two including sides.'

In the great circle problem that we wish to solve now, however, we are not given the three sides of the triangle $PAB$. We know that lat. $A$ is 15° 00′ N. Therefore, $PA = 75° 00′$. We know that lat. $B$ is 60° 00′ N. Therefore, $PB = 30° 00′$. Long. $A$ is 45° 00′ W and long. $B$ is 60° 00′ E. Therefore, angle $P$, the angle at the Pole between the two meridians, is 45° 00′ + 60° 00′ = 105° 00′.

Therefore, in the spherical triangle $PAB$, we are given $PA$, $PB$ and angle $P$, i.e. we are given two sides and their included angle. We can still solve the triangle, however, and find the third side, $AB$, by simple transposition of formula (i) above:

$$\text{hav } P = \frac{\text{hav } AB - \text{hav } (PA \sim PB)}{\text{sine } PA . \text{sine } PB},$$

$\therefore$ hav $P$.sine $PA$.sine $PB$
$$= \text{hav } AB - \text{hav } (PA \sim PB),$$
$\therefore$ hav $AB = $ hav $P$.sine $PA$.sine $PB$
$$+ \text{hav } (PA \sim PB) \quad . \quad . \quad . \quad \text{(iv)}$$

Similarly, from formula (ii), we obtain:

hav $PB = $ hav $A$.sine $PA$.sine $AB$
$$+ \text{hav } (PA \sim AB) \quad . \quad . \quad . \quad \text{(v)}$$

and, from formula (iii), we obtain:

hav $PA = $ hav $B$.sine $PB$.sine $AB$
$$+ \text{hav } (PB \sim AB) \quad . \quad . \quad . \quad \text{(vi)}$$

We shall not require to use formulae (v) and (vi) here, but we will now see how to use formula (iv) to find the great circle distance between the points $A$ and $B$ on the earth's surface. And then we shall see how to use formulae (ii) and (iii) to find the Initial and Final courses respectively.

### To find the Great Circle Distance AB

hav $AB = $ hav $P$.sine $PA$.sine $PB +$ hav $(PA \sim PB)$.

We are given that $P = 105°\ 00'$, $PA = 75°\ 00'$, $PB = 30°\ 00'$, and thence $(PA \sim PB) = 45°\ 00'$.

Since we lack Haversine Tables, we must first find hav $105°\ 00'$ and hav $45°\ 00'$, as follows:

$$\text{hav } 105°\ 00' = \frac{1 - \cos 105°\ 00'}{2}.$$

But $\cos 105° = -\cos 75°$ and $-\cos 75° = -0.2588$ from the Cosine Table in this book.

$$\therefore \text{ hav } 105° = \frac{1 - (-0.2588)}{2} = \frac{1 + 0.2588}{2}$$
$$= \frac{1.2588}{2} = 0.6294.$$

Similarly, hav $45° = \dfrac{1-\cos 45°}{2}$. Cos $45° = 0.7071$ from Cos Table,

$$\therefore \text{ hav } 45° = \frac{1-0.7071}{2} = \frac{0.2929}{2} = 0.146\ 45.$$

We also require sine 75° and sine 30°, which are 0.9659 and 0.5 respectively, from the Sine Table in this book.

If we now put these values into the above formula, we have:

$$\text{hav } AB = 0.6294 \times 0.9659 \times 0.5 + 0.146\ 45.$$

This rather cumbersome calculation must be worked to an accuracy of four places of decimals. The multiplication may be done by logarithms, but it can be done by long multiplication, as follows:

$$
\begin{array}{rl}
0.6294 & \\
0.9659 & \times
\end{array}
\qquad
\begin{array}{rl}
0.60794 & \\
0.5 & \times
\end{array}
$$

$$
\begin{array}{rl}
56646 & \\
31470 & + \\
37764 & \\
56646 & =
\end{array}
\qquad
\begin{array}{r}
0.303970 \\
0.146450 \\
\hline
0.450420
\end{array}
$$

$$0.60793746$$

$$\therefore \text{ hav } AB = 0.4504.$$

But
$$\cos\ AB = 1 - 2\text{ hav } AB,$$
$$\therefore \cos\ AB = 1 - 0.9008,$$
$$\therefore \cos\ AB = 0.0992.$$

Whence, from the Cosine Table, $AB = 84° 18'$.

The cosine is positive, so this is the angle we require.

Since each degree equals 60 n. miles and each minute equals 1 n. mile, the great circle distance from $A$ to $B$ = 5058 n. miles. *Ans.*

It will be noted, therefore, that since the rhumb line distance between the two places is 5438·6 n. miles, there is a considerable saving of distance by following the great circle track.

We will now see how to find the Initial and Final courses on the great circle track. In order to do this, we must find angle $A$ and angle $B$ in the triangle $PAB$.

Angle $A$ is found by formula (ii) above, as follows:

$$\text{hav } A = \frac{\text{hav } PB - \text{hav } (PA \sim AB)}{\text{sine } PA \cdot \text{sine } AB}.$$

In this formula we are given $PB = 30° \ 00'$, $PA = 75° \ 00'$ and $AB$ (which we have just found) $= 84° \ 18'$. Therefore $(PA \sim AB) = 9° \ 18'$.

Since we lack Haversine Tables, we must find hav $30° 00'$ and hav $9° \ 18'$, as follows:

$$\text{hav } 30° \ 00' = \frac{1 - \cos 30°}{2}.$$

But cosine $30° = 0·866$, from the Cosine Table.

$$\therefore \ \underline{\text{hav } 30° \ 00'} = \frac{1 - 0·866}{2} = \frac{0·134}{2} = \underline{0·067}.$$

$$\text{hav } 9° \ 18' = \frac{1 - \cos 9° \ 18'}{2}.$$

But cosine $9° \ 18' = 0·9869$, from the Cosine Table.

$$\therefore \ \underline{\text{hav } 9° \ 18'} = \frac{1 - 0·9869}{2} = \frac{0·0131}{2} = 0·006 \ 55.$$

Also, sine $75° \ 00' = 0·9659$ and sine $84° \ 18' = 0·9951$, from the Sine Table.

$$\text{Therefore, hav } A = \frac{0·067 - 0·006 \ 55}{0·9659 \times 0·9951}.$$

The working, by long methods, is as follows:

$$
\begin{array}{ccc}
0 \cdot 06700 & 0 \cdot 9659 & 0 \cdot 06289 \\
0 \cdot 00655 & 0 \cdot 9951 & 9 \cdot 6117) \overline{0 \cdot 604500} \\
\hline
0 \cdot 06045 & & 576702
\end{array}
$$

$$-$$  $$\times$$  $$\div$$

```
0·06700      0·9659          0·06289
0·00655      0·9951    9·6117)0·604500
-------                        576702
0·06045        9659          -------
-------       48295          277980
              86931          192234
              86931          -------
            ---------        857460
            0·96116709       768936
            ---------        -------
                             885240
```

$$\therefore \text{ hav } A = 0 \cdot 062 \ 89.$$

But

$$
\begin{aligned}
\cos A &= 1 - 2 \text{ hav } A, \\
&= 1 - 0 \cdot 125 \ 78, \\
&= 0 \cdot 874 \ 22.
\end{aligned}
$$

Therefore, from Cosine Table, angle $A = 29° \ 03'$. The cosine is again positive, so this is the angle required. Therefore, the initial course on the great circle track from $A$ to $B$ is N 29° 03' (True). *Ans.*

It will now be left as an exercise for the reader to work out angle $B$ in the triangle $PAB$, using formula (iii) above. He should find that the angle comes to 69° 40'. By studying Fig. 20, and remembering that the Final course is in the direction $BX$, it should be apparent that the Final course at $B$ is S 69° 40' E, since angle $Y\hat{B}X$ is equal to angle $P\hat{B}A$.

We have shown, therefore, how to calculate the great circle distance between $A$ and $B$, and also the Initial and Final courses.

Finally, some reference must be made to the special chart that is used to determine the positions of the intermediate points $c, d, e, f,$ etc., in Fig. 20.

This chart is called a 'Gnomonic Chart', and on this

type of chart all great circles are represented as straight lines.

The simplest type of Gnomonic chart is the one that is constructed for Polar regions, and this is often used for navigation in high latitudes, where the Mercator's chart is useless because of the infinite distance between parallels of latitude near the Poles on the Mercator's projection.

The Polar Gnomonic chart has the Pole in the centre, and the meridians radiate from the Pole like the spokes of a wheel. They are, of course, straight lines, because they are arcs of great circles, and any other straight line drawn on the chart is also the arc of a great circle.

But a Gnomonic chart can be constructed for any part of the world, such as that part of the world traversed by the great circle track $AB$ in Fig. 20. Such a Gnomonic chart is called an 'Oblique' Gnomonic chart, because it is neither Polar nor Equatorial.

On the Gnomonic chart of this area, therefore, if we draw a straight line from $A$ to $B$, then the line is an arc of a great circle; i.e. it is the great circle track from $A$ to $B$. And we can read off the latitudes at which the line crosses each meridian in turn. In other words, we can read off the latitude and longitude of each of the points $c, d, e, f$, etc.

Knowing the latitude and longitude of each of these points, we can then plot them on a Mercator's chart and join them by a series of short straight lines, which are rhumb lines.

By steering each of these short rhumb line courses in turn, the ship or aircraft is kept very close to the great circle track, i.e. she follows the dotted line $AnB$ or $A_1 n_1 B_1$ of Figs. 2 (a) and 2 (b) respectively.

As stated before, the positions of the points $c, d, e, f$, etc., in Fig. 20, *can* be calculated, if so desired.

When this is done, it is customary to first find the position of the 'Vertex' of the great circle, which is that point on it that is nearest to the Pole. The meridian which passes through the vertex makes a right angle with the great circle, and a right-angled spherical triangle is thus formed. The positions of $c$, $d$, $e$, $f$, etc., can then be calculated by right-angled spherical trigonometry. This is not a difficult process, but it is beyond the scope of this book. Most practical navigators, however, prefer to use the Gnomonic chart instead of making such a lengthy trigonometrical calculation.

## Examples for Exercise

### Exercise 16

(1) In lat. 44° 49′ N, the departure made good was 36·5 n. miles. Find the difference of longitude.

(2) In lat. 25° 25′ N, a vessel steams 125 n. miles due West from long. 58° 29′ W. Find the longitude arrived at.

(3) How far must a ship sail due East in lat. 60° 28′ S to change her longitude from 36° 29′ E to 42° 20′ E?

(4) A vessel steams due West at 24 knots in lat. 52° 00′ N. At what rate per hour is she changing her longitude?

(5) The difference of longitude between two places on the same parallel of latitude is 5° 49·5′, and their distance apart is 185 n. miles. What is the latitude of the two places?

### Exercise 17

(1) Find, by Plane Sailing, the True course and distance between $A$ in 51° 15′ N 5° 05′ W and $B$ in 51° 30′ N 3° 55′ W.

(2) If a vessel leaves point $A$ in 34° 20′ S 174° 40′ E and steers 240° True for a distance of 60 n. miles, find, by Plane Sailing, the latitude and longitude of the position arrived at.

(3) A vessel leaves position $A$ in 48° 23·5′ N 7° 02·8′ W and steers N 5½° W True for 175 n. miles and then S 83½°

E True for 125 n. miles. Find, by Plane Sailing, the latitude and longitude of the position arrived at.

(4) An aircraft leaves position 52° 28′ N 2° 22′ W and flies North True for 150 n. miles, West True for 150 n. miles, South True for 150 n. miles and East True for 150 n. miles in still air. What is her final position?

(5) Find, by Plane Sailing, the True course and distance from A in 38° 00′ N 10° 00′ W to B in 40° 00′ N 8° 00′ W.

## Exercise 18

(1) Find the rhumb line course and distance, by Mercator's Sailing, from A in 57° 10′ N 12° 13′ W to B in 25° 00′ N 62° 33′ W, given that the D.M.P. between latitudes 57° 10′ N and 25° 00′ N is 2641·2 units.

(2) Find the rhumb line course and distance by Mercator's Sailing from A in 42° 13′ S 149° 49′ E to B in 55° 56′ S 94° 32′ W, given that the D.M.P. between latitudes 42° 13′ S and 55° 56′ S is 1263·9 units.

(3) Find, by Great Circle Sailing, the Initial course and the distance along the great circle track from A in 32° 15′ N 64° 45′ W to B in 49° 52′ N 5° 12′ W.

(4) Find, by Great Circle Sailing, the Initial course and the distance along the great circle track from A in 46° 00′ N 45° 00′ W to B in 51° 00′ N 9° 30′ W.

(5) (a) Find, by Mercator's Sailing, the rhumb line course and distance from Cape Horn, in 55° 58½′ S 67° 17½′ W, to the Cape of Good Hope, in 34° 21′ S 18° 29½′ E, given that the D.M.P. between the two latitudes is 1868·15 units.

(b) Find also the great circle distance between the two places, and the Initial great circle course to steer from Cape Horn.

# CHAPTER 5

# Astronomy and Navigation

We have so far been concerned with finding position either by 'dead reckoning' or by taking observations of terrestrial objects—the kind of position finding that is practised by the navigators of coastwise vessels that do not venture far from the sight of land.

Needless to say, these are not the only methods of fixing position that are available to the navigator. For when a ship leaves the land behind her, or when an aircraft flies for thousands of miles above the clouds, other methods have to be used.

This chapter, and also the three that follow it, will therefore be devoted to the principles and methods of astronomical navigation. This is the kind of navigation that is practised on board 'deep sea' ships and is also used by air navigators when they are out of range of radio and radar stations.

In order to understand astronomical navigation, however, we must start off with some discussion of elementary astronomy; and here, as elsewhere, it will be as well to start at the beginning.

The ancients believed that the earth was at the centre of the universe, and that all the heavenly bodies revolved round it. This was a very natural belief, because if you or I stand on the earth's surface today, and watch the sun and stars continuously for a long enough period of time, we shall see that these heavenly bodies do indeed *appear* to revolve round the earth from East to West. Also, the sun and planets appear to occupy different positions in the sky at different times of the year, and the moon changes its position in the sky from night to night.

In the year 1543, however, the astronomer Copernicus demonstrated conclusively that the heavenly bodies (except the moon) do *not* revolve round the earth. He showed that, on the contrary, the earth and the other planets revolve in orbits round the sun, which is at the centre of our 'solar system'. Other famous men such as Kepler, Galileo, Tycho Brahe and Newton made further discoveries which augmented the findings of Copernicus. Today, therefore, we know a great deal about the real motion of the earth and its associated bodies, and the main features of this motion are as follows.

The earth spins on its axis once in approximately 24 hours, the direction of spin being from West to East. It also rolls along its orbit round the sun, and completes a circuit of the orbit in a year.

The earth's Equator is inclined to the plane of the orbit at an angle of $23\frac{1}{2}°$. The orbit is not a true circle but an ellipse, with the sun situated at one of the two focii of the ellipse; because of these last two facts, the speed of the earth in its orbit varies slightly from day to day.

The moon revolves round the earth in the same direction as the earth's direction of spin, and takes a month to complete one circuit of the earth.

The planets, of which the earth is one, all revolve round the sun at varying speeds and at different distances from the sun. Venus and Mercury are in orbits that are nearer to the sun than the earth's orbit; all the other planets are farther from the sun than the earth.

The sun is a star, and is relatively small as stars go. Apart from the sun, the nearest star to the earth is so far away that its light takes $4\frac{1}{2}$ years to reach us, travelling at a speed of 186 000 statute miles (300 000 km) per second. Other stars besides the sun *may* have planets, but we do not know if this is so, because if such planets are there, they are far too distant to be seen by our most powerful telescopes.

The above, then, is a brief summary of what we know

about the *real* motion of the heavenly bodies. But the navigator wishes to observe these bodies with his sextant, and therefore he is more interested in how the bodies *appear* to move than in how they actually move. In other words, astronomical navigation deals more with the

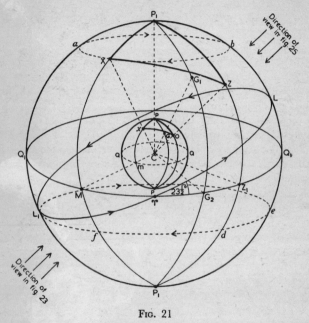

FIG. 21

*apparent motion* of heavenly bodies than with their real motion.

But a knowledge of the real motion helps us to understand the apparent motion, as we shall see when we come to explain the following astronomical terms, which are illustrated in Fig. 21.

Note that this figure is deliberately drawn out of perspective in order to show important features more clearly. It is, perhaps, unfortunate, that so many definitions have to be given all together; but if the reader does not master them all at once, he can always turn back and refresh his memory as he goes on.

*The Celestial Sphere* is considered to be a huge hollow sphere with the earth at its centre. To an observer on the earth, the heavenly bodies (the sun, moon, stars and planets) all appear to be situated on the inside surface of the sphere.

*The Equinoctial* ($Q_1Q_1$ in Fig. 21) is a great circle in the celestial sphere in the same plane as the earth's Equator ($QQ$). You may prefer to think of the equinoctial as 'a projection of the earth's Equator on to the inside surface of the celestial sphere'.

*The Celestial Poles* ($P_1P_1$ in Fig. 21) are points in the celestial sphere immediately above the Poles of the earth ($PP$). You may prefer to think of them as 'projections of the earth's Poles on to the inside surface of the celestial sphere'.

*A Celestial Meridian* ($P_1G_1P_1$ in Fig. 21) is a semi-great circle in the celestial sphere joining the celestial poles. $G$, which represents Greenwich on the earth, is on the terrestrial meridian of Greenwich *PGP*. $P_1G_1P_1$ is the corresponding celestial meridian, and $G_1$ is the celestial position of Greenwich. Note that $G_1$ is directly above $G$, so that a straight line can be drawn from $G_1$ through $G$ to $C$, the centre of the earth.

*The Ecliptic* ($LL_1$ in Fig. 21) is a great circle in the celestial sphere inclined to the Equinoctial at an angle of $23\frac{1}{2}°$. It is the path which the sun *appears* to follow as it makes its apparent annual journey round the earth. It will be noted that this path crosses the Equinoctial from South to North at ♈. This symbol is supposed to look like a pair of ram's horns, and it represents the position of 'The First Point of Aries'. Early astronomy was closely related to astrology, and Aries, the Ram, is one of the 'Signs of the Zodiac'. The sun enters Aries in March, and is actually at ♈ on 21st March.

All this really means is that the earth is tilted in its orbit in such a way that, on 21st March, the Equator is directly underneath the sun. But in terms of apparent motion, it means that, on 21st March, the sun is on the Equinoctial, and after that date it appears to move slowly northwards. By 21st June it has reached $L$, and it then has maximum northerly 'declination'. It then appears to start moving southwards, crosses the Equinoctial from North to South on 23rd September, and reaches its maximum southerly 'declination' on 22nd December, at $L_1$. It then starts to move northwards again.

*The Declination of a Heavenly Body* is the arc of a celestial meridian intercepted between the Equinoctial and the body, and measured in degrees and minutes North or South of the Equinoctial. Thus, when the sun is at $L$, its declination is the arc $Q_1L$ ($23\frac{1}{2}°$ N). When the sun is at $\Upsilon$, its declination is zero. When the sun is at $L_1$, its declination is the arc $Q_1L_1$ ($23\frac{1}{2}°$ S). Similarly, the declination of star $X$, on the celestial meridian $P_1PX_1$, is the arc $MX$ (about 60° N).

*Parallel of Declination* (the dotted circle $Xab$ in Fig. 21) is a small circle in the celestial sphere, parallel to the Equinoctial, and it is the path which a heavenly body appears to describe during the course of a day. Because the earth spins on its axis from West to East once in approximately 24 hours, the star $X$ appears to describe the circle $Xab$, from East to West, in approximately 24 hours, and the declination of the star at any point on its path remains constant. The declinations of the sun, moon and planets change gradually from hour to hour, because they are so relatively close to the earth. We nevertheless speak of a 'parallel of declination' of sun, moon or planet, although the apparent path of such a body is not really parallel to the Equinoctial. Thus, $L_1fde$ is the parallel of declination of the sun on 22nd December, when the sun's declination is $23\frac{1}{2}°$ S, i.e. the arc of any celestial meridian from the Equinoctial to this parallel of declination is $23\frac{1}{2}°$ approximately.

*The Observer's Zenith* is the point in the celestial sphere immediately above the observer's head. One might say that it is the observer's celestial position. The observer is shown in Fig. 21 at $O$, in East longitude on the earth, on the terrestrial meridian $POP$. A line drawn vertically upwards from $O$ strikes the inside of the celestial sphere at $Z$, which is the observer's zenith, on the celestial meridian $P_1ZP_1$.

*The Sub-stellar Point (or Geographical Position) of a Heavenly Body* is the point on the earth's surface immediately below a heavenly body. Thus, in the case of the star $X$, a line drawn from $X$ to the centre of the earth at $C$ passes through the earth's surface at point $x$ on the terrestrial meridian $PxmP$. It should be noted that the latitude of the sub-stellar point of the star $X$ is the arc $mx$ on the earth. This arc subtends the same angle at the centre of the earth as the arc $MX$ in the celestial sphere. Thus it follows that the latitude of the sub-stellar point of a heavenly body has the same value in degrees and minutes as the declination of the body in the celestial sphere.

*The Zenith Distance of a Heavenly Body* is the arc of a great circle in the celestial sphere intercepted between the observer's zenith and the given heavenly body. In Fig. 21, $ZX$ is the zenith distance of the star $X$. It should be noted that this arc subtends the same angle at the centre of the earth as the arc $ox$ on the surface of the earth. A very important principle follows from this fact.

Since 1 minute of arc, measured along a great circle on the earth, equals 1 nautical mile, the zenith distance of a heavenly body, in minutes of arc, is equal to the distance, in nautical miles, between the observer and the sub-stellar point of the body.

*Hour Angle* is a generic term used to describe arcs of the Equinoctial in the celestial sphere, measured in an easterly or westerly direction. Most hour angles are measured in a westerly direction, as follows:

The Sidereal Hour Angle of a Star (S.H.A.*) is the arc of the Equinoctial intercepted between the celestial meridian of Aries and that of the given star. It is measured westwards from Aries from 0° to 360°. ♈ M is the S.H.A. of the star X in Fig. 21, and is approximately equal to 45°. Since the star is so far away, its sidereal hour angle, like that of all stars, is almost constant, and only changes slightly from year to year.

The Greenwich Hour Angle of Aries (G.H.A. ♈) is the arc of the Equinoctial intercepted between the celestial meridian of Greenwich and that of Aries. It is measured westward from Greenwich from 0° to 360°. $G_2$♈ is the G.H.A. ♈ in Fig. 21. Note that, because the earth is spinning on its axis from West to East, the G.H.A. ♈ is changing all the time. At the instant shown in the figure its value is about 30°. An hour later it will have increased to about 45°, because of the movement of Greenwich to the eastwards.

The Greenwich Hour Angle of a Heavenly Body (G.H.A. Star, Sun, Moon or Planet) is the arc of the Equinoctial intercepted between the celestial meridian of Greenwich and that of the given heavenly body. It is measured westward from Greenwich from 0° to 360°. $G_2M$ is the G.H.A. of the star X in Fig. 21. As will be seen from the figure, for a star, such as X:

$$\text{G.H.A.*} = \text{G.H.A.} ♈ + \text{S.H.A.*}$$

and, since the value of G.H.A. ♈ is constantly changing as the earth spins on its axis, so also does the value of G.H.A.* change at the same rate. In the case of the sun, when it is at $L_1$, its G.H.A. is thus $G_2Q_1$.

The Local Hour Angle of a Heavenly Body (L.H.A. Star, Sun, Moon or Planet) is the arc of the Equinoctial intercepted between the celestial meridian of the observer and that of the given heavenly body. It is usually measured westward from the observer from 0° to 360°. $Z_1 M$ is the L.H.A. of the star $X$ in Fig. 21. As will be seen from the figure, where the arc $G_2 Z_1$ is the East longitude of the observer:

$$L.H.A.* = G.H.A.* + E \text{ long. of observer.}$$

If the observer were in West longitude, then:

$$L.H.A.* = G.H.A.* - W \text{ long. of observer,}$$

and similarly for other heavenly bodies.

The above are the basic definitions of astronomical navigation, and they should be thoroughly understood before proceeding further.

## The Nautical and Air Almanacs

The Nautical Almanac is published annually and the Air Almanac at four-monthly intervals, in advance, by Her Majesty's Stationery Office in Britain; and similar almanacs are published by the corresponding State publishers in other countries. They are indispensable to the astronomical navigator, because in them is tabulated everything that he needs to know about the positions of all the heavenly bodies used in navigation.

By consulting the Nautical or Air Almanac for the current period, the navigator can obtain the following information, and much else besides:

(a) The declinations of sun, moon, stars and planets for every minute of every hour of Greenwich Mean Time on every day of the period covered by the almanac.

(b) The G.H.A.♈ for every second of G.M.T. throughout the period.

(c) The S.H.A. of every star used in navigation.

(d) The G.H.A. of the sun, moon and principal planets for every second of G.M.T. throughout the period.

Some of the other information contained in these almanacs will be referred to, as required, later in this book. The almanacs are simple to use, because they contain a full explanation of their contents, and worked examples are given. The interested reader will perhaps obtain a copy of one of these almanacs, so that he can study it for himself. But so far as this book is concerned, all the data that is required from the Nautical or Air Almanacs will be given when it is needed.

# CHAPTER 6

# The Sextant

This chapter deals with the sextant, which is the principal instrument of astronomical navigation, since it can be used to measure angles in the vertical plane as well as those in the horizontal plane.

It is called a 'sextant' because its arc, on which the observed angle is read, is the sixth part of a circle. One of its most recent ancestors was a quadrant, with an arc equal to a quarter of a circle, and another was an octant, with an arc of only 45 degrees.

In earlier times, an astrolabe was used to measure angles in the vertical plane; and it is interesting to note that, in the year 1391, the poet Chaucer, who was far from being a specialist in his own particular field, wrote a treatise on the astrolabe for the edification of his 'litel sonne Lewis'.

The modern sextant, however, is the instrument with which we are chiefly concerned; and whether it is a 'marine' sextant, as used at sea, or a 'bubble' sextant, as used in the air, its construction is based on two simple optical principles. These are as follows:

(1) When a ray of light is reflected at the surface of a plane mirror, the angle of incidence is equal to the angle of reflection.

(2) When a ray of light suffers two reflections at the surfaces of two plane mirrors in succession, the angle between the first ray and the last reflection is double the angle of the inclination of the mirrors.

Fig. 22 shows how these two optical principles are applied to the construction of the marine sextant.

*VW* is the arc of the sextant, which forms the lower part of a rigid frame that is not shown in the diagram. *I* is the index glass, or index mirror, which is pivoted into the frame at *L*, and is attached to the index arm, *LB*. The lower end of this arm moves along the arc, *L* being the centre of curvature of the arc.

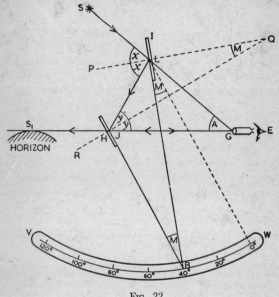

Fig. 22

*H* is the horizon glass, which is also fixed to the frame, and which is half mirror and half plain glass (in two vertical sections, as viewed through the telescope). The observer, with his eye at *E*, can see the horizon through the plain glass part of the horizon glass.

*S* is a star of which the observer wishes to measure the altitude. This altitude, known as the 'sextant altitude', is the angle $S\hat{A}S_1$. It approximates closely to that which geometry books call the 'angle of elevation' of the star.

Let us now consider what happens to the ray of light from the star:

It strikes the index glass at $L$, and is reflected, as shown, to the horizon glass. It strikes the mirror portion of the horizon glass at $J$, and is reflected towards the observer's eye in the direction $JG$. But the observer, looking through the eyepiece of his telescope, sees two things simultaneously. He sees the horizon through the plain part of the horizon glass, and he also sees the reflected image of the star, which appears to be at $S_1$.

He adjusts the arm of the sextant until the reflection of the star exactly coincides with the horizon, and he then reads his sextant; i.e. he determines, by means of the micrometer or vernier, with which the sextant is fitted, the exact position of the index arm on the arc of the sextant.

The instrument is so constructed that when the altitude is zero the index glass and index arm are parallel to the horizon glass. When observing an altitude, such as that indicated by angle $A$ in Fig. 22, the index glass and horizon glass are inclined to each other at angle $M$.

Let $PQ$ and $QR$ be lines perpendicular to the two mirrors at $L$ and $J$ respectively. Then, by geometry, angle $P\hat{Q}R$ equals angle $M$. Angle $B\hat{L}o°$ also equals $M$.

Because of the first optical principle given above,

angle $S\hat{L}P$ = angle $P\hat{L}J$; let these equal $x$,
and   angle $L\hat{J}Q$ = angle $Q\hat{J}G$; let these equal $y$.

Now consider the triangle $QJL$, with exterior angle $J\hat{L}P$:

$x = M + y$ (Exterior = Sum of Interior Opposites),
$\therefore M = x - y$ .   .   .   .   .   .   .   (i)

Then consider the triangle $GJL$, with the exterior angle $J\hat{L}S$:

$2x = A + 2y$ (Exterior = Sum of Interior Opposites),
$\therefore A = 2x - 2y$ .   .   .   .   .   .   (ii)

From equations (i) and (ii), therefore, it follows that $A = 2M$.

This demonstrates the second optical principle on which the sextant is constructed. It also shows that when a given altitude, such as angle $A$, is observed, the distance the index arm moves along the arc is equal to angle $M$, and this is only half the altitude. For this reason, although the arc of a sextant is only about 60° in length, it can measure angles up to 120°. Most modern sextants have slightly longer arcs and can measure angles up to about 130°.

The bubble sextant, used in air navigation, is constructed on exactly the same basic principle as the marine sextant, but the application of the principle is different. Instead of viewing the horizon through the horizon glass (because, at great altitudes, and at night, the horizon cannot be seen) a bubble, just like the bubble in a spirit-level, is used to determine the horizontal plane. The altitude of the body observed is measured relative to this horizontal plane. Because the bubble dances about a great deal in a fast-moving aircraft, the bubble sextant is fitted with a device which automatically averages a large number of observations, taken over a period of one or two minutes. Even with this attachment, however, the bubble sextant cannot give results which are as accurate as those obtained by the marine sextant, which makes use of the natural or visible horizon.

## The Sextant Altitude and its Correction

The marine or bubble sextant is used to obtain the Sextant altitude of a heavenly body, and the method of using either of these instruments is best learnt by practical tuition from an experienced observer. Considerable practice is required before good results can be obtained. Under average conditions, experienced navigators, observing simultaneously, will find that their observations agree to within half a minute of arc when using a marine sextant, and to within 2 or 3 minutes of arc when using a bubble sextant. Practical astronomical navigation, therefore, is not an exact science; but under the conditions that it is normally used, it is exact enough. In the absence of anything more accurate, it is quite satisfactory to have a position line at sea which is correct to within half a mile, or a position line in the air which is correct to within 2 or 3 miles of the real position.

Before we can begin to find a position line, however, we must first convert the Sextant altitude into a True altitude; and the first part of this procedure is to apply index error (if any) to the Sextant altitude. Index error is merely an instrumental error, due to the index arm of the sextant not being exactly at zero on the arc when the index glass and horizon glass are parallel to each other. The simplest way to find the value of this error is to set the index arm approximately at zero and then look through the telescope at the horizon, or at any distant horizontal line, such as the ridge of a distant roof, which will serve as an horizon for this particular purpose. Then adjust the tangent screw of the instrument, which moves the index arm very slowly, until the true and reflected horizons appear to be in line. Then note the reading. If this is more than zero, then the reading is 'on the arc', and if it is less than zero, then the reading is 'off the arc'. An 'on the arc' reading means that the index error must be subtracted from all Sextant altitudes, and an 'off the arc' reading means that the index error must be added. In practice, the index error and certain other instrumental errors of the sextant can be removed by turning the appropriate adjustment screws on the instrument, but this operation, like the art of taking observations, must be learnt by actual practice.

When the index error of the sextant has been found, it is applied, plus or minus, to the Sextant altitude, and the result is known as the 'Observed altitude'. It is, in fact, the altitude that would be observed by a sextant that had no index error. It is not surprising if the intelligent layman finds this terminology a little confusing; but a navigator knows what is meant by the terms 'Sextant altitude' and 'Observed altitude', and that is what matters to him.

The Observed altitude is shown in Fig. 23, which also shows the relationship between the Observed altitude and the True altitude that we ultimately require.

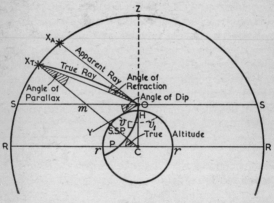

FIG. 23

This figure represents the earth and the celestial sphere from a somewhat different point of view than that of Fig. 21. The reader should imagine that he is looking at Fig. 21 from a position slightly downwards and to the left of the sphere, so that the line joining $C$, $O$ and $Z$ appears to be vertical, as it is shown in Fig. 23.

In this diagram the observer is viewing the earth in the plane of the great circle which joins the observer to the sub-stellar point of the star; and he is viewing the celestial sphere in the plane of the great circle which joins the observer's zenith to the star itself.

## Angle of Dip

The observer, $O$, in Fig. 23, has an 'Height of Eye' ($H$) and the arc of the circle $vv_1$ (shown dotted) is the observer's visible horizon, i.e. his sea horizon. He uses this as a datum for measuring Sextant altitudes with a marine sextant. $OY$ is a line from the observer's eye tangential to the sea horizon. $SOS$ is a horizontal plane through the observer's eye, known technically as the 'Sensible Horizon', and angle $Y\hat{O}S$ is the Angle of Dip of the sea horizon. This is usually called, briefly, 'the Dip', and it can be seen that its value depends on the height of the observer's eye. The navigator on the bridge of a liner, 100 feet (30·48 metres) above sea-level, uses a different angle of dip to that used by the navigator of a yacht, whose eye is, perhaps, only 10 feet (3·05 metres) above sea-level. Nautical Tables give the value of the Dip for different heights of eye, but if you lack tables, you can use the formula:

Angle of dip in minutes = $0.98 \times \sqrt{\text{Ht. of eye in feet.}}$

If the height of eye is given in metres, the formula must be amended to read:

Angle of dip in minutes
$$= 0.98 \times \sqrt{\text{Ht. of eye in metres} \times 3.28.}$$

## The Apparent and Real Position of a Heavenly Body; Atmospheric Refraction

In Fig. 23, $X_T$ is the real position of the star $X$. It will be seen, however, that the line joining $X_T$ to the observer at $O$ is bent near to $O$. This is due to effect of atmospheric refraction, whereby a ray of light, as it passes through layers of atmosphere of different densities, becomes bent, or 'refracted', in the manner shown. The observer, how-ever, can only see the ray of light in the direction in which it is travelling when it strikes his eye, and he therefore sees it in a direction which is tangential to the line $OX_T$ at $O$. This has the effect of making the observer see the star at $X_A$, which is called the 'apparent' position of the star, instead of seeing it at $X_T$, where the star is really situated. The angle $X_A\hat{O}X_T$ is called the Angle of Atmospheric Refraction, or, briefly, 'the refraction'.

## The Observed Altitude and the True Altitude

The above considerations, therefore, should make it clear that, in Fig. 23, the Observed altitude is the angle $X_A\hat{O}Y$.

In Fig. 23, $RR$ is called the 'Celestial' or 'Rational' horizon, and it is defined as 'a great circle in the celestial sphere, the plane of which passes through the centre of the earth, and which is parallel to the observer's sensible horizon'. If one views the celestial sphere downwards, from a point above $Z$, $RR$ appears to be a circle, with $Z$ in the middle, just as the sea horizon on the earth is a circle with the observer in the middle.

The True altitude of a heavenly body is defined as follows:

'The True altitude of a body is the arc of the great circle, passing through the observer's zenith and perpendicular to the horizon, which is intercepted between the horizon and the body.'

In Fig. 23 it is the arc $RX_T$, or the corresponding angle $X_T\hat{C}R$ at the centre of the earth. It is also the arc $r$ — S.S.P. on the surface of the earth.

## Astronomical Parallax

In order to convert the Observed altitude of a star into True altitude, therefore, we must apply Dip and Refraction first of all. That is to say, from the Observed altitude

$X_A\hat{O}Y$ we subtract Dip (angle $Y\hat{O}S$) and Refraction (angle $X_A O X_T$). This leaves us with angle $X_T\hat{O}S$.

But we have said that the True altitude is angle $X_T\hat{C}R$. What, then, must we do to convert angle $X_T\hat{O}S$ into angle $X_T\hat{C}R$?

The answer is that, in the case of a star, we must do nothing. This is because stars are so far away that the radius of the earth is, relatively speaking, an infinitesimal quantity, and the directions $X_T O$ and $X_T C$ are parallel to each other. In other words, the angle of astronomical parallax $O\hat{X}_T C$, shown in Fig. 23, is nil for a star, and therefore angle $X_T\hat{O}S$ equals angle $X_T\hat{C}R$.

When observing the moon, which is relatively close to the earth, the angle of parallax is appreciable (it can be about 1° at low altitudes, decreasing to zero at altitude 90°) and it must therefore be applied.

By geometry, angle $X_T\hat{m}S$ = angle $X_T\hat{C}R$ = True latitude.

But angle $X_T\hat{m}S$ = angle $X_T\hat{O}S$ + angle $O\hat{X}_T C$ (Exterior Angle = sum of Interior Opposites).

Therefore, astronomical parallax, when it is applicable, must be added. As we have seen, it is negligible for stars. For the moon it is considerable, and must always be applied. For the sun and the planets it is small, but should be applied when great accuracy is required.

## Semi-diameter

When observing the sun or the moon, greater accuracy can be obtained with the marine sextant if the reflected image of the object's 'lower limb' or 'upper limb' is brought into contact with the horizon. Fig. 24 shows what the observer sees through his sextant telescope and horizon glass in each case.

It is the altitude of the sun or moon's *centre* that is required. A little thought, therefore, should make it clear that when the lower limb is observed, the semi-diameter (or radius) of the body in minutes of arc, as viewed from the earth, must be added. When the upper limb is observed, the semi-diameter must be subtracted.

The value of the semi-diameter of both the sun and the moon, for each day of the year, is found in the Nautical Almanac. Like the value of parallax of the sun, moon and planets, the value of the semi-diameter of the sun and

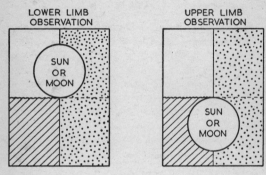

FIG. 24

moon changes each day, on account of the varying distance of the bodies from the earth.

## Summary of Corrections

Summarizing, therefore, the navigator, using a marine sextant, starts with a Sextant altitude of a heavenly body. He applies index error, if any, and obtains the Observed altitude. If the body is a star, he must then subtract Dip and Refraction to obtain the True altitude. If the body is moon, sun or planet, he must add Parallax, in addition to subtracting Dip and Refraction. And if, with a marine sextant, he observes the lower or upper limb of the sun or moon, he must add or subtract the semi-diameter of the body. If he is using a bubble sextant, he applies all the above corrections except Dip and semi-diameter, since the bubble sextant measures altitudes relative to the sensible horizon ($SOS$ in Fig. 23), and the centre of the sun or moon is brought into coincidence with the bubble.

All the above corrections can be obtained, with little difficulty, from a set of nautical tables, but when they are required in this book they will be given. Most nautical tables, and also the Nautical Almanac, contain a table of 'Total Corrections' in which all the above corrections are combined together into one or two larger corrections. This, of course, makes the work of correcting an Observed altitude much quicker; but the beginner is advised to use the individual corrections, so that he will understand better what he is about.

## True Altitude and Zenith Distance

Why have we gone to all this bother to obtain the True altitude?

If we now refer back to Fig. 23, it will be seen that the True altitude is the angle $X_T\hat{C}R$, and it is also the corresponding arc $RX_T$ in the celestial sphere.

But arc $RX_T$ + arc $ZX_T = 90°$, and arc $ZX_T$, by definition, is the zenith distance of the star $X$ from the observer's zenith $Z$. But we have explained already, in Chapter 5, that the zenith distance of a heavenly body, in minutes of arc, is equal to the distance, in nautical miles, between the observer and the sub-stellar point of the body. Therefore, if we subtract the True altitude from 90°, we obtain the True zenith distance, and that gives us the distance from $O$ to S.S.P. in Fig. 23. The reader will notice that this is the same angular measurement as the arc $X_T$ to $Z$, since it subtends the same angle at the centre of the earth.

When an observer uses his sextant, therefore, to obtain the altitude of a heavenly body, he first corrects it, and thus obtains the True altitude. He subtracts this from 90° and this gives him the True zenith distance, which is the distance, measured in degrees and minutes, from his own position on the earth to the position of the sub-stellar point of the body that he has observed.

## The Position Circle and Position Line

If one had a model of the earth and a pair of compasses, one could place one leg of the compasses on S.S.P. in Fig. 23 and describe the circle PLO of radius O − S.S.P. But O, the observer, is on this circle. Therefore, we say that PLO is a 'position circle' somewhere on which the observer is situated.

The True zenith distance, obtained with the sextant, gives us the radius of this circle. And if we know the geographical position (or sub-stellar point) of the body that has been observed, at the instant of observation, we can find out how to draw the position circle. When the zenith distance is small, we can, in fact, draw the circle on our chart. But the zenith distance is usually too great for this method to be practicable, so we use a method whereby we can draw on our chart that part of the position circle that passes through the observer's position. This portion of the position circle is known as the observer's 'position line', and, since any point on the circumference of a circle is at right angles to its radius, it follows that the observer's position line is always at right angles to the bearing (or 'Azimuth', as it is sometimes called) of the body observed. In Fig. 23, the line PLO, at O, is at right angles to the line O − S.S.P.

The application of these principles to the various methods of astronomical position finding will be explained in the next two chapters.

## EXAMPLES FOR EXERCISE

### Exercise 19

Find the True altitude corresponding to each of the following Sextant altitudes observed with a marine sextant:

| | Body Observed and Sextant Altitude | Index Error | Dip. | Refraction | Palx. | S. Dmtr. |
|---|---|---|---|---|---|---|
| 1 | Star 31° 40′ | +1·2′ | 5·4′ | 1·6′ | — | — |
| 2 | Star 62° 08·2′ | +2·2′ | 4·8′ | 0·5′ | — | — |
| 3 | Sun (L.L.) 67° 56·3′ | −1·7′ | 5·8′ | 0·4′ | 0·05 | 16·2′ |
| 4 | Sun (U.L.) 74° 28·85′ | +3·0′ | 5·35′ | 0·3′ | 0·05′ | 16·3′ |
| 5 | Moon (L.L.) 58° 17·5′ | +1·4′ | 5·35′ | 0·6′ | 28·5′ | 15·1′ |
| 6 | Planet 50° 32·5′ | +2·35′ | 6·2′ | 0·8′ | — | — |

# CHAPTER 7

# Finding the Latitude

The simplest problem in astronomical navigation is to find the parallel of latitude on which the observer is situated; i.e. to find the observer's latitude.

But although the actual working of the problem is simple enough, its understanding requires a little thought.

The reader must first imagine that he is looking down on the celestial sphere in such a way that the observer's zenith is directly below him and that the observer's celestial meridian runs North and South through the zenith. If you turn back to Fig. 21 and imagine that you are looking down from a point on $COZ$ produced, you will have the right idea. Fig. 25 illustrates what the celestial sphere looks like when viewed from this angle. It should be noted that, unlike the diagram in Fig. 21, this diagram and those which follow it are drawn in perspective, so far as it is possible to do so.

It should be observed, first of all, that, since $Z$ is in the centre of the diagram, the circumference of the circle represents the observer's celestial or rational horizon. In order to appreciate this a little better, you should turn to Fig. 23 and imagine that you are looking down on that figure from a point above $Z$. The rational horizon ($RR$) would then appear as a circle round $Z$, as it does in Fig. 25. Always remember that these diagrams represent spheres, so that $Z$ is raised above the level of the rational horizon, the plane of which passes through the centre of the earth. The earth is not shown here, because it is unnecessary to do so.

$NZS$ in Fig. 25 is the observer's celestial meridian, so that $N$ is the northern point of the celestial horizon and $S$

is the southern point. *WZE* is known as the 'Prime Vertical' and is a great circle in the celestial sphere which passes through the observer's zenith and also through the East and West points of the horizon. Its principal function in Fig. 25 is to determine these East and West points of the celestial horizon.

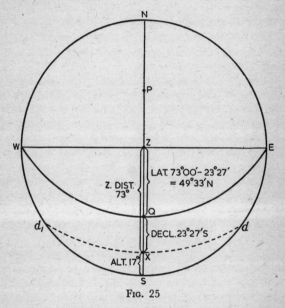

FIG. 25

Let us now suppose that a navigator, wishing to find his latitude, observes the sun at noon on 23rd December. He observes it at noon, because the sun then bears due South if the observer is North of the sun, and due North if the observer is South of the sun. It follows, therefore, as explained at the end of the last chapter, that the observer's line of position will lie in an East-West direction, i.e. it will be a parallel of latitude.

Let us suppose that the sun bears due South in this case, and that its Sextant altitude, when corrected, gives a True altitude of 17° 00'. If the True altitude is 17° 00', then the zenith distance must be 73° 00', since altitude and zenith distance are complementary.

This information enables us to mark the position of the sun in Fig. 25. For if the sun were on the meridian, bearing South, at an altitude of 0° 00', it would be at $S$, and its zenith distance would be 90° 00'. But $ZS$ is an arc of 90° 00' in the celestial sphere. Therefore, a body with an altitude of 45° 00' would be halfway between $S$ and $Z$, and one with an altitude of 90° 00' would be at $Z$, and its zenith distance would be nil.

The sun that we have observed, however, has an altitude of 17° 00' and a zenith distance of 73° 00', so we place it at $X$, 17° 00' from $S$ and 73° 00' from $Z$. When you are drawing your figure, it is advisable to make the radius of the circle ($ZS$) equal to 90 units, to some suitable scale that will fit the paper, and then it is easy to mark in points such as $X$ with reasonable accuracy.

But the sun has been observed on 23rd December, and if we consult the Nautical Almanac we shall find that on that date the sun's declination is 23° 27' S, i.e. its parallel of declination is 23° 27' South of the Equinoctial. There- fore, as it rises in the East and sets in the West, it appears to cross the observer's meridian at a point 23° 27' South of the Equinoctial. This means, of course, that when the sun is on the observer's meridian its sub-solar point is 23° 27' South of the Equator. In other words, the sun rises above the celestial horizon at $d$ in Fig. 25 and follows the apparent path or parallel of declination $dXd_1$, being on the meridian at $X$ and setting at $d_1$. It is observed at $X$.

But we know that $X$ is 23° 27' South of the Equinoctial, and this enables us to plot the point $Q$, 23° 27' North of $X$, in Fig. 25. Then join $WQE$ to represent the Equinoctial, and if you have a sphere or globe available, satisfy your- self that the Equinoctial will, in fact, appear as it does in Fig. 25, when it is viewed from a point above $Z$. In this type of diagram, which is drawn to represent the celestial sphere in the plane of the observer's rational horizon, the Equinoctial always passes through the East and West points, as well as through $Q$.

You have now found the observer's latitude. Latitude, by definition, is the arc of the meridian intercepted between the Equator and the observer. It is, therefore, the arc of the celestial meridian intercepted between the Equinoctial and the observer's zenith. This is the arc $QZ$ in Fig. 25, and it is not difficult to see that the arc $QZ$ is equal to $73°\ 00' - 23°\ 27' = 49°\ 33'$. And the latitude is North, because $Z$ is North of the Equinoctial, so the observer on the earth must be North of the Equator by the same number of degrees and minutes.

To complete the diagram you should insert $P$, the Celestial Pole, which is $90°$ away from the Equinoctial. If $QZ$ is the latitude, then $PZ$ is the co-latitude or $(90° -$ latitude$)$. $PX$ is the Polar distance, i.e. the angular distance of the body observed from the Celestial Pole, and in this case it is $(90° +$ declination $= 113°\ 27'$, because the latitude is North and the declination is South. When the latitude and declination are both North or both South, then the Polar distance $= (90° -$ declination$)$.

The above method of finding the latitude dates from very early times, because, in practice, it has always been easy to know when the sun or other heavenly body was on the meridian. A glance at Fig. 25 will show you that, when the sun is on the meridian, its altitude is greatest, i.e. it is at its highest point above the horizon. All the early navigator had to do, therefore, was to watch the sun through the eyepiece of his astrolabe, as the modern navigator now watches it through the telescope of his sextant, until it reached its maximum altitude, and he then knew that it was on the meridian. It should be noted that this is not strictly correct if the observer is travelling at high speed, as in a very fast ship or in an aircraft; under these circumstances, a suitable correction must be

applied to convert the maximum altitude to the meridian
altitude. But for a stationary observer, or for the navigator of a surface vessel steaming at anything less than
about 30 knots, no correction is necessary.

The beginner who wishes to understand the principles
of navigation should draw a diagram like the one in Fig.
25 and use simple reasoning, on the lines indicated above,
to find the latitude. It must be noted that, if the observer
is in South latitude, $Q$ will be North of $Z$ and $P$ will be
South of $Z$, but the Equinoctial will still pass through
$WQE$.

For those who prefer to follow a set pattern of work,
however, the following 'drill' gives the steps to be taken
in finding the latitude:

(1) Observe the heavenly body concerned with a sextant when it attains its maximum altitude, and note
if it bears North or South.

(2) Correct this Observed meridian altitude and thus
obtain the True meridian altitude of the body.

(3) Subtract the True meridian altitude from 90° 00'.
This gives the meridian zenith distance, which must be
named opposite to the altitude. Thus, if the altitude is
obtained with the body bearing South, then the zenith
distance must be named North, and vice versa.

(4) Extract the declination of the body from the
Nautical or Air Almanac using the date and G.M.T.
of observation. Full details of this process are given in
the explanatory parts of the almanacs, together with
worked examples. You will understand these much
better if you remember that the declinations of sun,
moon and planets are changing all the time, because of
their proximity to the earth, whilst the declinations of
stars are almost constant in any one year.

(5) Apply the declination to the zenith distance, using
the rules:

(a) Like names, add and name the same.

(b) Unlike names, subtract lesser from greater and name according to the greater.

The above example, worked according to this 'drill', appears as follows:

| | | |
|---|---|---|
| True altitude | = | 17° 00' South |
| | | 90° 00' |
| Zenith distance | = | 73° 00' North |
| Declination | = | 23° 27' South |
| Latitude | = | 49° 33' North |

If the reader gives the matter a little thought, he will appreciate that this 'drill' is derived from the basic reasoning that was employed in the first instance to find the latitude, as illustrated in Fig. 25.

## Latitude by Pole Star

Fig. 26 is similar to Fig. 25 insofar as it shows the celestial sphere in the plane of the observer's rational horizon, for an observer in North latitude. The Celestial Pole, $P$, is also shown.

Now let us suppose that there is a star situated exactly at $P$. Then it will be agreed that the arc $NP$ is the True altitude of the star when it is on the observer's meridian bearing North. $PZ$ will be the star's zenith distance, since $NP + PZ = 90°\ 00'$. But $QZ$ is the observer's latitude, and $QZ + PZ = 90°\ 00'$, since it is 90° 00' of arc along any meridian from Equinoctial to Pole. From the above equations, therefore, we see that $NP = QZ$. In other words, the True altitude of the Celestial Pole is equal to the observer's latitude.

If there were a star exactly at the Pole, therefore, it would only be necessary to observe its altitude at any time, apply the usual corrections to obtain True altitude, and the result would be the observer's latitude.

Now, there is no star or other heavenly body *exactly* at either Pole of the heavens; but in the northern hemisphere there is a star, called 'Polaris' or the 'Pole Star', which has a declination of about 89° 00′ North. Its

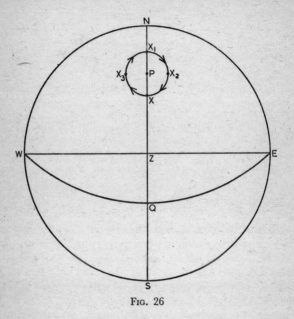

Fig. 26

parallel of declination is shown in Fig. 26 as the small dotted circle round *P*. It follows that the Polar distance of this star is 1° 00′ (90° 00′ − declination).

It will be appreciated that, as the earth spins on its axis, the Pole Star will appear to move along its parallel of declination in the direction shown, i.e. the star will appear to make a complete circuit of the Pole once in approximately 24 hours. If the star is observed at *X*, we say that it is on the meridian 'above the Pole', because its altitude is then greater than the altitude of the Pole. Its altitude is then $NX$, but if we subtract $PX$, the Polar distance, which is $1°\ 00'$, we shall obtain $NP$, the True altitude of the Pole, which is also the observer's latitude. The star will then bear due North, and it will be at its maximum altitude.

If, however, the Pole Star is observed when it is at $X_1$, we say that it is on the observer's meridian 'below the Pole', because its altitude is less than that of the Pole. Its True altitude is then $NX_1$, but if we now add $PX$, the Polar distance, which is $1°\ 00'$, we shall again obtain $NP$, the True altitude of the Pole, which is also the observer's latitude. The star will again bear due North, but it will now be at its minimum altitude.

From the above reasoning, therefore, it can be seen that there are two occasions during each period of approximately 24 hours when the Pole Star can be observed in the Northern Hemisphere bearing due North; and the latitude of the observer can then be obtained by applying a correction of $1°\ 00'$ to the star's True altitude.

The early navigators, who found their way across the great oceans, knew all about this method of obtaining the latitude, and they could also tell approximately when the Pole Star was on the meridian by the relative positions of other stars near it.

The modern navigator, however, has the advantage of having a Nautical or Air Almanac at his disposal. This enables him to observe the Pole Star at any time that is convenient, since, by consulting a table in the Almanac, called the 'Pole Star' Table, he can find the correction to apply to the True altitude that will give him his latitude. He can, for example, observe the Pole Star when it is at $X_2$ or $X_3$ in Fig. 26. The correction will then be small, and the star will bear slightly East, or slightly West of North. A subsidiary table in the Almanac gives the True bearing of the Pole Star, and this is never more than about $3°\ 00'$ to the East or West of the meridian. By taking a Compass

bearing of the Pole Star, a navigator can use this subsidiary table to find its True bearing, and thus check the
error of his compass, if he wishes to do so.

It should be appreciated that, if the Pole Star is
observed at $X_2$, when it bears, say, 003° True, then the
observer's line of position, instead of being a parallel of
latitude in an East-West direction, will be a line which
lies in the direction 093°-273°, at right angles to the True
bearing of the star. For practical purposes, however, it is
usually considered to be accurate enough to regard the
position line as a parallel of latitude.

The Pole Star Table is very easy to use, and a worked
example is given in the Nautical Almanac. The reader
will realize, of course, that the correction to apply
depends on the position of the star on the small circle in
Fig. 26. It depends, in fact, on the star's 'Hour Angle',
and in the Almanac it is found convenient to tabulate the
correction against the value of the Local Hour Angle of
Aries. Also, the correction in the Almanac is given in
several different parts, but in the examples in this book
these are combined into one, for simplicity.

Having given sufficient of the theory for the reader to
understand what he is about, let us now summarize the
practical steps to be taken in obtaining a latitude by Pole
Star observation.

(1) Observe the Pole Star at any time that is convenient and note the Greenwich Mean Time of
observation.

(2) Apply the usual corrections to the Sextant altitude
of the star to obtain the True altitude.

(3) Enter the Almanac for the date and G.M.T. of
observation, and extract the G.H.A. ♈. Add the East
longitude, or subtract the West longitude of the
observer to obtain the L.H.A. ♈.

(4) Enter the Pole Star Table with L.H.A. ♈, month
and D.R. latitude of the observer, and extract the

corrections to apply to the True altitude to obtain the observer's latitude. At the same time, the True bearing of the Pole Star can be obtained from the subsidiary table, if it is required, in order to find the error of the compass.

*Example.* On a certain evening the Pole Star was observed to have a Sextant altitude which, when corrected, gave a True altitude of 49° 10′. The date and G.M.T. of observation were noted, and from the Almanac the G.H.A. ♈ was found to be 120° 10′. The observer's longitude was 30° 00′ W. Find the observer's latitude.

From the above information, it follows that the L.H.A. ♈ = 120° 10′ − 30° 00′ = 90° 10′. The observer's D.R. latitude must be near to 49° 10′—a glance at Fig. 26 will show that it cannot be more than 2° different from this.

Now enter the Pole Star Table with the arguments L.H.A. ♈, month and D.R. latitude, and it will be found that the combined correction to apply is −25·9′. The latitude is then found, very simply, as follows:

> True altitude         = 49° 10′
> Combined correction =     −25·9′
>
> Latitude            = 48° 44·1′ N

Needless to say, the latitude is North. If the observer were in the Southern Hemisphere, the Pole Star would always be below the northern horizon.

If, at the same time, it were required to find the True bearing of the Pole Star, the navigator would enter the subsidiary table with the arguments L.H.A. ♈ (90° 10′), and D.R. latitude (49° 10′). This gives the True bearing of the Pole Star as 1·3° to the West of North.

### EXAMPLES FOR EXERCISE

## Exercise 20

(1) An observer takes an observation of the sun when it is on his meridian, and finds that its True altitude is 39° 48·8′, bearing North. Its declination is 15° 29·2′ N. What is the observer's latitude?

(2) An observer takes an observation of the sun when it is on his meridian, and finds that its True altitude is 68° 04·6′, bearing South. Its declination is 12° 25′ S. What is the observer's latitude?

(3) An observer takes an observation of a star when it is on his meridian, and finds that its True altitude is 47° 32·5′, bearing North. Its declination is 31° 59·7′ N. What is the observer's latitude?

(4) An observer takes an observation of the Pole Star and finds its True altitude to be 26° 02·8′. The combined correction from the Pole Star Table is +55·7′. What is the observer's latitude?

(5) An observer takes an observation of the Pole Star when it is on his meridian below the Pole, and he finds that its True altitude is 35° 15·3′. If its declination is 89° 02·3′ N, find the observer's latitude.

# CHAPTER 8

# The Astronomical 'Fix'

There are several methods employed by navigators to find a position line from the observation of a heavenly body that is not on the observer's meridian. In this book it is intended to deal with one of these methods only; but it is the one that is generally considered to be the best available, since its principles can be applied to any observation that is made, even when the body observed is very close to the meridian.

This method is known as the 'Marq St. Hilaire Method', and is named after the Frenchman who invented it. The underlying principle of the method was discovered by Captain Sumner, an American seaman, but the Marq St. Hilaire method of calculation is an improvement on that practised by Sumner.

At the end of Chapter 6, it was explained that if we had a model of the earth we could mark on it the geographical position, or sub-stellar point, of the heavenly body observed and use this point as the centre of a position circle, the radius of which would be the True zenith distance of the body, as obtained by sextant observation.

This was illustrated in Fig. 23, where $PLO$ is part of such a position circle of radius $O-$S.S.P. The arc $O-$S.S.P., on the earth, is the same as the arc $ZX_T$ in the celestial sphere. But on the earth, 1 minute of arc, measured along a great circle, is equal to 1 nautical mile. Therefore, the True zenith distance of a heavenly body, if it is expressed in minutes of arc, gives the distance in nautical miles from the observer to the sub-stellar point of the body. Or, as we have said before, it gives the radius of the position circle on which the observer is situated.

Furthermore, that part of the position circle which passes through the observer is at right angles to the bearing, or azimuth, of the body, since the circumference of a circle is always at right angles to its radius.

Now, as we shall see, the sub-stellar point of any heavenly body can be found for any given second of Greenwich Mean Time, on any given date in the year, by reference to the Nautical or Air Almanac. All ships and aircraft are equipped with chronometers or chronometer watches which are set to G.M.T., and nowadays these are kept accurate by means of constant checking against radio time-signals. Before the days of radio, chronometers were often in error, and this gave rise to inaccuracies in position finding. And before chronometers were invented, latitude could be found accurately enough, as described in the last chapter, but longitude could not be found with any degree of accuracy at all, i.e. it was most difficult to find an accurate position line by observation of a body that was not on the observer's meridian. But today we have accurate chronometers, and any good watch with a second hand can be used as a chronometer, provided that it does not gain or lose more than a few seconds a day, which can be allowed for in the calculation.

The earth spins on its axis once in approximately 24 hours. That is to say, it rotates through 360° in about 24 hours, which is 15° per hour. This means that it rotates through 1° of arc in 4 minutes of time, which is the same as 1 minute of arc in 4 seconds of time.

When we enter the Nautical Almanac, one of the essential elements that we extract, either directly or indirectly, is the Greenwich Hour Angle of the body that we have observed at the given G.M.T. This G.H.A. of the body is the number of degrees, minutes and seconds of arc that the celestial meridian of the body is to the westward of the meridian of Greenwich. It is also the number of degrees, minutes and seconds of arc that the sub-stellar point of the body is to the westward of Greenwich.

From this it follows that if the G.M.T. we use is 4 seconds of time in error, the position of the sub-stellar point that we obtain from the Almanac will be 1 minute of arc in error, which is 1 n. mile, if it is measured along the Equator. Similarly, 4 minutes error in time of observation will mean 1° of arc in error for the position of the sub-stellar point, and this will be an error of 60 n. miles if it is measured along the Equator.

It follows from this that if the position of the sub-stellar point of the observed body is in error, owing to using the incorrect time, then the resulting position line, which is part of the circumference of the circle round the sub-stellar point of the observed body, will be in error by the same amount.

In other words, for every second of time that the chronometer is in error, the observer's position can be as much as a quarter of a mile in error. The moral, therefore, is obvious: Always have accurate G.M.T. on your chronometer, and your position will be accurate too—provided that you don't make any mistakes in your calculations.

Summarizing, therefore, we see that the Greenwich Hour Angle of the body observed, obtained from the Almanac for the accurate G.M.T. of observation, gives the longitude of the sub-stellar point in degrees and minutes West of Greenwich. And, as can be seen by studying Fig. 21, the declination of the body observed, also obtained from the Almanac, gives the latitude of its sub-stellar point.

We can, therefore, by reference to the Nautical or Air Almanac, find the Geographical position of the sub-stellar point of the body that we observe. So, *if* we had a model world constructed accurately enough, we *could* take the True zenith distance, obtained from the sextant observation, in our compasses, and, with sub-stellar point as centre, we *could* describe a circle of position somewhere on which the observer would be situated.

But, needless to say, it is not feasible to have such a model world on board ship, and certainly not on board an aircraft. The sphere would have to be very large indeed, and very accurately constructed, to give the degree of accuracy that is required in position finding. Such a sphere would also be very cumbersome to use. For this reason, the Marq St. Hilaire calculation method is used as a means of obtaining data from which the observer's position line can be drawn on an ordinary navigation chart. And now that some of the basic principles have been explained, this method will not be found difficult to understand.

If the reader now turns back to Fig. 21, he will see that $O$, the observer, is shown as being in North latitude and East longitude, whilst the star $X$ has northern declination and a local hour angle west of the observer's meridian.

He will also see that $P_1 Z X$ is a spherical triangle on the surface of the celestial sphere which is exactly similar to the spherical triangle $POx$ on the surface of the earth. This is because arc $P_1 X$ and arc $Px$ both subtend the same angle at the centre of the earth, and, similarly, arc $P_1 Z$ subtends the same angle as arc $PO$ and arc $ZX$ subtends the same angle as arc $Ox$. That is to say, in angular measurement, $P_1 X = Px$, $P_1 Z = PO$ and $ZX = Ox$.

In the Marq St. Hilaire Method, the observer starts off by observing the altitude of a suitable heavenly body, and he notes the exact G.M.T. of the observation by means of his chronometer or chronometer watch. He converts the Sextant altitude to True altitude, subtracts this from 90° and thus obtains the True zenith distance of the body observed.

He makes a note of this True zenith distance, but he does not use it yet. Before he can use it, there is considerable calculation to be done.

By plotting on the chart, or by Plane or Mercator's Sailing, the Dead Reckoning position must now be determined, because this is used in the calculation which follows.

$O$, in Fig. 21, is the *Dead Reckoning position* of the observer who has observed the altitude of the star $X$. It is not his true position, because this has yet to be found.

The observer, then, works out his D.R. position in latitude and longitude, and then makes use of it as follows: By subtracting the latitude from 90°, he obtains $PO$, the co-latitude of the D.R. position, and this is the same as $P_1Z$ in the celestial sphere. He thus knows the side $P_1Z$ of the spherical triangle $P_1ZX$.

He now enters the Almanac with the date and G.M.T. of observation, and extracts the exact declination of the body observed. In Fig. 21, $MX$ is the declination of the star $X$. By subtracting this from 90°, $P_1X$ is obtained, and this is the Polar distance of the star. The side $P_1X$ of the spherical triangle $P_1ZX$ is now known.

It should be noted that if the star observed has Southerly declination its Polar distance for an observer in North latitude is 90° + declination. Similarly, for an observer in South latitude, the Polar distance of a star which has North declination is also 90° + declination.

The observer then enters the Almanac again, and, with the date and exact G.M.T. of observation, he now extracts (i) the G.H.A. ♈ and (ii) the S.H.A.*. These two, added together, as explained in Chapter 5, give the G.H.A.*. For sun, moon and planet, the G.H.A. is extracted directly from the Almanac for the given G.M.T.

But we know that

$$\text{L.H.A.*} = \text{G.H.A.*} \begin{array}{l} + \text{E. long.} \\ - \text{W. long.} \end{array}$$

The observer knows that his D.R. longitude is, shall we say, so many degrees and minutes East of Greenwich. He therefore adds this East longitude to the G.H.A.* and he now has (see Fig. 21) the arc $Z_1M$ of the Equinoctial, which is of the same value as the corresponding angle $Z\hat{P}_1X$ at the celestial pole, between the meridians of $Z$ and $X$.

Thus, in the spherical triangle $P_1ZX$, the observer now knows the angle $Z\hat{P}_1X$, or, as it is usually called, the angle $P_1$, which is the L.H.A. of the body observed relative to the observer's D.R. position.

Therefore, he now knows the values of two sides and the included angle in the spherical triangle $P_1ZX$, which is known to be similar in all respects to the triangle $POx$ on the earth.

But if two sides and the included angle of a spherical triangle are known, the third side may be calculated by the spherical haversine formula, in exactly the same way as the great circle distance was calculated in Chapter 4. And once the third side of the triangle has been found, the haversine formula can be used, in its other form, to calculate either of the two remaining angles.

In brief, therefore, we can now calculate side $ZX$ of the triangle $P_1ZX$, and, when found, this side is known as the 'Calculated Zenith Distance'. It will be seen from Fig. 21 that, in degrees and minutes of arc, $ZX$ is exactly the same value as the great circle distance from $O$ to $x$ on the earth's surface.

Having found side $ZX$ in the triangle, we can now find angle $P_1\hat{Z}X$, or, to be brief, angle $Z$. This gives us the azimuth or bearing of the star from the observer's zenith, and it can be seen from Fig. 21 that this corresponds to the bearing of $x$ from $O$ on the surface of the earth.

We will now give some values to the generalized terms referred to in Fig. 21.

Let us suppose that the True altitude of the star $X$, obtained from its Sextant altitude, is 50° 44′. This gives True zenith distance 39° 16′. Make a note of this. It will be needed later.

Let us suppose that the observer's D.R. position is 50°

10' N 10° 15' E. This D.R. latitude gives us a co-latitude of 39° 50', i.e. side $P_1Z = 39°\ 50'$.

On entering the Almanac with the date and G.M.T. of observation, let us suppose that we obtain:

(i) Declination of star $X = 60°\ 20'$ N. Therefore, the Polar distance of the star is 29° 40', i.e. side $P_1X = 29°\ 40'$.

(ii) G.H.A. ♈ $= 20°\ 05'$.

(iii) S.H.A.* $= 40°\ 20'$.

From this it follows that G.H.A.* $= 60°\ 25'$.

But the observer's D.R. longitude is 10° 15' E.

Therefore, the L.H.A.* $= 70°\ 40'$ West of the observer, so that angle $P_1 = 70°\ 40'$.

In the spherical triangle $P_1ZX$, therefore, we have angle $P_1 = 70°\ 40'$, side $P_1Z = 39°\ 50'$ and side $P_1X = 29°\ 40'$.

It is first required to find side $ZX$. By the spherical haversine formula, we have:

$$\text{hav } ZX = \text{hav } P_1 . \text{sine } P_1Z . \text{sine } P_1X + \text{hav } (P_1Z \sim P_1X).$$

*To find hav $P_1$ (70° 40') by use of Tables at end of this book:*

$$\text{hav } 70°\ 40' = \frac{1 - \cos 70°\ 40'}{2}$$

$$= \frac{1 - 0\cdot3311}{2} = \frac{0\cdot6689}{2} = 0\cdot334\ 45.$$

*To find hav $P_1Z \sim P_1X$ (10° 10'):*

$$\text{hav } 10°\ 10' = \frac{1 - \cos 10°\ 10'}{2}$$

$$= \frac{1 - 0\cdot9843}{2} = \frac{0\cdot0157}{2} = \underline{0\cdot007\ 85}.$$

Also, from the Tables:

$$\text{sine } P_1Z, \ 39° \ 50' = \underline{0{\cdot}6405}$$

and $\qquad$ $\text{sine } PX, \ 29° \ 40' = \underline{0{\cdot}4949}$

$\therefore$ hav $ZX = 0{\cdot}334\ 45 \times 0{\cdot}6405 \times 0{\cdot}4949 + 0{\cdot}007\ 85,$

$\therefore$ hav $ZX = 0{\cdot}106\ 02 + 0{\cdot}007\ 85,$

$\qquad$ hav $ZX = 0{\cdot}113\ 87.$

But

$\qquad \cos ZX = 1 - 2\ \text{hav } ZX = 1 - 0{\cdot}227\ 74 =$

$0{\cdot}772\ 26$

$\qquad \therefore \ \underline{ZX = 39° \ 26'.}$

It is now required to find angle $Z$. By spherical haversine formula, we have:

$$\text{hav } Z = \frac{\text{hav } P_1X - \text{hav } (P_1Z \sim ZX)}{\text{sine } P_1Z \cdot \text{sine } ZX}.$$

*To find hav $P_1X$ (29° 40′):*

$$\text{hav } 29° \ 40' = \frac{1 - \cos 29° \ 40'}{2}$$

$$= \frac{1 - 0{\cdot}8689}{2} = \frac{0{\cdot}1311}{2} = \underline{0{\cdot}0655.}$$

*To find hav $(P_1Z \sim ZX)$ (0° 24′):*

$$\text{hav } 0° \ 24' = \frac{1 - \cos 0° \ 24'}{2}$$

$$= \frac{1 - 1{\cdot}000}{2} = \frac{0}{2} = \underline{0{\cdot}0000.}$$

Also, from the Tables:

$$\text{sine } P_1Z \ (39° \ 50') = \underline{0{\cdot}6405}$$

and $\qquad$ $\text{sine } ZX \ (39° \ 26') = \underline{0{\cdot}6351}$

$\therefore$ hav $Z = \dfrac{0{\cdot}0655 - 0{\cdot}0000}{0{\cdot}6405 \times 0{\cdot}6351} = \dfrac{\underline{0{\cdot}0655}}{0{\cdot}406\ 78} = 0{\cdot}16102.$

But
$$\cos Z = 1 - 2 \text{ hav } Z = 1 - 0 \cdot 322\,04 = 0 \cdot 677\,96$$
$$\therefore \text{ Angle } Z = 47° \, 19'.$$

We have now found the *Calculated* zenith distance of the heavenly body from the zenith of the observer's D.R. position, and also the azimuth or bearing of the body from the same D.R. position.

Needless to say, professional navigators can, and do, make the above calculation much easier by the use of Nautical Tables, which contain the natural and logarithmic values of the haversines, etc. But their results, although obtained more quickly, will be the same as ours, if we take into account the degree of accuracy that is obtainable with the four-figure tables that we have used.

Many navigators use various 'Short Tables' that can be purchased and give very rapid solutions of the $P_1ZX$ triangle. These Tables will be referred to again later; but it must be emphasized here that, whatever methods or tables are used to do the job, the $P_1ZX$ triangle *must* be solved, so as to obtain the Calculated zenith distance and azimuth, before it is possible to proceed further with the finding of a position line.

You should now refer to Fig. 27. *abcd* represents a chart of that part of the world in which the observer is situated. *O* on the chart is the observer's D.R. position; *x* is the sub-stellar point of the body observed; and *Ox* (not to scale) is the great circle distance from *O* to *x*, i.e. it is the Calculated zenith distance of the observed body from the observer's D.R. position. The angle at *O*, between *Ox* and the meridian, is the azimuth of the observed body.

The dotted line *eOf* is part of the circle of position round *x* on which the observer would be situated if he were exactly at *O*.

In the example that we have just worked, the value of the Calculated zenith distance is 39° 26'. If the True

zenith distance were also 39° 26′, then the observer
would be on the position line *eOf*.

But the True zenith distance is *not* 39° 26′. It is 39° 16′.
Therefore the observer is 10 n. miles nearer to *x* than he
thought he was by Dead Reckoning. In other words, the
radius of the True position circle round *x* is 10 n. miles
less than the Calculated radius, and the observer is
therefore on the position line *gTh*. *OT* is called the
'Intercept', and, in this case, we say that it is 10 n. miles
'Towards' the body observed.

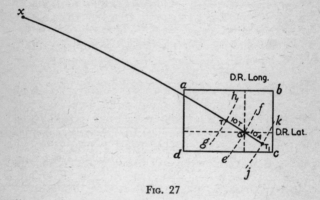

FIG. 27

If the True zenith distance had been 39° 36′, then the
intercept would have been 10 n. miles 'Away' from the
body observed, and the observer would have been on the
position line $jT_1k$.

It should now be apparent that there is no need, in
practice, to show *x* on the diagram at all, provided that
we know the direction in which it lies.

The procedure for plotting the position line, which will
now be described, should make this point clear.

(1) Plot the observer's D.R. position on the chart.
(2) Through the D.R. position draw a line in the
direction of the azimuth of the body observed.

(3) Find the difference between the True and the Calculated zenith distance. This is the intercept, called 'Towards' if the True zenith distance is less than the Calculated and called 'Away' if the True zenith distance is more than the Calculated.

(4) Mark the intercept off along the line of azimuth to $T$, which is called the 'Intercept Terminal Point', and through $T$ draw a line at right angles to the azimuth. It should be appreciated that the position circle round the sub-stellar point is so large that no harm is done by regarding part of its circumference as a straight line.

In the example that we have just worked, we shall find, by following the above procedure, that the observed position is somewhere on the line $gTh$.

If we wish to state our result clearly, as for an entry in a ship's log book, we proceed as follows:

$T$ is N 47° W (True) distant 10 n. miles from $O$. By plotting to scale on a chart, or by a Plane Sailing calculation, we can determine the position of $T$. For this purpose it is quite accurate enough to use an azimuth correct to the nearest degree. The outline of the Plane Sailing calculation is shown below, although in practice it is much easier to find the position of $T$ by plotting.

N 47° W dist. 10 n. miles gives D. lat. 6·8′ N, Dep. 7·3′ W.

Mean lat. is 50° 13′ N.    ∴. D. long. is 11·2′ W.

| $O$ is in position | 50° 10′ N | | 10 15′ E |
| | D. lat. | 6·8′ N | D. long. | 11·2′ W |
| $T$ is in position | 50° 16·8′ N | | 10° 03·8′ E |

The position line $gTh$ is at right angles to the azimuth. The azimuth, in Three Figure Notation, is 313° T. Therefore, the position line lies in a direction 223°/043° T.

We can summarize our result, therefore, by saying that the observed position is *somewhere* on a position line which lies in a direction 223°/043° T and which passes through a point in lat. 50° 16·8′ N long. 10° 03·8′ E.

Such a position line, drawn on his chart, is very useful to a navigator who has no other information about his position, but, of course, it does not tell him *where* he is on the position line. One observation of a heavenly body only gives a position *line*. It does not give a position, or 'Fix'.

In order to obtain a Fix, another observation must be taken, which will produce another position line at a suitable inclination or 'angle of cut' to the first one. Where the second position line intersects the first one will be the observer's exact position or Fix.

## Procedure for Obtaining a Fix

Let us suppose that the star observation, from which we have just obtained the above position line, was made on board a ship at morning twilight, when star observations are usually made. Let us further suppose that, after taking the above observation, the ship steamed S 70° W (T) at 12 knots. After steaming for 3 hours on this course, it having become daylight in the meantime, the sun was observed through a break in the clouds to have a Sextant altitude, which, when corrected, gave a True altitude of 19° 11′. The G.M.T. of the observation was noted, and, on entering the Nautical Almanac with the date and G.M.T. of observation, the G.H.A. sun was found to be 340° 40′ and its declination 20° 10′ S.

We now have the necessary information to obtain another position line, which can be 'crossed' with our first position line in order to give a Fix.

The procedure is as follows:

First of all, the D.R. position at the time of the second observation must be obtained, and this may be done either by a Plane Sailing calculation or by plotting on a chart. The outline of the Plane Sailing calculation is given here, although it is, of course, much easier to plot it on the chart. Course and distance between observations is S 70° W (T) 36 n. miles.

This gives D. lat. 12·3′ S, Dep. 33·8′ W.

Mean lat. is 50° 04′ N. ∴ D. long. is 52·5′ W.

| 1st D.R. position | 50° 10′ N | | 10° 15′ E |
|---|---|---|---|
| D. lat. | 12·3′S | D. long. | 52·5′ W |
| 2nd D.R. position | 49° 57·5′ N | | 9° 22·5 E |

As in the first observation, we must now use our information to name the parts of the $P_1ZX$ triangle that has to be solved.

$$P_1Z = 90° - \text{lat.} = 90° \ 00′ - 49° \ 57·7′ = 40° \ 02·3′.$$

Since latitude is North and declination is South,

$$P_1X = 90° + \text{dec.} = 90° \ 00′ + 20° \ 10′ = 110° \ 10′.$$

In this observation, however, it must be remembered that the sun has been observed in the forenoon. Therefore, the sun's celestial meridian must be to the East of the observer's meridian, i.e. the sun's hour angle must be East.

We have, from the Almanac, that G.H.A. sun is 340° 40′ and this is West, as are all hour angles that are taken from the Almanac. Also, the observer's D.R. longitude is now 9° 22·5′ E.

$$\therefore \text{L.H.A. sun} = \text{G.H.A. sun} + \text{E. long.}$$
$$= 340° \ 40′ + 9° \ 22·5′$$
$$= 350° \ 02·5′.$$

This L.H.A. is also West, by the definition of L.H.A. as applied to quantities taken from the Almanac.

But we know that the sun has been observed East of the meridian, and apart from this, in our $P_1ZX$ triangle, an angle of 350° at the Pole would be awkward, to say the least.

To overcome this difficulty we subtract the above westerly hour angle from 360° and call the result East. This means that angle $P_1$ in our $P_1ZX$ triangle will be $360° - 350° 02·5' = 9° 57·5'$ East.

Since naming of the L.H.A. correctly is so important, the principles involved are illustrated in Fig. 28 (a), (b) and (c). In these diagrams, the reader should imagine that he is looking down on the celestial sphere from above the North Celestial Pole. The circumference of each circle, therefore, will represent the Equinoctial, and the radial lines will represent the meridians of Greenwich, the observer and the body observed, respectively.

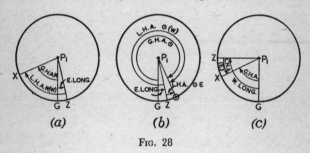

(a)          (b)          (c)

FIG. 28

Fig. 28 (a) shows the conditions of our first observation, i.e. G.H.A.* = 60° 25', long. 10° 15' E. ∴ L.H.A.* = 70° 40' W.

Therefore, angle $P_1$ = 70° 40' West (of the observer).

Fig. 28 (b) shows the conditions of our second observation, i.e. G.H.A. sun 340° 40', long. 9° 22·5' E.

Therefore, L.H.A. sun = 350° 02·5' West.

But this is clearly $360° - 350° 02·5' = 9° 57·5'$ *East* of the observer.

The general rule to apply in these circumstances is 'When the local hour angle comes to more than 180°, subtract it from 360°, and call it East.'

Fig. 28 (c) shows a case that sometimes arises when the D.R. longitude of the observer is West and is numerically greater than the G.H.A. taken from the Almanac. In this instance, the diagram shows a G.H.A. of 60° 00′ and a D.R. longitude of 90° 00′ West. From the diagram it will be seen that the L.H.A. is 30° 00′, and it is *East*.

Again, it sometimes happens that, when you are adding together G.H.A. $\gamma$, S.H.A.* and longitude, in order to obtain the L.H.A., the sum of these quantities comes to *more* than 360°.

This shouldn't worry you. It only means that the addition of these arcs has gone more than once round the circle, so you merely have to subtract 360° to obtain the answer; and the resultant hour angle will still be West, because all hour angles taken from the Almanac are West. If the resultant hour angle is more than 180°, however, it must be subtracted from 360° and called East before you can use it in the $P_1ZX$ triangle.

*Example*

G.H.A. $\gamma$ = 300°, S.H.A.* = 310°, long. = 20° East.
∴ L.H.A. = 300° + 310° + 20° = 630°
= 630° − 360°
= 270° West
= 090° East.

But when in doubt about how to name the hour angle, *draw a diagram*, and you can't very well go wrong.

Reverting now to the $P_1ZX$ triangle for our second observation, we now have all the information that we require.

The triangle is shaped as in Fig. 29, and we know that $P_1Z$ = 40° 02·5′, $P_1X$ = 110° 10′ and angle $P_1$ = 9° 57·5′, the meridian of $X$ being to the eastward of the observer's meridian.

Before proceeding further, however, the reader should study Fig. 29 (*a*), which is inserted to show how the $P_1ZX$ triangle should be drawn for an observer in South latitude.

This diagram shows an observer in D.R. latitude 50° 00′ S. The declination of the body observed is 20° 00′ N, and the L.H.A. of the body is 350° W, i.e. 10° E. Note that $P_1 Z$ is 40° 00′, and that it is measured from the South Celestial Pole. Similarly, $P_1 X$ is 110° 00′, and this is also measured from the South Celestial Pole, because the observer is in South latitude.

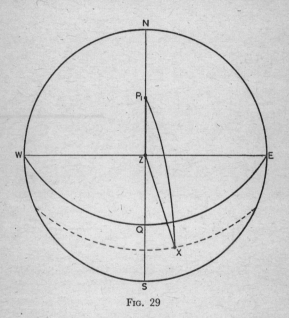

Fig. 29

Returning again to our $P_1 Z X$ triangle in Fig. 29, we have to find $Z X$, which is the Calculated zenith distance of sun from the observer's new D.R. position, and angle $P_1 \hat{Z} X$, which is the azimuth of the sun at the time of observation.

This calculation must be done by using the haversine formula, and it is left as an exercise for the reader. The only difficulty that he is likely to encounter is the fact that

$P_1X$ is more than 90°. It must be remembered, therefore, that sine $A$ = sine $(180° - A)$, i.e. in order to find the sine of 110° 10' you must look up the sine of 69° 50'. Also, it can be seen from the diagram that angle $P_1\hat{Z}X$ is more than 90°; but if it is remembered that the cosine of an angle between 90° and 180° is negative, this should cause no trouble.

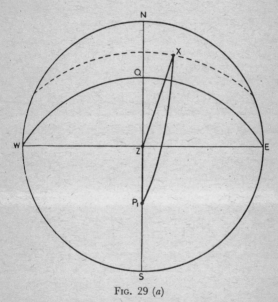

FIG. 29 (a)

The reader, then, should work out for himself that, in the triangle $P_1\hat{Z}X$ of Fig. 29, $ZX$, the Calculated zenith distance, is 70° 41' and angle $P_1\hat{Z}X$, the azimuth, is 170° 04'. This means that, when observed, the sun's bearing was S 10° E, to the degree of accuracy required for an azimuth.

Since the True altitude, obtained by correcting the Sextant altitude, is 19° 11', it follows that the True zenith distance of the sun is 70° 49'.

Therefore, at the second observation, when the sun bears S 10° E, the intercept is 8 n. miles 'Away', because the True zenith distance is 8′ more than the Calculated zenith distance.

The final plotting of the Fix is shown in Fig. 30.

In this plot, the scale used in the book is about $\frac{1}{20}$ inch (0·127 cm) to 1 n. mile. In practice, of course, a much larger scale would be used, or the plotting would be done on the chart.

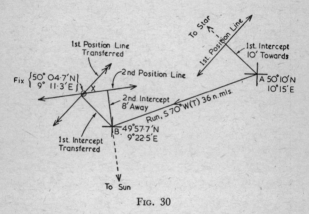

FIG. 30

*A* is the first D.R. position, from which *B*, the second D.R. position, is found by plotting. We have already found this D.R. position by Plane Sailing calculation, however, so there is really no need to do the plotting from *A* to *B*. It is only shown here in order to demonstrate the principle used, which is that of the 'transferred position line' which has already been described in the chapter on chartwork.

*B*, then, is the second D.R. position; and from it we plot *both* the intercepts and the position lines that we have obtained. The position line with the two arrows at each end is the first position line, transferred for the run. The ship must be somewhere on this line at the time of the second observation. But she is also on the position line obtained by the second observation. The ship's position, or Fix, therefore, is where these two lines intersect at $X$.

We know the latitude and longitude of $B$, so even if we are not using a chart we can find the position of $X$. To the scale used in this book, $X$ is 7 n. miles North of $B$, which is in lat. 49° 57·7′ N. Therefore, $X$ is in lat. 50° 04·7′ N. Also, by measurement, $X$ is 7·2 n. miles to the West of $B$. This, of course, is Departure, which must be changed into D. long., i.e.:

D. long. = Dep. × secant mean lat.,

∴ D. long. = 7·2 × sec 50° 01′,

∴ D. long. = 7·2 × 1·5557 = 11·2 minutes of long.

$B$ is in long. 9° 22·5′ E, and therefore $X$ is in long. 9° 11·3′ E. The final Fix, therefore, is in

latitude 50° 04·7′ N. longitude 9° 11·3′ E. *Ans.*

## Checking the Compass Deviation by Astronomical Observation

Part of the process of obtaining both the above position lines was to find the azimuths, or True bearings, of the bodies observed.

The fact that the azimuth is calculated from the D.R. position instead of from the True position does not lead to any appreciable error in the azimuth, unless the D.R. position is wildly inaccurate. If, after calculating the azimuth of a heavenly body, a navigator subsequently finds that the D.R. position which he used was very much in error, he should re-calculate the azimuth, using a more correct position. This caveat also applies to finding a position line by the Marq St. Hilaire Method. If, after calculating an intercept, it is found to be very large—say more than 100 n. miles—it will be obvious that the D.R. position used was wildly inaccurate. In these circumstances, the calculation should be done again, using the intercept terminal point as a D.R. position.

Returning again to the question of the azimuth, it should be apparent that, if at the time of taking the sextant observation of a heavenly body, in order to find a position line, a Compass bearing of the body is also obtained, the Deviation can be found as well as a position line.

For example, let us suppose that, at the time of the second observation above, the sun was observed to bear 168° by compass and that the local Variation was 5° W. The True bearing, or azimuth, of the sun was found by calculation to be 170° True.

170° T, Variation 5° W   = 175° Magnetic
But Compass bearing       = 168° Compass

∴ Deviation of compass for
    direction of ship's head =    7° East.

It has been stated before that, in a well-run ship, the Compass Deviation is checked once in every watch, and on all occasions when the course is altered. The ship may be in sight of land, so there is no need to find an astronomical position line. Under these circumstances, therefore, and whenever the Deviation only has to be checked, the $P_1ZX$ triangle is solved for angle $Z$ only, in order to find the True bearing of the heavenly body of which the Compass bearing has been taken. Local Variation is applied to the True bearing, so as to give the Magnetic bearing, and this, compared with the Compass bearing, gives the Deviation, as in the above example.

## Short Tables

In practice, Short Tables are used to solve the $P_1ZX$ triangle for angle $Z$. These tables, of which there are several types available, are easy to use by following the instructions given in the front of the book in which the tables are bound. The procedure is as follows:

(i) Note the G.M.T. at the time of taking the Compass bearing of the heavenly body. Enter the Almanac with the date and G.M.T., and extract the G.H.A. and declination of the body. Apply the D.R. longitude to find the L.H.A. of the body.

(ii) Enter the Short Tables with the three arguments, Latitude, Declination and Hour Angle, and by following the instructions, extract the True azimuth of the body.

The reader will realize that these Short Tables are merely solving the $P_1ZX$ triangle. The argument Latitude corresponds to side $P_1Z$, Declination corresponds to side $P_1X$ and Local Hour Angle corresponds to angle $P_1$.

Short Tables are also frequently used to find the Calculated zenith distance, i.e. the side $ZX$ of the $P_1ZX$ triangle. These tables effect a great saving of time in working out a position, and consequently they are always used by air navigators, to whom speed is essential. And their use is becoming increasingly popular amongst sea navigators now that it is realized that they give results that are as accurate as any practical navigator could wish for.

When using Short Tables for zenith distance, however, a slight difficulty arises. In order to keep the size of the tables reasonably small, latitudes and hour angles are only tabulated for an integral number of degrees in most types of Short Tables. For this reason, the D.R. position of the observer has to be changed slightly to what is called a 'chosen' or 'selected' position, which is so adjusted as to make the side $P_1Z$ (co-latitude) and angle $P_1$ (hour angle) of the $P_1ZX$ triangle an integral number of degrees. The azimuths and intercepts obtained are then plotted from the chosen positions, instead of plotting them from the D.R. position. A little thought about the principle of the Marq St. Hilaire Method will convince you that this makes no difference whatever to the final results that are obtained. The azimuths and intercepts worked by the Tables relative to the chosen positions will be slightly different to those worked by full calculation relative to the D.R. position, but the resulting position lines will be exactly the same.

## Finding Position on Land by Astronomical Observation

Explorers and surveyors, not to mention other dry-land navigators, often wish to find their position on land by astronomical observation, and the reader of this book may wish to apply his knowledge in order to find the latitude and longitude of his home.

If he wishes to do this, he will need to have a current Nautical or Air Almanac and a watch set to G.M.T. He will also need to borrow either a theodolite, a bubble sextant or a marine sextant with which to make his observations. As we have said before, he will need a little practical tuition in the operation of whichever instrument he decides to use.

The theodolite and the bubble sextant will both give the altitude of the observed body relative to the sensible horizon so that the only corrections to apply will be index error (if any), refraction and parallax (if the body observed is sun, moon or a planet).

If the instrument used is a marine sextant, however, it will have to be used in conjunction with an artificial horizon. This consists, basically, of some liquid in a flat container, so placed that the reflection of the sun, or of any other heavenly body, can be clearly seen in the reflecting surface. Treacle, heavy oil or glycerine, contained in a soup plate, will make an excellent artificial horizon, the principle of which is illustrated in Fig. 31.

$SS_1$ is the reflecting surface. *Before* using the sextant, the eye must be placed in such a position (1) that, with the naked eye, the reflected image of the sun or other body

is seen at *B*. The path of the light rays which make this
possible is shown in dotted lines in Fig. 31.

The marine sextant is then brought into action, and
with the eye in position (2) *B* can still be seen through the
clear portion of the horizon glass.

The reflected image of the lower limb of the sun (*C*), as
seen in the mirror portion of the horizon glass, is now
brought into coincidence with the upper limb of *B* by

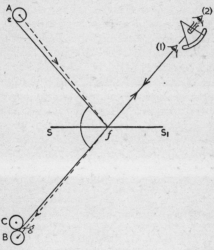

FIG. 31

adjusting the index arm, and the reading of the sextant is
taken. The angle that has been measured in this manner
is the angle *e f g*, which is clearly twice angle *e f s*.

But angle *e f s* is the apparent altitude of the lower limb
of the sun above the sensible horizon.

It should be pointed out, at this stage, that the fact of
holding the sextant at position (2) makes no difference to
the angle observed. The heavenly body is so far away
from the observer, compared with the distance between *f*

and the sextant, that the ray of light from the body to $f$ is in exactly the same direction as the ray of light from the body to the sextant.

To summarize, therefore, the method of obtaining a True altitude, when using an artificial horizon, is as follows:

(1) Use the sextant, as described above, and apply index error, if any, to the observed angle. This gives angle $e\hat{f}g$.

(2) Divide angle $e\hat{f}g$ by 2. This gives angle $e\hat{f}s$.

(3) Subtract the atmospheric refraction appropriate to angle $e\hat{f}s$.

(4) Add the semi-diameter of the sun or moon. In the case of a star or planet, this step is unnecessary, since, with a star or planet, which has no appreciable diameter, the sextant image $(C)$ is made to coincide exactly with the reflected image $(B)$, and the original angle observed is angle $A\hat{f}B$.

(5) Add parallax of sun, moon or planet.

The result of these operations is the True altitude.

Having seen how to find the True altitude of a heavenly body from a position on land, the procedure for finding the position follows simply from our knowledge of the Marq St. Hilaire Method.

(1) By using a map, first determine the approximate latitude and longitude of some point within about 50 miles of your position, and call this point your Dead Reckoning position. If you think this at all odd, you should remember that the navigator on the sea, or in the air, starts his Marq St. Hilaire calculation from a D.R. position, so the navigator on land must do likewise. Since the navigator on land is stationary, however, he will not have any run between sights to deal with and will not have to transfer any position lines.

(2) If you decide to use the sun, it should be observed

in the morning at about 9 a.m. If you live in the Northern Hemisphere, it will then bear in a south-easterly direction, and if you live in the Southern Hemisphere it will bear north-easterly. Use your instruments to find its True zenith distance from its True altitude, and for the G.M.T. of observation work out its Calculated zenith distance, its azimuth and intercept relative to the assumed D.R. position; and plot the resultant position line on a chart of the area if you have one, or otherwise on plain paper.

(3) Wait until near noon, and then watch the sun carefully through the sextant and note the maximum altitude that it reaches. Correct this altitude to give the True meridian altitude, and calculate your latitude by the meridian altitude method. Plot the parallel of latitude obtained, as a position line in an East-West direction, and the point where this position line cuts the one obtained by the morning observation gives you your position. The latitude and longitude of this position is determined by measurement from the D.R. position, not forgetting, of course, to change the Departure into D. long. for the latitude of the place.

The position can be checked by waiting until about 3 p.m., when the sun will be considerably West of the meridian, and then observing it again. Obtain a third position line from this observation, and the third position line should pass through the point of intersection of the other two. If the three lines do not intersect, or nearly intersect, in one point, there is something wrong with your observations or your calculations.

Stars, moon or planets can be used instead of the sun, but these are rather more difficult to observe with an artificial horizon. But whatever bodies are observed, the important point to remember is that there must be a good 'angle of cut' between your position lines. Since each position line is at right angles to each azimuth, it follows that there must be an angle of 30° or more between the bearings of the bodies when they are observed. It should also be noted that, if the altitude of the body observed is more than about 65°, it cannot be observed with a marine sextant and an artificial horizon. This is because the arc of a sextant only reads up to 130°. Under these circumstances, a bubble sextant or a theodolite must be used.

## Some Limitations of Astronomical Navigation

Astronomical navigation, in one form or another, has been used by the navigators of ships, when out of sight of land, for centuries; and today it is also used by the navigators of long-range aircraft. Observing instruments and methods of calculation have been considerably improved, and they are probably as perfect now as they ever will be.

But this age-old method of position finding has always had certain limitations, which will be briefly mentioned here, so that the reader will be better able to form an opinion of the value of astronomical navigation compared with some of the more modern methods that are now available.

In the first place, the marine sextant is an instrument which, under good conditions and in the hands of a practised observer, will give a position line that is accurate to within 1 sea mile. But in order to achieve this degree of accuracy, the sky and the sea horizon must both be clear of cloud and haze. Now, one has only to make a few Atlantic crossings in winter months to realize that it is frequently possible to steam for several days and nights on end without catching a glimpse of the sun, moon or stars, and with the horizon completely shrouded in mist, fog, rain, sleet or snow. Furthermore, even when observing conditions are good as regards visibility, observations can only be made with a marine sextant during daylight hours, or at twilight, when the horizon is visible. It is for this reason that star observations on board ship are nearly always taken during morning or evening twilight, when the stars and the sea horizon can be seen together. Sometimes the moon will illuminate the horizon sufficiently for an observation to be taken by moonlight, but, generally speaking, star sights cannot be taken during hours of darkness.

In air navigation, a bubble sextant of one form or another is used; and since it is possible for aircraft to fly over the clouds, and for the bubble chamber of the sextant to be illuminated so that observations can be taken in complete darkness, it would appear that astronomical navigation can be more widely used in the air than at sea. Unfortunately, however, this is not so, because of the difficulty that arises in determining the sensible horizon accurately with the aid of a bubble—a difficulty that becomes more and more serious as the speeds of aircraft increase. If you have any cause to doubt this statement, you should try taking an ordinary carpenter's spirit level for a ride in a fast motor-car and notice what happens to the bubble. And, in an aircraft, the spirit in the bubble chamber is not only subjected to accelerations, decelerations, centrifugal and centripetal forces but is also subjected to geostrophic deflection, or 'Coriolis Effect', caused by the rotation of the earth. The greater the speed of the aircraft, the greater these errors become. And, finally, when astronomical observations are taken in the air, it takes at least 10 minutes for the navigator to plot the resulting 'Fix' on the chart, and by that time the modern aircraft is probably 100 miles beyond the point at which the observations were made.

In recent years, several projects have been initiated to overcome some, or all, of the above limitations of astronomical navigation. One hears that a radar sextant has been invented that will enable observations to be taken through cloud, by obtaining radar echoes from the sun or the moon. One also hears of an 'inter-continental ballistic missile' which can navigate itself across half the world, its instruments being 'tied' to a heavenly body by radar or by a photo-electric cell.

It remains to be seen, however, whether these ingenious devices, which, it should be realized, only depend for their operation on complicated applications of already known principles, will ever come into general use. In all probability, they will always be too expensive to be used by merchant ships in peace time, and we can only hope that there will be no need to use them in war.

It seems likely, therefore, that ordinary 'bread and butter' astronomical navigation will continue to suffer its present limitations for a long time to come. And it is for this reason that some of the more practical modern aids to navigation, which do not depend on astronomical observations, are to be briefly described in the last chapter of this book.

## EXAMPLES FOR EXERCISE

### Exercise 21

(1) From a ship in D.R. position 47° 05′ N 59° 55′ W, an observation of the sun is taken in the early morning, and the True altitude is found to be 26° 42′. From the Almanac, G.H.A. sun is 344° 56·1′ and Decl. 23° 16·8′ N. The ship then steams 044° (T) for 30 n. miles, and then a second observation of the sun is taken, which gives a True altitude of 64° 36′. The sun's G.H.A. is now 50° 26·1′ and its Decl. 23° 16·3′ N.

Calculate the azimuth and intercept from the appropriate D.R. position at each observation, and thence find the position of the ship at the time of the second observation, by plotting to scale.

(2) From a ship in D.R. position 4° 46′ N 63° 45′ E, an observation of the star Capella is taken when it is to the eastward of the observer, and its True altitude is found to be 45° 43·1′. At the time of observation, G.H.A. ♈ is

355° 59·4′, S.H.A.* is 281° 42·3′ and the Decl. of the star is 45° 57·3′ N. The ship steams S 55° W (T) for 29 n. miles, and then a second observation of the same star is taken, the star being now to the westward of the observer. Its True altitude is now found to be 35° 09·3′. The G.H.A. ♈ is now 56° 35·5′ and the S.H.A.* is unchanged at 281° 42·3′. The Decl. is still 45° 57·3′ N. Find the azimuths and intercepts, and the position of the ship at the time of the second observation, as in Question 1.

(3) From a ship in D.R. position 41° 10′ S 92° 30·4′ E, an observation of the star Sirius is taken when it is to the eastward of the observer, and its True altitude is found to be 52° 06·6′. At the G.M.T. of observation, G.H.A. ♈ is 334° 49′, S.H.A.* is 259° 14·1′ and the Decl. of star is 16° 39′ S. The ship then steams 090° (T) for 40 n. miles, and then an observation of the star Rigel is taken, this star being to the westward of the observer. Its True altitude is found to be 46° 51·3′. The G.H.A. ♈ is now 16° 17·1′, S.H.A.* is 281° 56·2′ and the Decl. of the star is 8° 15·3′ S. Find the azimuths and intercepts, and the position of the ship at the time of the second observation, as in Question 1.

(4) A stationary observer in D.R. position 34° 30′ N 160° 10′ E wishes to find his position accurately, so he takes observations of the sun and moon, using a marine sextant and an artificial horizon. He first observes the moon to the westward of his meridian and finds its True altitude to be 44° 41·3′. At the G.M.T. of observation, G.H.A. moon is 238° 55·5′ and Decl. moon is 6° 46′ N. He then observes the sun to the eastward of his meridian, and finds that its True altitude is 54° 29·9′. At the G.M.T. of this observation, G.H.A. sun is 161° 11·1′, and Decl. sun is 23° 20·6′ N. Find the azimuths and intercepts for each observation, and thence determine the observer's latitude and longitude, by plotting to scale.

(5) A stationary observer in D.R. position 43° 15′ S 35° 30′ W wishes to find his accurate position by the use

of marine sextant and artificial horizon, so he decides to take observations of the moon and of the planet Venus. His observation of the moon, to the eastward of the meridian, gives a True altitude of 35° 49·6'. At the G.M.T. of observation, G.H.A. moon is 357° 32·6' and Decl. moon is 1° 05·3' S. His observation of Venus, to the westward of the meridian, gives a True altitude of 60° 06'. At the G.M.T. of this observation, G.H.A. Venus is 64° 21·4' and Decl. Venus is 25° 00·7' S. Find the azimuth and intercept for each observation, and thence determine the observer's latitude and longitude, by plotting to scale.

# CHAPTER 9

# Modern Navigation Instruments

## The Gyro Compass

This instrument was mentioned in Chapter 2, and, as stated there, its great advantage is that it gives True directions instead of the approximately Magnetic directions indicated by the magnetic compass. It has the further advantage that its directive force is very much greater than that of the magnetic compass, and this enables it to be used for operating automatic steering devices, or 'Iron Mikes' as they are colloquially termed by seamen.

A gyroscope is a rapidly spinning wheel which has 'three degrees of freedom'. That is to say, the wheel, or rotor, is so mounted that, in addition to being able to revolve about its axis of rotation, it can turn about the horizontal and vertical axes. Such a 'free' gyroscope has two important properties, known respectively as 'rigidity in space' and 'precession'. Both these properties are utilized in the construction of the gyro compass, in which a free gyroscope is 'gravity controlled' and 'damped' so as to make it into a direction-indicating instrument.

The type of gyro compass fitted in most ships today consists of a 'master unit', which is preferably housed somewhere near the centre of gravity of the ship, where the effect of rolling and pitching is reduced to a minimum, and several repeaters are connected electrically to the master unit. The repeaters on the bridge enable True courses to be steered and True bearings to be observed. An automatic helmsman may also be actuated by the master unit.

The type of gyro compass used in ships is too heavy to be fitted in aircraft, in which a much lighter gyro-magnetic compass is often installed. This consists of a small gyroscope, which is monitored by means of a powerful magnetic needle. Some aircraft are fitted with a 'flux-gate' compass, in which the magnetic field of the earth is detected electrically and the flux-gate unit is stabilized in the horizontal plane by means of a gyro-scope. Both these aircraft instruments indicate magnetic directions, but they also incorporate a device by means of which the local Variation can be applied mechanically. This enables True courses to be steered—so long as the navigator remembers to turn the Variation Setting Knob as the aircraft crosses each isogonal.

## The Patent Sounding Machine and Echo Sounder

In addition to ensuring that his ship is proceeding in the right direction, an obvious essential of the sea navigator's job is to ensure that his ship remains afloat at all times.

Even if visibility is poor, and the actual position of the vessel is unknown, a ship will not come to much harm so long as she continues to have sufficient water under her keel.

The oldest instrument used by mariners to measure the depth of water was the 'deep sea lead', which consisted of a heavy billet of lead attached to a long line. When this was used in a sailing ship, the ship had to be hove to, so as to reduce her headway. The lead was carried forward and the line was led aft, outside the rail, with men stationed at intervals along its length. On the signal being given, the lead was released, and the first man to feel it touch bottom noted the depth of water by means of marks on the line.

This effective but tiresome method of 'sounding' was superseded by the patent sounding machine invented by Lord Kelvin. This consists of a very long, thin and strong wire, on a reel, with a 28-lb (12·7-kg) lead attached to the end of the wire. The reel has a brake, which can be released so that the lead on the end of the wire sinks rapidly to the bottom. An officer stands by the wire as it is running out and holds a metal 'feeler' that touches the wire. He can thus detect the instant that the lead touches bottom, because the wire slackens, and he then applies the brake. The wire, with the lead attached, is then wound back on board.

It will occur to the reader that the amount of wire that has been run out will give a rough approximation of the depth; but since the ship is going ahead at full speed, the wire will trail far astern as it is running out, so that this method of finding the depth is not used.

Instead, a tube, closed at the top end and open at the bottom end, is attached to the wire, just above the lead. The tube is coated on the inside with a chemical which discolours when in contact with salt water. As the lead and the tube sink lower in the water, the air in the tube is compressed by the increasing pressure, and the salt water rises further and further up the tube. Students of physics will recognize that this is an application of Boyle's Law. After the lead has touched bottom, and the tube has been brought back on board, the length of that part of the tube which has been discoloured is measured against a suitably calibrated scale, and this gives the depth of water in which the ship is floating.

In addition, there is a hemispherical cavity in the bottom end of the lead into which a lump of tallow can be pressed. This strikes the bottom of the sea first and collects some particles of sand, or some small shells, or some mud—whatever, in fact, is on the bottom in the particular locality in which the sounding has been taken.

Having 'taken a cast of the lead', as the above operation is termed, the navigator then consults his Admiralty chart. If you examine such a chart yourself, you will see lots of small figures and letters scattered all over the sea area of the chart, and also rows of dotted and pecked lines, like contour lines on a map of the land. Each of these small figures represents the depth of water at the point where the figure is situated, and the small letters indicate the 'nature of the bottom'. Thus, 's' means 'sand' and 'm' means 'mud'. And the dotted and pecked lines *are* contour lines, but they represent depths instead of heights.

It is important to realize, however, that the depths given on the chart are the depths below 'Chart Datum'. This is a particular level of water which approximates to that of Mean Low Water Spring Tides. Thus, when a sounding is taken at any other time but the time of Mean Low Water Spring Tides, a correction must be applied to the depth of water obtained by the lead before the depth can be compared with that given on the chart. Full instructions for doing this are contained in the Admiralty Tide Tables, and a copy of these Tables is carried in all ships. The depths or 'soundings' on Admiralty Charts are at present mainly given in fathoms (1 fathom equals 6 feet) but it is intended that, in due course, these units of measurement will be changed to metres.

It will be appreciated, therefore, that if a series of soundings is taken, at known distances apart, when a ship is proceeding on a straight course, such a 'line of soundings' as it is called can be used to estimate the ship's position by 'matching' the spacing of the depths obtained with those on the chart and also by comparing the nature of the bottom at successive soundings with those shown on the chart.

In recent years, the Patent Sounding Machine has itself been superseded by the 'Echo Sounder', which enables the depth of water under a ship to be ascertained much more easily and quickly than before.

This modern instrument is based on the fact that sound travels at a known speed through water; and the interval of time that it takes for a sound wave to travel from the bottom of the ship to the sea-bed and back again determines the depth of water under the ship. In practice, a transmitter at the bottom of the ship sends out a supersonic sound wave, which, when it comes back as an echo from the sea-bed, is received by a receiver, which is specially tuned for the purpose. The weak signal that has been received is then amplified by an amplifier, and the stronger signal thus produced operates a recorder, which shows the depth of water. In this manner, when the instrument is switched on, a constant record of the depth of water under the ship is shown in the chart room. The only disadvantage of this instrument, compared with the older sounding machine, is that it does not show the precise nature of the ocean bed. Apart from this, however, it is an ideal instrument for 'running a line of soundings' and can often be used in this way to determine the ship's position in thick weather.

## Radio and Radar Aids to Navigation

Having discussed some modern direction-indicating and depth-recording instruments, let us now turn to some of the position-finding and collision-avoiding devices that are at the disposal of today's sea and air navigator.

### Radar

'Radar' is an abbreviation for 'Radio Detection and Ranging', and a 'radar set' in a ship or aircraft is an instrument that does precisely this, i.e. it detects the bearing and range of coastal objects, and of other ships or aircraft, not only when the visibility is good but also in fog, mist, falling snow or heavy rainstorms.

Basically, a radar set works on much the same principle as an echo sounder, i.e. the time that a pulse of very short wave radio energy takes to go from the ship to the shore and back, or to any distant object, such as another ship, and back, can be measured; and this interval of time determines the distance of the shore, or of the other object, from the ship. In the case of the echo sounder, it is the speed of sound in water that is measured, and this is approximately 5000 feet (1524 metres) per second. In the case of the radar set, however, it is the speed of radio waves in air that is being measured. This speed is the same as that of light, about 186 000 statute miles (300 000 km) per second, so it follows that a very accurate and precise measuring instrument must be used.

The instrument that is used for this purpose is the cathode-ray tube, similar to the one in a television set. As the reader probably knows, the picture in a television set is made by electrons impinging on the inside of the screen. The stream of electrons flies along the tube at an enormous speed, and in a radar set the stream is deflected by a pulse of energy that is sent out from the ship, and is again deflected by the same pulse as it is echoed back. The distance through which a particular group of electrons in the stream has travelled between the two deflections determines the distance of the ship from the object from which the echo has been obtained.

The pulses of energy, which are sent out at regular intervals, travel in the form of a narrow beam which emanates from a rotating 'scanner', and the echo is received back by the same scanner. The direction in which the scanner is facing when it receives an echo determines the bearing of the object from which the echo has come.

If one looks at the face of the P.P.I., or Plan Position Indicator, as the screen of the radar set is called, one sees a set of concentric circles and a narrow beam of light rotating about the centre. As the beam rotates, it momentarily illuminates a spot or patch on the screen, and it is this illuminated spot that is the distant object which the radar set has 'picked up'. The distance of the spot from the centre can be measured on an appropriate scale, and, since the centre of the circle represents the position of the ship, the bearing and distance of the spot from the centre represents the bearing and distance of the distant object from the ship.

Most radar sets have three range-scales, the greatest being 30 n. miles and the smallest 1 n. mile, the latter being used for close and accurate navigation in rivers and harbours. It must be emphasized that radar cannot be made to work from a ship at a range of much over 30 n. miles, because the radio waves that are sent out are of very short wavelength and of very high frequency, like those of light, so they can't bend round corners or go very far over the horizon. A radar set in an aircraft, of course, will have a much greater range than that of a ship-borne set, for exactly the same reason that an aviator, on a clear day, can see much farther than a seaman on the not very high bridge of his ship.

Radar has proved itself to be an invaluable aid to navigation when it has been intelligently used; but, like many other of the blessings of modern science, it can be misused, with the most unfortunate results. In order to use radar intelligently, it must be appreciated that, in many radar sets, the picture that is seen on the screen is one that shows the *relative* motion of other ships. If this fact is not fully appreciated, and if the principles of relative motion are not fully understood by the observer, then accidents are likely to happen.

A radar set has now been developed, however, which shows the *real* motion of other ships on the screen, and which also shows the motion of the ship which is carrying the radar set. The mechanism of this 'true motion' radar is, of necessity, very complicated, but in many respects it is a great improvement on the 'relative motion' type of instrument.

## The Radio Position Line and Fix
Radio bearings could be taken from ships and from shore stations long before the advent of radar, and such bearings are still used as a very helpful aid to navigation. They

enable the position of a ship to be fixed with reasonable accuracy when she is beyond visual and radar range of the land, and when astronomical observations cannot be obtained because of overcast conditions. Radio bearings and fixes are also used extensively by air navigators under corresponding circumstances in the air.

Most people are familiar with the phenomenon whereby, if a portable radio set is twisted round on its axis, the music or speech is louder when the set is facing in one direction than when it is facing in another direction. This is because the aerial of a portable radio set consists of a loop set in the vertical plane, and radio waves emanating from a transmitter have a vertical component, like the advancing front of an ocean wave. When the loop is set with its two sides in line with the direction of the advancing wave, the wave hits one side of the loop at one level and the other side at another level. This causes a potential difference between the two sides of the loop which produces a loud signal in the radio set. But when the loop is turned so that its face is parallel to the advancing wave front, both sides of the loop are hit by the wave at the same level and no signal results.

When using a radio direction-finding set (or D/F set, as it is usually called), the aerial is rotated until the direction of the minimum signal is ascertained. This is done because the minimum signal can be detected more accurately than the maximum. The operator who is rotating the loop then knows that its face is at right angles to the direction, or bearing, of the transmitter.

This does not tell him, however, on which side of the loop the station lies, but he usually knows this from his D.R. position. If he is doubtful about the '180° ambiguity', as it is termed, there is a device incorporated in the set which resolves the ambiguity for him. By depressing a 'sense' switch, which brings another aerial into operation, he can determine on which side of the loop the transmitting station lies.

Bearings that are taken with a D/F set in a ship or aeroplane are usually taken as bearings relative to the ship's or aircraft's head. Thus, if a ship is steering 030° T, and a D/F bearing of a radio station is taken which is found to be 080° Relative, then the navigator knows that the True great circle bearing of the station is 030° + 080° = 110°. Note that the bearing obtained is a great circle bearing, because radio waves, like light waves, travel along the arcs of great circles and not along rhumb lines.

Before discussing this any further, however, it should be mentioned why relative bearings are taken. This is done because the varying angles at which the incoming radio waves strike the structure of the ship or aircraft cause the waves to be deflected by varying amounts. This gives rise to what is known as 'Quadrantal Error', which depends for its value on the *relative* bearing of the station from the vessel. For a given ship or aircraft, the quadrantal error is tabulated in graphical form, something like a Deviation graph, and it is applied to the relative bearing before it is used.

A D/F set is not a very complicated piece of apparatus by present-day standards, and small sets are manufactured for use in yachts and coastal vessels. There is little doubt that an enthusiastic amateur builder of radio sets could make one for himself, and it would be reasonably accurate if he calibrated it carefully for the vessel in which it was to be used.

Most D/F sets in use at sea are designed to take bearings from medium wavelength stations which transmit signals that can be detected, at sea-level, at great distances from the station. Such stations are plotted on Admiralty charts, and they are also listed in the Admiralty List of Wireless Signals. In the air, there is a tendency for v.h.f. transmitters to be used, because there is less interference at these frequencies, although the range of such stations is much less than that of medium wavelength transmitters.

In the air, too, the air navigator often makes use of a Radio Compass, which is a type of D/F set that finds the minimum signal automatically and indicates it on a dial in the navigator's compartment.

D/F sets, or 'goniometers', are also installed at many radio stations ashore, so that the operators at these stations can, on request, take bearings of ships at sea or of aircraft in the air.

There are thus two methods open to the navigator by which he can fix his position by radio bearings if he wishes to do so.

If his vessel is equipped with a radio transmitter, he may radio to a D/F station ashore and ask 'What is my True bearing from you?' The operator at the D/F station will take a bearing of the ship's transmission and then radio back to her 'Your True bearing from me is $xyz°$'.

On the other hand, if a vessel is equipped with a D/F set (and nearly all ships and aircraft are so equipped nowadays), the navigator can himself take a bearing of the transmission from any shore station that he cares to select, provided that it is within the range of his set.

But it must be remembered that the bearing, however it is taken, is a great circle bearing, and it must be changed into a rhumb line bearing before it can be plotted on a Mercator's chart. Fig. 32 shows how radio bearings are plotted on such a chart.

Let us suppose, first of all, that the operator at the shore D/F station at $A$ takes a bearing of a ship and finds it to be 260°. This is the curved line G.C. (1) in the diagram. At the same time, the operator at the shore D/F station at $B$ takes a bearing of the same ship and finds it to be 300°. This is the curved line G.C. (2). The ship is told by radio what these two great circle bearings are. How does the navigator in the ship plot his position?

The procedure is as follows:

The navigator notes his D.R. position and also notes the position of each radio station. He uses this information to calculate the 'Conversion Angle' appropriate to each bearing. The conversion angle is the angle between the great circle and the rhumb line on a Mercator's chart, and is labelled $CA$ in Fig. 32.

The formula which gives conversion angle is:

Conversion angle $= \frac{1}{2}$ D. long $\times$ sine mean latitude.

Thus, if the D.R. position of the ship in Fig. 32 is 30° 00′ N 10° 00′ W and the position of the radio station

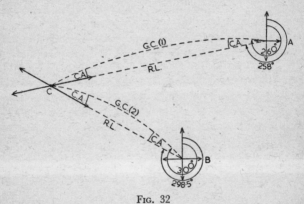

FIG. 32

$A$ is 30° 20′ N 02° 00′ W, then the conversion angle to apply to G.C. (1) is 4° × sine 30° 10′, i.e. it is 4° × 0·5, which equals 2°. Also, if the position of the radio station at $B$ is 29° 40′ N 04° 00′ W, then the conversion angle to apply to G.C. (2) is 3° × sine 29° 50′ = 3° × 0·5 = 1·5°.

Having found the conversion angle, the navigator applies it to the great circle bearing in the following manner. He imagines himself to be situated at the position of the person who is taking the bearing and then applies the conversion angle *towards the Equator*. Thus, at $A$, the G.C. bearing is 260°, so the rhumb line bearing is 258°. At $B$, the G.C. bearing is 300°, so the R.L. bearing is 298·5°.

These two rhumb-line bearings are now laid off from $A$ and $B$ respectively, and they will intersect at $C$, which is the ship's position.

Alternatively, suppose the navigator in the ship takes the bearings, using his own D/F set. Let us suppose that the ship's head is 030° T when the bearings are taken. The bearing of $A$ will then be found to be 046° Relative, i.e. relative to the ship's head. Now, $030° + 046° = 076°$. This means that the great circle bearing of $A$ from the ship is 076°. But the conversion angle, calculated as above, is 2°, and it is the ship that is taking the bearing on this occasion. Therefore, in order to apply the conversion angle correctly, the navigator must imagine himself to be situated at the ship (where he actually is) and he must apply the conversion angle towards the Equator, i.e. G.C. bearing = 076°; C.A. = 2°. Therefore, the rhumb-line bearing of the station $A$ from the ship is 078°. This means, of course, that the rhumb-line bearing of the ship from $A$ is the reciprocal of 078°, which equals 258°, as before.

Similarly, the relative bearing of $B$ from the ship will be 087°. Now, $030° + 087° = 117°$. This is the great circle bearing of $B$ from the ship. But C.A. = $1\frac{1}{2}°$. Therefore, the rhumb-line bearing of $B$ from the ship is $118\frac{1}{2}°$. This means, of course, that the R.L. bearing of the ship from $B$ is $298\frac{1}{2}°$, as before.

Sometimes it happens that only one radio bearing can be obtained, but this is better than nothing because it gives a position line somewhere on which the ship or aircraft is situated. And it is always possible that another position line can be obtained by astronomical means, so that this, combined with the radio bearing, will give the navigator his position.

In Chapter 4, mention has been made of the gnomonic chart, on which great circles appear as straight lines. It follows, therefore, that if a gnomonic chart is used to plot radio bearings, conversion angle need not be applied to the bearings. There are certain difficulties to be overcome when employing this technique, but such charts are, in fact, used to plot radio bearings in certain parts of the world.


*Consol*

Consol was invented by the Germans during the Second World War, and it was used by their submarines and aircraft to navigate across the Atlantic and the North Sea. Allied ships and aircraft also made use of it, although they didn't then know exactly how it worked. The principle of this device is quite complicated, but it is delightfully simple to use, because all the equipment that is required to take a bearing is an ordinary radio receiver.

A Consol station sends out a pattern of signals like the rays of light from a central source. (It was originally called 'Sonne', or Sun, by the Germans.) Each ray, or sector, is of about 15° angular measurement. Dots and dashes are transmitted into each sector, but the dots are transmitted first into one sector, and dashes are transmitted first into the sector adjacent to it. This means that a suitably tuned receiver will pick up the dots first in one sector, called the dot sector, and the dashes first in the next sector, which is called the dash sector. Since there is a similar dot or dash sector, 15° wide, some few miles away, the navigator must ascertain his approximate bearing from the station, either by D.R. or by the use of his D/F loop, so that he will know in which of the several dot or dash sectors he is situated. In addition to the dots and dashes, a continuous note is also transmitted, and the navigator who wishes to obtain a bearing listens for this. Immediately following the continuous note he hears either dots first or dashes first, and this tells him whether he is in a 'dot sector' or a 'dash sector' respectively. He counts the dots or dashes which follow the continuous note, observing a simple counting procedure; then, by reference to a specially constructed chart or to a special table, he can use the 'count' that he has obtained to determine the great circle bearing of his ship or aircraft from the position of the Consol station.

An example of the simple counting procedure referred to above is as follows:

A navigator finds by D.R., or by D/F loop, and by reference to a Consol chart or table, that he is in a certain dot sector of a Consol station. He listens to the transmission from the station and he first hears the station's call sign, followed by a continuous note. There is a short break, and then the dots begin, each lasting for one second, or for half a second, depending on the 'keying cycle' of the station.

After counting, say, 27 dots, they begin to fade, and an indefinite mixture of dots and dashes, called the 'equi-signal', is heard. This occurs in the 'twilight zone' between dots and dashes. Then dashes are heard, faintly at first but becoming clearer, and these dashes must also be counted. Suppose they amount to 29, and then there is silence until the next cycle begins.

There is a total of 60 characters in the keying cycle, and, in this case, 56 characters have been counted. This indicates that 4 characters have been lost in the twilight zone between the dots and dashes. Because the observer is in a dot sector, the first two lost characters must be dots, and thus the 'count' obtained is $27 + 2 = 29$ dots.

The appropriate sector of the Consol chart or table is now inspected, and the exact great circle bearing of the observer from the statioins obtained against a reading of 29 dots.

### Gee, Loran and Decca

These three aids to navigation are all called 'hyperbolic' aids, because, in order to use them, a navigator has to refer to special charts, on which patterns of hyperbolic position lines are superimposed.

An hyperbola is a line which maintains a constant difference in distance from two fixed points. All the lines, except $AB$ and $AC$, in Fig. 33 are hyperbolae. The firm lines are the hyperbolae drawn relative to the fixed points $A$ and $B$, and the pecked lines are the hyperbolae drawn relative to the fixed points $A$ and $C$.

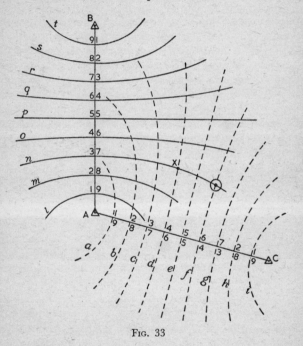

Fig. 33

If you take the point on the firm line which passes through 3-7 on $AB$, you will see that it is 3 units from $A$ and 7 units from $B$. The difference between 3 and 7 is 4. But if you take any other point, such as $X$, on the same curved line, you will find that $XB - XA$ also equals 4 units. Thus, this particular line is the locus of points which are all 4 units of distance nearer to $A$ than $B$. Therefore, if signals are transmitted simultaneously from $A$ to $B$, the navigator of a vessel situated anywhere on the hyperbola which passes through 3-7 will receive the signal from $A$ 4 units of time earlier than he will receive the signal from $B$. And if he had a device on board which can measure the time interval of 4 units between the receipt of the two signals, he will know that his position is somewhere on the particular hyperbola which passes through 3-7 and $X$, and which is labelled $n$. Similarly, if his device were to receive a signal from $B$ 2 units of time earlier than a simultaneously transmitted signal from $A$, then he would know that he was somewhere on the firm line which passes through 6-4, and which is labelled $q$.

The pecked lines, drawn relative to $A$ and $C$, give similar results. A navigator who receives a signal from $A$ 2 units of time later than he receives a simultaneously transmitted signal from $C$ knows that he is somewhere on the hyperbola labelled $f$, and if, at the same time, he has ascertained, by recording the signals from $A$ and $B$, that he is also on the hyperbola marked $n$, then he knows the exact position of his ship or aircraft. It is at the Fix, where the hyperbolae $n$ and $f$ intersect.

'Gee' is a relatively short-range device, which, in effect, measures the time interval between the receipt of simultaneously transmitted signals from two or more stations. 'Loran' is a long-range device, which does the same.

'Decca' makes use of the phase difference between radio waves from two stations, instead of the time difference between them, but it works on the same hyperbolic principle as Gee and Loran. In all these systems, the main station, such as $A$ in Fig. 33, is called the Master Station, and the subsidiary stations, such as $B$ and $C$, are called Slave Stations, because their signals are controlled by the Master Station.

An arrangement of stations, such as $A$, $B$ and $C$, is called a Chain. In recent years, a group of Decca Chains has been established round the British Isles, and similar

Chains are being established in other areas. Decca is now used extensively by ships and aircraft, and all a navigator has to do in order to fix his position is to read two or three dials, which tell him on which hyperbolae he is situated. The positions that are obtained in this manner are very accurate indeed, and they are reliable in all weather conditions.

In addition to the Decca system described above, which entails the reading of dials and subsequent reference to the hyperbolae of a chart, there is today a more advanced Decca instrument available for the use of ships and aircraft engaged on regular services, such as those across the English Channel.

In this latest device, the incoming signals, instead of actuating dials, are made to operate mechanism which pin-points a spot of light on a specially designed chart. The spot of light travels across the chart, and traces out every movement of the ship or aircraft which carries the instrument. In this manner, the navigator can see, at a glance, the exact position of his craft at any moment during the flight or passage.

# Appendices

## NATURAL SINES

| Angle. | 0' | 6' | 12' | 18' | 24' | 30' | 36' | 42' | 48' | 54' | 1' | 2' | 3' | 4' | 5' |
|---|---|---|---|---|---|---|---|---|---|---|---|---|---|---|---|
| 0° | ·0000 | ·0017 | ·0035 | ·0052 | ·0070 | ·0087 | ·0105 | ·0122 | ·0140 | ·0157 | 3 | 6 | 9 | 12 | 15 |
| 1° | ·0175 | ·0192 | ·0209 | ·0227 | ·0244 | ·0262 | ·0279 | ·0297 | ·0314 | ·0332 | 3 | 6 | 9 | 12 | 15 |
| 2° | ·0349 | ·0366 | ·0384 | ·0401 | ·0419 | ·0436 | ·0454 | ·0471 | ·0488 | ·0506 | 3 | 6 | 9 | 12 | 15 |
| 3° | ·0523 | ·0541 | ·0558 | ·0576 | ·0593 | ·0610 | ·0628 | ·0645 | ·0663 | ·0680 | 3 | 6 | 9 | 12 | 15 |
| 4° | ·0698 | ·0715 | ·0732 | ·0750 | ·0767 | ·0785 | ·0802 | ·0819 | ·0837 | ·0854 | 3 | 6 | 9 | 12 | 14 |
| 5° | ·0872 | ·0889 | ·0906 | ·0924 | ·0941 | ·0958 | ·0976 | ·0993 | ·1011 | ·1028 | 3 | 6 | 9 | 12 | 14 |
| 6° | ·1045 | ·1063 | ·1080 | ·1097 | ·1115 | ·1132 | ·1149 | ·1167 | ·1184 | ·1201 | 3 | 6 | 9 | 12 | 14 |
| 7° | ·1219 | ·1236 | ·1253 | ·1271 | ·1288 | ·1305 | ·1323 | ·1340 | ·1357 | ·1374 | 3 | 6 | 9 | 12 | 14 |
| 8° | ·1392 | ·1409 | ·1426 | ·1444 | ·1461 | ·1478 | ·1495 | ·1513 | ·1530 | ·1547 | 3 | 6 | 9 | 12 | 14 |
| 9° | ·1564 | ·1582 | ·1599 | ·1616 | ·1633 | ·1650 | ·1668 | ·1685 | ·1702 | ·1719 | 3 | 6 | 9 | 12 | 14 |
| 10° | ·1736 | ·1754 | ·1771 | ·1788 | ·1805 | ·1822 | ·1840 | ·1857 | ·1874 | ·1891 | 3 | 6 | 9 | 11 | 14 |
| 11° | ·1908 | ·1925 | ·1942 | ·1959 | ·1977 | ·1994 | ·2011 | ·2028 | ·2045 | ·2062 | 3 | 6 | 9 | 11 | 14 |
| 12° | ·2079 | ·2096 | ·2113 | ·2130 | ·2147 | ·2164 | ·2181 | ·2198 | ·2215 | ·2233 | 3 | 6 | 9 | 11 | 14 |
| 13° | ·2250 | ·2267 | ·2284 | ·2300 | ·2317 | ·2334 | ·2351 | ·2368 | ·2385 | ·2402 | 3 | 6 | 8 | 11 | 14 |
| 14° | ·2419 | ·2436 | ·2453 | ·2470 | ·2487 | ·2504 | ·2521 | ·2538 | ·2554 | ·2571 | 3 | 6 | 8 | 11 | 14 |
| 15° | ·2588 | ·2605 | ·2622 | ·2639 | ·2656 | ·2672 | ·2689 | ·2706 | ·2723 | ·2740 | 3 | 6 | 8 | 11 | 14 |
| 16° | ·2756 | ·2773 | ·2790 | ·2807 | ·2823 | ·2840 | ·2857 | ·2874 | ·2890 | ·2907 | 3 | 6 | 8 | 11 | 14 |
| 17° | ·2924 | ·2940 | ·2957 | ·2974 | ·2990 | ·3007 | ·3024 | ·3040 | ·3057 | ·3074 | 3 | 6 | 8 | 11 | 14 |
| 18° | ·3090 | ·3107 | ·3123 | ·3140 | ·3156 | ·3173 | ·3190 | ·3206 | ·3223 | ·3239 | 3 | 6 | 8 | 11 | 14 |
| 19° | ·3256 | ·3272 | ·3289 | ·3305 | ·3322 | ·3338 | ·3355 | ·3371 | ·3387 | ·3404 | 3 | 5 | 8 | 11 | 14 |
| 20° | ·3420 | ·3437 | ·3453 | ·3469 | ·3486 | ·3502 | ·3518 | ·3535 | ·3551 | ·3567 | 3 | 5 | 8 | 11 | 14 |
| 21° | ·3584 | ·3600 | ·3616 | ·3633 | ·3649 | ·3665 | ·3681 | ·3697 | ·3714 | ·3730 | 3 | 5 | 8 | 11 | 14 |
| 22° | ·3746 | ·3762 | ·3778 | ·3795 | ·3811 | ·3827 | ·3843 | ·3859 | ·3875 | ·3891 | 3 | 5 | 8 | 11 | 14 |
| 23° | ·3907 | ·3923 | ·3939 | ·3955 | ·3971 | ·3987 | ·4003 | ·4019 | ·4035 | ·4051 | 3 | 5 | 8 | 11 | 14 |
| 24° | ·4067 | ·4083 | ·4099 | ·4115 | ·4131 | ·4147 | ·4163 | ·4179 | ·4195 | ·4210 | 3 | 5 | 8 | 11 | 13 |
| 25° | ·4226 | ·4242 | ·4258 | ·4274 | ·4289 | ·4305 | ·4321 | ·4337 | ·4352 | ·4368 | 3 | 5 | 8 | 11 | 13 |
| 26° | ·4384 | ·4399 | ·4415 | ·4431 | ·4446 | ·4462 | ·4478 | ·4493 | ·4509 | ·4524 | 3 | 5 | 8 | 10 | 13 |
| 27° | ·4540 | ·4555 | ·4571 | ·4586 | ·4602 | ·4617 | ·4633 | ·4648 | ·4664 | ·4679 | 3 | 5 | 8 | 10 | 13 |
| 28° | ·4695 | ·4710 | ·4726 | ·4741 | ·4756 | ·4772 | ·4787 | ·4802 | ·4818 | ·4833 | 3 | 5 | 8 | 10 | 13 |
| 29° | ·4848 | ·4863 | ·4879 | ·4894 | ·4909 | ·4924 | ·4939 | ·4955 | ·4970 | ·4985 | 3 | 5 | 8 | 10 | 13 |
| 30° | ·5000 | ·5015 | ·5030 | ·5045 | ·5060 | ·5075 | ·5090 | ·5105 | ·5120 | ·5135 | 3 | 5 | 8 | 10 | 13 |
| 31° | ·5150 | ·5165 | ·5180 | ·5195 | ·5210 | ·5225 | ·5240 | ·5255 | ·5270 | ·5284 | 3 | 5 | 7 | 10 | 12 |
| 32° | ·5299 | ·5314 | ·5329 | ·5344 | ·5358 | ·5373 | ·5388 | ·5402 | ·5417 | ·5432 | 2 | 5 | 7 | 10 | 12 |
| 33° | ·5446 | ·5461 | ·5476 | ·5490 | ·5505 | ·5519 | ·5534 | ·5548 | ·5563 | ·5577 | 2 | 5 | 7 | 10 | 12 |
| 34° | ·5592 | ·5606 | ·5621 | ·5635 | ·5650 | ·5664 | ·5678 | ·5693 | ·5707 | ·5721 | 2 | 5 | 7 | 10 | 12 |
| 35° | ·5736 | ·5750 | ·5764 | ·5779 | ·5793 | ·5807 | ·5821 | ·5835 | ·5850 | ·5864 | 2 | 5 | 7 | 9 | 12 |
| 36° | ·5878 | ·5892 | ·5906 | ·5920 | ·5934 | ·5948 | ·5962 | ·5976 | ·5990 | ·6004 | 2 | 5 | 7 | 9 | 12 |
| 37° | ·6018 | ·6032 | ·6046 | ·6060 | ·6074 | ·6088 | ·6101 | ·6115 | ·6129 | ·6143 | 2 | 5 | 7 | 9 | 12 |
| 38° | ·6157 | ·6170 | ·6184 | ·6198 | ·6211 | ·6225 | ·6239 | ·6252 | ·6266 | ·6280 | 2 | 5 | 7 | 9 | 11 |
| 39° | ·6293 | ·6307 | ·6320 | ·6334 | ·6347 | ·6361 | ·6374 | ·6388 | ·6401 | ·6414 | 2 | 4 | 7 | 9 | 11 |
| 40° | ·6428 | ·6441 | ·6455 | ·6468 | ·6481 | ·6494 | ·6508 | ·6521 | ·6534 | ·6547 | 2 | 4 | 7 | 9 | 11 |
| 41° | ·6561 | ·6574 | ·6587 | ·6600 | ·6613 | ·6626 | ·6639 | ·6652 | ·6665 | ·6678 | 2 | 4 | 7 | 9 | 11 |
| 42° | ·6691 | ·6704 | ·6717 | ·6730 | ·6743 | ·6756 | ·6769 | ·6782 | ·6794 | ·6807 | 2 | 4 | 6 | 9 | 11 |
| 43° | ·6820 | ·6833 | ·6845 | ·6858 | ·6871 | ·6884 | ·6896 | ·6909 | ·6921 | ·6934 | 2 | 4 | 6 | 8 | 11 |
| 44° | ·6947 | ·6959 | ·6972 | ·6984 | ·6997 | ·7009 | ·7022 | ·7034 | ·7046 | ·7059 | 2 | 4 | 6 | 8 | 10 |

## NATURAL SINES

| Angle. | 0′ | 6′ | 12′ | 18′ | 24′ | 30′ | 36′ | 42′ | 48′ | 54′ | 1′ | 2′ | 3′ | 4′ | 5′ |
|---|---|---|---|---|---|---|---|---|---|---|---|---|---|---|---|
| 45° | ·7071 | ·7083 | ·7096 | ·7108 | ·7120 | ·7133 | ·7145 | ·7157 | ·7169 | ·7181 | 2 | 4 | 6 | 8 | 10 |
| 46° | ·7193 | ·7206 | ·7218 | ·7230 | ·7242 | ·7254 | ·7266 | ·7278 | ·7290 | ·7302 | 2 | 4 | 6 | 8 | 10 |
| 47° | ·7314 | ·7325 | ·7337 | ·7349 | ·7361 | ·7373 | ·7385 | ·7396 | ·7408 | ·7420 | 2 | 4 | 6 | 8 | 10 |
| 48° | ·7431 | ·7443 | ·7455 | ·7466 | ·7478 | ·7490 | ·7501 | ·7513 | ·7524 | ·7536 | 2 | 4 | 6 | 8 | 10 |
| 49° | ·7547 | ·7559 | ·7570 | ·7581 | ·7593 | ·7604 | ·7615 | ·7627 | ·7638 | ·7649 | 2 | 4 | 6 | 8 | 9 |
| 50° | ·7660 | ·7672 | ·7683 | ·7694 | ·7705 | ·7716 | ·7727 | ·7738 | ·7749 | ·7760 | 2 | 4 | 6 | 7 | 9 |
| 51° | ·7771 | ·7782 | ·7793 | ·7804 | ·7815 | ·7826 | ·7837 | ·7848 | ·7859 | ·7869 | 2 | 4 | 5 | 7 | 9 |
| 52° | ·7880 | ·7891 | ·7902 | ·7912 | ·7923 | ·7934 | ·7944 | ·7955 | ·7965 | ·7976 | 2 | 4 | 5 | 7 | 9 |
| 53° | ·7986 | ·7997 | ·8007 | ·8018 | ·8028 | ·8039 | ·8049 | ·8059 | ·8070 | ·8080 | 2 | 3 | 5 | 7 | 9 |
| 54° | ·8090 | ·8100 | ·8111 | ·8121 | ·8131 | ·8141 | ·8151 | ·8161 | ·8171 | ·8181 | 2 | 3 | 5 | 7 | 8 |
| 55° | ·8192 | ·8202 | ·8211 | ·8221 | ·8231 | ·8241 | ·8251 | ·8261 | ·8271 | ·8281 | 2 | 3 | 5 | 7 | 8 |
| 56° | ·8290 | ·8300 | ·8310 | ·8320 | ·8329 | ·8339 | ·8348 | ·8358 | ·8368 | ·8377 | 2 | 3 | 5 | 6 | 8 |
| 57° | ·8387 | ·8396 | ·8406 | ·8415 | ·8425 | ·8434 | ·8443 | ·8453 | ·8462 | ·8471 | 2 | 3 | 5 | 6 | 8 |
| 58° | ·8480 | ·8490 | ·8499 | ·8508 | ·8517 | ·8526 | ·8536 | ·8545 | ·8554 | ·8563 | 2 | 3 | 5 | 6 | 8 |
| 59° | ·8572 | ·8581 | ·8590 | ·8599 | ·8607 | ·8616 | ·8625 | ·8634 | ·8643 | ·8652 | 1 | 3 | 4 | 6 | 7 |
| 60° | ·8660 | ·8669 | ·8678 | ·8686 | ·8695 | ·8704 | ·8712 | ·8721 | ·8729 | ·8738 | 1 | 3 | 4 | 6 | 7 |
| 61° | ·8746 | ·8755 | ·8763 | ·8771 | ·8780 | ·8788 | ·8796 | ·8805 | ·8813 | ·8821 | 1 | 3 | 4 | 6 | 7 |
| 62° | ·8829 | ·8838 | ·8846 | ·8854 | ·8862 | ·8870 | ·8878 | ·8886 | ·8894 | ·8902 | 1 | 3 | 4 | 5 | 7 |
| 63° | ·8910 | ·8918 | ·8926 | ·8934 | ·8942 | ·8949 | ·8957 | ·8965 | ·8973 | ·8980 | 1 | 3 | 4 | 5 | 6 |
| 64° | ·8988 | ·8996 | ·9003 | ·9011 | ·9018 | ·9026 | ·9033 | ·9041 | ·9048 | ·9056 | 1 | 3 | 4 | 5 | 6 |
| 65° | ·9063 | ·9070 | ·9078 | ·9085 | ·9092 | ·9100 | ·9107 | ·9114 | ·9121 | ·9128 | 1 | 2 | 4 | 5 | 6 |
| 66° | ·9135 | ·9143 | ·9150 | ·9157 | ·9164 | ·9171 | ·9178 | ·9184 | ·9191 | ·9198 | 1 | 2 | 3 | 5 | 6 |
| 67° | ·9205 | ·9212 | ·9219 | ·9225 | ·9232 | ·9239 | ·9245 | ·9252 | ·9259 | ·9265 | 1 | 2 | 3 | 4 | 6 |
| 68° | ·9272 | ·9278 | ·9285 | ·9291 | ·9298 | ·9304 | ·9311 | ·9317 | ·9323 | ·9330 | 1 | 2 | 3 | 4 | 5 |
| 69° | ·9336 | ·9342 | ·9348 | ·9354 | ·9361 | ·9367 | ·9373 | ·9379 | ·9385 | ·9391 | 1 | 2 | 3 | 4 | 5 |
| 70° | ·9397 | ·9403 | ·9409 | ·9415 | ·9421 | ·9426 | ·9432 | ·9438 | ·9444 | ·9449 | 1 | 2 | 3 | 4 | 5 |
| 71° | ·9455 | ·9461 | ·9466 | ·9472 | ·9478 | ·9483 | ·9489 | ·9494 | ·9500 | ·9505 | 1 | 2 | 3 | 4 | 5 |
| 72° | ·9511 | ·9516 | ·9521 | ·9527 | ·9532 | ·9537 | ·9542 | ·9548 | ·9553 | ·9558 | 1 | 2 | 3 | 3 | 4 |
| 73° | ·9563 | ·9568 | ·9573 | ·9578 | ·9583 | ·9588 | ·9593 | ·9598 | ·9603 | ·9608 | 1 | 2 | 2 | 3 | 4 |
| 74° | ·9613 | ·9617 | ·9622 | ·9627 | ·9632 | ·9636 | ·9641 | ·9646 | ·9650 | ·9655 | 1 | 2 | 2 | 3 | 4 |
| 75° | ·9659 | ·9664 | ·9668 | ·9673 | ·9677 | ·9681 | ·9686 | ·9690 | ·9694 | ·9699 | 1 | 1 | 2 | 3 | 4 |
| 76° | ·9703 | ·9707 | ·9711 | ·9715 | ·9720 | ·9724 | ·9728 | ·9732 | ·9736 | ·9740 | 1 | 1 | 2 | 3 | 3 |
| 77° | ·9744 | ·9748 | ·9751 | ·9755 | ·9759 | ·9763 | ·9767 | ·9770 | ·9774 | ·9778 | 1 | 1 | 2 | 3 | 3 |
| 78° | ·9781 | ·9785 | ·9789 | ·9792 | ·9796 | ·9799 | ·9803 | ·9806 | ·9810 | ·9813 | 1 | 1 | 2 | 2 | 3 |
| 79° | ·9816 | ·9820 | ·9823 | ·9826 | ·9829 | ·9833 | ·9836 | ·9839 | ·9842 | ·9845 | 1 | 1 | 2 | 2 | 3 |
| 80° | ·9848 | ·9851 | ·9854 | ·9857 | ·9860 | ·9863 | ·9866 | ·9869 | ·9871 | ·9874 | 0 | 1 | 1 | 2 | 2 |
| 81° | ·9877 | ·9880 | ·9882 | ·9885 | ·9888 | ·9890 | ·9893 | ·9895 | ·9898 | ·9900 | 0 | 1 | 1 | 2 | 2 |
| 82° | ·9903 | ·9905 | ·9907 | ·9910 | ·9912 | ·9914 | ·9917 | ·9919 | ·9921 | ·9923 | 0 | 1 | 1 | 2 | 2 |
| 83° | ·9925 | ·9928 | ·9930 | ·9932 | ·9934 | ·9936 | ·9938 | ·9940 | ·9942 | ·9943 | 0 | 1 | 1 | 1 | 2 |
| 84° | ·9945 | ·9947 | ·9949 | ·9951 | ·9952 | ·9954 | ·9956 | ·9957 | ·9959 | ·9960 | 0 | 1 | 1 | 1 | 1 |
| 85° | ·9962 | ·9963 | ·9965 | ·9966 | ·9968 | ·9969 | ·9971 | ·9972 | ·9973 | ·9974 | 0 | 0 | 1 | 1 | 1 |
| 86° | ·9976 | ·9977 | ·9978 | ·9979 | ·9980 | ·9981 | ·9982 | ·9983 | ·9984 | ·9985 | 0 | 0 | 1 | 1 | 1 |
| 87° | ·9986 | ·9987 | ·9988 | ·9989 | ·9990 | ·9990 | ·9991 | ·9991 | ·9993 | ·9993 | 0 | 0 | 0 | 1 | 1 |
| 88° | ·9994 | ·9995 | ·9995 | ·9996 | ·9996 | ·9997 | ·9997 | ·9997 | ·9998 | ·9998 | 0 | 0 | 0 | 0 | 1 |
| 89° | ·9998 | ·9999 | ·9999 | ·9999 | ·9999 | 1·000 | 1·000 | 1·000 | 1·000 | 1·000 | 0 | 0 | 0 | 0 | 0 |

## NATURAL COSINES

Subtract Differences.

| | 0′ | 6′ | 12′ | 18′ | 24′ | 30′ | 36′ | 42′ | 48′ | 54′ | 1′ | 2′ | 3′ | 4′ | 5′ |
|---|---|---|---|---|---|---|---|---|---|---|---|---|---|---|---|
| 0° | 1·0000 | 1·000 | 1·000 | 1·000 | 1·000 | 1·000 | ·9999 | ·9999 | ·9999 | ·9999 | 0 | 0 | 0 | 0 | 0 |
| 1° | ·9998 | ·9998 | ·9998 | ·9997 | ·9997 | ·9997 | ·9996 | ·9996 | ·9995 | ·9995 | 0 | 0 | 0 | 0 | 0 |
| 2° | ·9994 | ·9993 | ·9993 | ·9992 | ·9991 | ·9990 | ·9990 | ·9989 | ·9988 | ·9987 | 0 | 0 | 0 | 0 | 0 |
| 3° | ·9986 | ·9985 | ·9984 | ·9983 | ·9982 | ·9981 | ·9980 | ·9979 | ·9978 | ·9977 | 0 | 0 | 1 | 1 | 1 |
| 4° | ·9976 | ·9974 | ·9973 | ·9972 | ·9971 | ·9969 | ·9968 | ·9966 | ·9965 | ·9963 | 0 | 0 | 1 | 1 | 1 |
| 5° | ·9962 | ·9960 | ·9959 | ·9957 | ·9956 | ·9954 | ·9952 | ·9951 | ·9949 | ·9947 | 0 | 1 | 1 | 1 | 1 |
| 6° | ·9945 | ·9943 | ·9942 | ·9940 | ·9938 | ·9936 | ·9934 | ·9932 | ·9930 | ·9928 | 0 | 1 | 1 | 1 | 2 |
| 7° | ·9925 | ·9923 | ·9921 | ·9919 | ·9917 | ·9914 | ·9912 | ·9910 | ·9907 | ·9905 | 0 | 1 | 1 | 2 | 2 |
| 8° | ·9903 | ·9900 | ·9898 | ·9895 | ·9893 | ·9890 | ·9888 | ·9885 | ·9882 | ·9880 | 0 | 1 | 1 | 2 | 2 |
| 9° | ·9877 | ·9874 | ·9871 | ·9869 | ·9866 | ·9863 | ·9860 | ·9857 | ·9854 | ·9851 | 0 | 1 | 1 | 2 | 2 |
| 10° | ·9848 | ·9845 | ·9842 | ·9839 | ·9836 | ·9833 | ·9829 | ·9826 | ·9823 | ·9820 | 1 | 1 | 2 | 2 | 3 |
| 11° | ·9816 | ·9813 | ·9810 | ·9806 | ·9803 | ·9799 | ·9796 | ·9792 | ·9789 | ·9785 | 1 | 1 | 2 | 2 | 3 |
| 12° | ·9781 | ·9778 | ·9774 | ·9770 | ·9767 | ·9763 | ·9759 | ·9755 | ·9751 | ·9748 | 1 | 1 | 2 | 3 | 3 |
| 13° | ·9744 | ·9740 | ·9736 | ·9732 | ·9728 | ·9724 | ·9720 | ·9715 | ·9711 | ·9707 | 1 | 1 | 2 | 3 | 3 |
| 14° | ·9703 | ·9699 | ·9694 | ·9690 | ·9686 | ·9681 | ·9677 | ·9673 | ·9668 | ·9664 | 1 | 1 | 2 | 3 | 4 |
| 15° | ·9659 | ·9655 | ·9650 | ·9646 | ·9641 | ·9636 | ·9632 | ·9627 | ·9622 | ·9617 | 1 | 2 | 2 | 3 | 4 |
| 16° | ·9613 | ·9608 | ·9603 | ·9598 | ·9593 | ·9588 | ·9583 | ·9578 | ·9573 | ·9568 | 1 | 2 | 2 | 3 | 4 |
| 17° | ·9563 | ·9558 | ·9553 | ·9548 | ·9542 | ·9537 | ·9532 | ·9527 | ·9521 | ·9516 | 1 | 2 | 3 | 4 | 4 |
| 18° | ·9511 | ·9505 | ·9500 | ·9494 | ·9489 | ·9483 | ·9478 | ·9472 | ·9466 | ·9461 | 1 | 2 | 3 | 4 | 5 |
| 19° | ·9455 | ·9449 | ·9444 | ·9438 | ·9432 | ·9426 | ·9421 | ·9415 | ·9409 | ·9403 | 1 | 2 | 3 | 4 | 5 |
| 20° | ·9397 | ·9391 | ·9385 | ·9379 | ·9373 | ·9367 | ·9361 | ·9354 | ·9348 | ·9342 | 1 | 2 | 3 | 4 | 5 |
| 21° | ·9336 | ·9330 | ·9323 | ·9317 | ·9311 | ·9304 | ·9298 | ·9291 | ·9285 | ·9278 | 1 | 2 | 3 | 4 | 5 |
| 22° | ·9272 | ·9265 | ·9259 | ·9252 | ·9245 | ·9239 | ·9232 | ·9225 | ·9219 | ·9212 | 1 | 2 | 3 | 4 | 6 |
| 23° | ·9205 | ·9198 | ·9191 | ·9184 | ·9178 | ·9171 | ·9164 | ·9157 | ·9150 | ·9143 | 1 | 2 | 3 | 5 | 6 |
| 24° | ·9135 | ·9128 | ·9121 | ·9114 | ·9107 | ·9100 | ·9092 | ·9085 | ·9078 | ·9070 | 1 | 2 | 4 | 5 | 6 |
| 25° | ·9063 | ·9056 | ·9048 | ·9041 | ·9033 | ·9026 | ·9018 | ·9011 | ·9003 | ·8996 | 1 | 3 | 4 | 5 | 6 |
| 26° | ·8988 | ·8980 | ·8973 | ·8965 | ·8957 | ·8949 | ·8942 | ·8934 | ·8926 | ·8918 | 1 | 3 | 4 | 5 | 6 |
| 27° | ·8910 | ·8902 | ·8894 | ·8886 | ·8878 | ·8870 | ·8862 | ·8854 | ·8846 | ·8838 | 1 | 3 | 4 | 5 | 7 |
| 28° | ·8829 | ·8821 | ·8813 | ·8805 | ·8796 | ·8788 | ·8780 | ·8771 | ·8763 | ·8755 | 1 | 3 | 4 | 6 | 7 |
| 29° | ·8746 | ·8738 | ·8729 | ·8721 | ·8712 | ·8704 | ·8695 | ·8686 | ·8678 | ·8669 | 1 | 3 | 4 | 6 | 7 |
| 30° | ·8660 | ·8652 | ·8643 | ·8634 | ·8625 | ·8616 | ·8607 | ·8599 | ·8590 | ·8581 | 1 | 3 | 4 | 6 | 7 |
| 31° | ·8572 | ·8563 | ·8554 | ·8545 | ·8536 | ·8526 | ·8517 | ·8508 | ·8499 | ·8490 | 2 | 3 | 5 | 6 | 8 |
| 32° | ·8480 | ·8471 | ·8462 | ·8453 | ·8443 | ·8434 | ·8425 | ·8415 | ·8406 | ·8396 | 2 | 3 | 5 | 6 | 8 |
| 33° | ·8387 | ·8377 | ·8368 | ·8358 | ·8348 | ·8339 | ·8329 | ·8320 | ·8310 | ·8300 | 2 | 3 | 5 | 6 | 8 |
| 34° | ·8290 | ·8281 | ·8271 | ·8261 | ·8251 | ·8241 | ·8231 | ·8221 | ·8211 | ·8202 | 2 | 3 | 5 | 7 | 8 |
| 35° | ·8192 | ·8181 | ·8171 | ·8161 | ·8151 | ·8141 | ·8131 | ·8121 | ·8111 | ·8100 | 2 | 3 | 5 | 7 | 8 |
| 36° | ·8090 | ·8080 | ·8070 | ·8059 | ·8049 | ·8039 | ·8028 | ·8018 | ·8007 | ·7997 | 2 | 3 | 5 | 7 | 9 |
| 37° | ·7986 | ·7976 | ·7965 | ·7955 | ·7944 | ·7934 | ·7923 | ·7912 | ·7902 | ·7891 | 2 | 4 | 5 | 7 | 9 |
| 38° | ·7880 | ·7869 | ·7859 | ·7848 | ·7837 | ·7826 | ·7815 | ·7804 | ·7793 | ·7782 | 2 | 4 | 5 | 7 | 9 |
| 39° | ·7771 | ·7760 | ·7749 | ·7738 | ·7727 | ·7716 | ·7705 | ·7694 | ·7683 | ·7672 | 2 | 4 | 6 | 7 | 9 |
| 40° | ·7660 | ·7649 | ·7638 | ·7627 | ·7615 | ·7604 | ·7593 | ·7581 | ·7570 | ·7559 | 2 | 4 | 6 | 8 | 9 |
| 41° | ·7547 | ·7536 | ·7524 | ·7513 | ·7501 | ·7490 | ·7478 | ·7466 | ·7455 | ·7443 | 2 | 4 | 6 | 8 | 10 |
| 42° | ·7431 | ·7420 | ·7408 | ·7396 | ·7385 | ·7373 | ·7361 | ·7349 | ·7337 | ·7325 | 2 | 4 | 6 | 8 | 10 |
| 43° | ·7314 | ·7302 | ·7290 | ·7278 | ·7266 | ·7254 | ·7242 | ·7230 | ·7218 | ·7206 | 2 | 4 | 6 | 8 | 10 |
| 44° | ·7193 | ·7181 | ·7169 | ·7157 | ·7145 | ·7133 | ·7120 | ·7108 | ·7096 | ·7083 | 2 | 4 | 6 | 8 | 10 |

# NATURAL COSINES

|  | 0′ | 6′ | 12′ | 18′ | 24′ | 30′ | 36′ | 42′ | 48′ | 54′ | 1′ | 2′ | 3′ | 4′ | 5′ |
|---|---|---|---|---|---|---|---|---|---|---|---|---|---|---|---|
| 45° | ·7071 | ·7059 | ·7046 | ·7034 | ·7022 | ·7009 | ·6997 | ·6984 | ·6972 | ·6959 | 2 | 4 | 6 | 8 | 10 |
| 46° | ·6947 | ·6934 | ·6921 | ·6909 | ·6896 | ·6884 | ·6871 | ·6858 | ·6845 | ·6833 | 2 | 4 | 6 | 8 | 11 |
| 47° | ·6820 | ·6807 | ·6794 | ·6782 | ·6769 | ·6756 | ·6743 | ·6730 | ·6717 | ·6704 | 2 | 4 | 6 | 9 | 11 |
| 48° | ·6691 | ·6678 | ·6665 | ·6652 | ·6639 | ·6626 | ·6613 | ·6600 | ·6587 | ·6574 | 2 | 4 | 7 | 9 | 11 |
| 49° | ·6561 | ·6547 | ·6534 | ·6521 | ·6508 | ·6494 | ·6481 | ·6468 | ·6455 | ·6441 | 2 | 4 | 7 | 9 | 11 |
| 50° | ·6428 | ·6414 | ·6401 | ·6388 | ·6374 | ·6361 | ·6347 | ·6334 | ·6320 | ·6307 | 2 | 4 | 7 | 9 | 11 |
| 51° | ·6293 | ·6280 | ·6266 | ·6252 | ·6239 | ·6225 | ·6211 | ·6198 | ·6184 | ·6170 | 2 | 5 | 7 | 9 | 11 |
| 52° | ·6157 | ·6143 | ·6129 | ·6115 | ·6101 | ·6088 | ·6074 | ·6060 | ·6046 | ·6032 | 2 | 5 | 7 | 9 | 12 |
| 53° | ·6018 | ·6004 | ·5990 | ·5976 | ·5962 | ·5948 | ·5934 | ·5920 | ·5906 | ·5892 | 2 | 5 | 7 | 9 | 12 |
| 54° | ·5878 | ·5864 | ·5850 | ·5835 | ·5821 | ·5807 | ·5793 | ·5779 | ·5764 | ·5750 | 2 | 5 | 7 | 9 | 12 |
| 55° | ·5736 | ·5721 | ·5707 | ·5693 | ·5678 | ·5664 | ·5650 | ·5635 | ·5621 | ·5606 | 2 | 5 | 7 | 10 | 12 |
| 56° | ·5592 | ·5577 | ·5563 | ·5548 | ·5534 | ·5519 | ·5505 | ·5490 | ·5476 | ·5461 | 2 | 5 | 7 | 10 | 12 |
| 57° | ·5446 | ·5432 | ·5417 | ·5402 | ·5388 | ·5373 | ·5358 | ·5344 | ·5329 | ·5314 | 2 | 5 | 7 | 10 | 12 |
| 58° | ·5299 | ·5284 | ·5270 | ·5255 | ·5240 | ·5225 | ·5210 | ·5195 | ·5180 | ·5165 | 2 | 5 | 7 | 10 | 12 |
| 59° | ·5150 | ·5135 | ·5120 | ·5105 | ·5090 | ·5075 | ·5060 | ·5045 | ·5030 | ·5015 | 3 | 5 | 8 | 10 | 13 |
| 60° | ·5000 | ·4985 | ·4970 | ·4955 | ·4939 | ·4924 | ·4909 | ·4894 | ·4879 | ·4863 | 3 | 5 | 8 | 10 | 13 |
| 61° | ·4848 | ·4833 | ·4818 | ·4802 | ·4787 | ·4772 | ·4756 | ·4741 | ·4726 | ·4710 | 3 | 5 | 8 | 10 | 13 |
| 62° | ·4695 | ·4679 | ·4664 | ·4648 | ·4633 | ·4617 | ·4602 | ·4586 | ·4571 | ·4555 | 3 | 5 | 8 | 10 | 13 |
| 63° | ·4540 | ·4524 | ·4509 | ·4493 | ·4478 | ·4462 | ·4446 | ·4431 | ·4415 | ·4399 | 3 | 5 | 8 | 10 | 13 |
| 64° | ·4384 | ·4368 | ·4352 | ·4337 | ·4321 | ·4305 | ·4289 | ·4274 | ·4258 | ·4242 | 3 | 5 | 8 | 11 | 13 |
| 65° | ·4226 | ·4210 | ·4195 | ·4179 | ·4163 | ·4147 | ·4131 | ·4115 | ·4099 | ·4083 | 3 | 5 | 8 | 11 | 13 |
| 66° | ·4067 | ·4051 | ·4035 | ·4019 | ·4003 | ·3987 | ·3971 | ·3955 | ·3939 | ·3923 | 3 | 5 | 8 | 11 | 13 |
| 67° | ·3907 | ·3891 | ·3875 | ·3859 | ·3843 | ·3827 | ·3811 | ·3795 | ·3778 | ·3762 | 3 | 5 | 8 | 11 | 13 |
| 68° | ·3746 | ·3730 | ·3714 | ·3697 | ·3681 | ·3665 | ·3649 | ·3633 | ·3616 | ·3600 | 3 | 5 | 8 | 11 | 14 |
| 69° | ·3584 | ·3567 | ·3551 | ·3535 | ·3518 | ·3502 | ·3486 | ·3469 | ·3453 | ·3437 | 3 | 5 | 8 | 11 | 14 |
| 70° | ·3420 | ·3404 | ·3387 | ·3371 | ·3355 | ·3338 | ·3322 | ·3305 | ·3289 | ·3272 | 3 | 5 | 8 | 11 | 14 |
| 71° | ·3256 | ·3239 | ·3223 | ·3206 | ·3190 | ·3173 | ·3156 | ·3140 | ·3123 | ·3107 | 3 | 6 | 8 | 11 | 14 |
| 72° | ·3090 | ·3074 | ·3057 | ·3040 | ·3024 | ·3007 | ·2990 | ·2974 | ·2957 | ·2940 | 3 | 6 | 8 | 11 | 14 |
| 73° | ·2924 | ·2907 | ·2890 | ·2874 | ·2857 | ·2840 | ·2823 | ·2807 | ·2790 | ·2773 | 3 | 6 | 8 | 11 | 14 |
| 74° | ·2756 | ·2740 | ·2723 | ·2706 | ·2689 | ·2672 | ·2656 | ·2639 | ·2622 | ·2605 | 3 | 6 | 8 | 11 | 14 |
| 75° | ·2588 | ·2571 | ·2554 | ·2538 | ·2521 | ·2504 | ·2487 | ·2470 | ·2453 | ·2436 | 3 | 6 | 8 | 11 | 14 |
| 76° | ·2419 | ·2402 | ·2385 | ·2368 | ·2351 | ·2334 | ·2317 | ·2300 | ·2284 | ·2267 | 3 | 6 | 8 | 11 | 14 |
| 77° | ·2250 | ·2233 | ·2215 | ·2198 | ·2181 | ·2164 | ·2147 | ·2130 | ·2113 | ·2096 | 3 | 6 | 9 | 11 | 14 |
| 78° | ·2079 | ·2062 | ·2045 | ·2028 | ·2011 | ·1994 | ·1977 | ·1959 | ·1942 | ·1925 | 3 | 6 | 9 | 11 | 14 |
| 79° | ·1908 | ·1891 | ·1874 | ·1857 | ·1840 | ·1822 | ·1805 | ·1788 | ·1771 | ·1754 | 3 | 6 | 9 | 11 | 14 |
| 80° | ·1736 | ·1719 | ·1702 | ·1685 | ·1668 | ·1650 | ·1633 | ·1616 | ·1599 | ·1582 | 3 | 6 | 9 | 11 | 14 |
| 81° | ·1564 | ·1547 | ·1530 | ·1513 | ·1495 | ·1478 | ·1461 | ·1444 | ·1426 | ·1409 | 3 | 6 | 9 | 12 | 14 |
| 82° | ·1392 | ·1374 | ·1357 | ·1340 | ·1323 | ·1305 | ·1288 | ·1271 | ·1253 | ·1236 | 3 | 6 | 9 | 12 | 14 |
| 83° | ·1219 | ·1201 | ·1184 | ·1167 | ·1149 | ·1132 | ·1115 | ·1097 | ·1080 | ·1063 | 3 | 6 | 9 | 12 | 14 |
| 84° | ·1045 | ·1028 | ·1011 | ·0993 | ·0976 | ·0958 | ·0941 | ·0924 | ·0906 | ·0889 | 3 | 6 | 9 | 12 | 14 |
| 85° | ·0872 | ·0854 | ·0837 | ·0819 | ·0802 | ·0785 | ·0767 | ·0750 | ·0732 | ·0715 | 3 | 6 | 9 | 12 | 14 |
| 86° | ·0698 | ·0680 | ·0663 | ·0645 | ·0628 | ·0610 | ·0593 | ·0576 | ·0558 | ·0541 | 3 | 6 | 9 | 12 | 15 |
| 87° | ·0523 | ·0506 | ·0488 | ·0471 | ·0454 | ·0436 | ·0419 | ·0401 | ·0384 | ·0366 | 3 | 6 | 9 | 12 | 15 |
| 88° | ·0349 | ·0332 | ·0314 | ·0297 | ·0279 | ·0262 | ·0244 | ·0227 | ·0209 | ·0192 | 3 | 6 | 9 | 12 | 15 |
| 89° | ·0175 | ·0157 | ·0140 | ·0122 | ·0105 | ·0087 | ·0070 | ·0052 | ·0035 | ·0017 | 3 | 6 | 9 | 12 | 15 |

## NATURAL TANGENTS

| Angle. | 0′ | 6′ | 12′ | 18′ | 24′ | 30′ | 36′ | 42′ | 48′ | 54′ | 1′ | 2′ | 3′ | 4′ | 5′ |
|---|---|---|---|---|---|---|---|---|---|---|---|---|---|---|---|
| 0° | 0·0000 | ·0017 | ·0035 | ·0052 | ·0070 | ·0087 | ·0105 | ·0122 | ·0140 | ·0157 | 3 | 6 | 9 | 12 | 15 |
| 1° | 0·0175 | ·0192 | ·0209 | ·0227 | ·0244 | ·0262 | ·0279 | ·0297 | ·0314 | ·0332 | 3 | 6 | 9 | 12 | 15 |
| 2° | 0·0349 | ·0367 | ·0384 | ·0402 | ·0419 | ·0437 | ·0454 | ·0472 | ·0489 | ·0507 | 3 | 6 | 9 | 12 | 15 |
| 3° | 0·0524 | ·0542 | ·0559 | ·0577 | ·0594 | ·0612 | ·0629 | ·0647 | ·0664 | ·0682 | 3 | 6 | 9 | 12 | 15 |
| 4° | 0·0699 | ·0717 | ·0734 | ·0752 | ·0769 | ·0787 | ·0805 | ·0822 | ·0840 | ·0857 | 3 | 6 | 9 | 12 | 15 |
| 5° | 0·0875 | ·0892 | ·0910 | ·0928 | ·0945 | ·0963 | ·0981 | ·0998 | ·1016 | ·1033 | 3 | 6 | 9 | 12 | 15 |
| 6° | 0·1051 | ·1069 | ·1086 | ·1104 | ·1122 | ·1139 | ·1157 | ·1175 | ·1192 | ·1210 | 3 | 6 | 9 | 12 | 15 |
| 7° | 0·1228 | ·1246 | ·1263 | ·1281 | ·1299 | ·1317 | ·1334 | ·1352 | ·1370 | ·1388 | 3 | 6 | 9 | 12 | 15 |
| 8° | 0·1405 | ·1423 | ·1441 | ·1459 | ·1477 | ·1495 | ·1512 | ·1530 | ·1548 | ·1566 | 3 | 6 | 9 | 12 | 15 |
| 9° | 0·1584 | ·1602 | ·1620 | ·1638 | ·1655 | ·1673 | ·1691 | ·1709 | ·1727 | ·1745 | 3 | 6 | 9 | 12 | 15 |
| 10° | 0·1763 | ·1781 | ·1799 | ·1817 | ·1835 | ·1853 | ·1871 | ·1890 | ·1908 | ·1926 | 3 | 6 | 9 | 12 | 15 |
| 11° | 0·1944 | ·1962 | ·1980 | ·1998 | ·2016 | ·2035 | ·2053 | ·2071 | ·2089 | ·2107 | 3 | 6 | 9 | 12 | 15 |
| 12° | 0·2126 | ·2144 | ·2162 | ·2180 | ·2199 | ·2217 | ·2235 | ·2254 | ·2272 | ·2290 | 3 | 6 | 9 | 12 | 15 |
| 13° | 0·2309 | ·2327 | ·2345 | ·2364 | ·2382 | ·2401 | ·2419 | ·2438 | ·2456 | ·2475 | 3 | 6 | 9 | 12 | 15 |
| 14° | 0·2493 | ·2512 | ·2530 | ·2549 | ·2568 | ·2586 | ·2605 | ·2623 | ·2642 | ·2661 | 3 | 6 | 9 | 12 | 16 |
| 15° | 0·2679 | ·2698 | ·2717 | ·2736 | ·2754 | ·2773 | ·2792 | ·2811 | ·2830 | ·2849 | 3 | 6 | 9 | 13 | 16 |
| 16° | 0·2867 | ·2886 | ·2905 | ·2924 | ·2943 | ·2962 | ·2981 | ·3000 | ·3019 | ·3038 | 3 | 6 | 9 | 13 | 16 |
| 17° | 0·3057 | ·3076 | ·3096 | ·3115 | ·3134 | ·3153 | ·3172 | ·3191 | ·3211 | ·3230 | 3 | 6 | 10 | 13 | 16 |
| 18° | 0·3249 | ·3269 | ·3288 | ·3307 | ·3327 | ·3346 | ·3365 | ·3385 | ·3404 | ·3424 | 3 | 6 | 10 | 13 | 16 |
| 19° | 0·3443 | ·3463 | ·3482 | ·3502 | ·3522 | ·3541 | ·3561 | ·3581 | ·3600 | ·3620 | 3 | 7 | 10 | 13 | 16 |
| 20° | 0·3640 | ·3659 | ·3679 | ·3699 | ·3719 | ·3739 | ·3759 | ·3779 | ·3799 | ·3819 | 3 | 7 | 10 | 13 | 17 |
| 21° | 0·3839 | ·3859 | ·3879 | ·3899 | ·3919 | ·3939 | ·3959 | ·3979 | ·4000 | ·4020 | 3 | 7 | 10 | 13 | 17 |
| 22° | 0·4040 | ·4061 | ·4081 | ·4101 | ·4122 | ·4142 | ·4163 | ·4183 | ·4204 | ·4224 | 3 | 7 | 10 | 14 | 17 |
| 23° | 0·4245 | ·4265 | ·4286 | ·4307 | ·4327 | ·4348 | ·4369 | ·4390 | ·4411 | ·4431 | 3 | 7 | 10 | 14 | 17 |
| 24° | 0·4452 | ·4473 | ·4494 | ·4515 | ·4536 | ·4557 | ·4578 | ·4599 | ·4621 | ·4642 | 4 | 7 | 11 | 14 | 18 |
| 25° | 0·4663 | ·4684 | ·4706 | ·4727 | ·4748 | ·4770 | ·4791 | ·4813 | ·4834 | ·4856 | 4 | 7 | 11 | 14 | 18 |
| 26° | 0·4877 | ·4899 | ·4921 | ·4942 | ·4964 | ·4986 | ·5008 | ·5029 | ·5051 | ·5073 | 4 | 7 | 11 | 15 | 18 |
| 27° | 0·5095 | ·5117 | ·5139 | ·5161 | ·5184 | ·5206 | ·5228 | ·5250 | ·5272 | ·5295 | 4 | 7 | 11 | 15 | 18 |
| 28° | 0·5317 | ·5340 | ·5362 | ·5384 | ·5407 | ·5430 | ·5452 | ·5475 | ·5498 | ·5520 | 4 | 8 | 11 | 15 | 19 |
| 29° | 0·5543 | ·5566 | ·5589 | ·5612 | ·5635 | ·5658 | ·5681 | ·5704 | ·5727 | ·5750 | 4 | 8 | 12 | 15 | 19 |
| 30° | 0·5774 | ·5797 | ·5820 | ·5844 | ·5867 | ·5890 | ·5914 | ·5938 | ·5961 | ·5985 | 4 | 8 | 12 | 16 | 20 |
| 31° | 0·6009 | ·6032 | ·6056 | ·6080 | ·6104 | ·6128 | ·6152 | ·6176 | ·6200 | ·6224 | 4 | 8 | 12 | 16 | 20 |
| 32° | 0·6249 | ·6273 | ·6297 | ·6322 | ·6346 | ·6371 | ·6395 | ·6420 | ·6445 | ·6469 | 4 | 8 | 12 | 16 | 20 |
| 33° | 0·6494 | ·6519 | ·6544 | ·6569 | ·6594 | ·6619 | ·6644 | ·6669 | ·6694 | ·6720 | 4 | 8 | 13 | 17 | 21 |
| 34° | 0·6745 | ·6771 | ·6796 | ·6822 | ·6847 | ·6873 | ·6899 | ·6924 | ·6950 | ·6976 | 4 | 9 | 13 | 17 | 21 |
| 35° | 0·7002 | ·7028 | ·7054 | ·7080 | ·7107 | ·7133 | ·7159 | ·7186 | ·7212 | ·7239 | 4 | 9 | 13 | 18 | 22 |
| 36° | 0·7265 | ·7292 | ·7319 | ·7346 | ·7373 | ·7400 | ·7427 | ·7454 | ·7481 | ·7508 | 5 | 9 | 14 | 18 | 23 |
| 37° | 0·7536 | ·7563 | ·7590 | ·7618 | ·7646 | ·7673 | ·7701 | ·7729 | ·7757 | ·7785 | 5 | 9 | 14 | 18 | 23 |
| 38° | 0·7813 | ·7841 | ·7869 | ·7898 | ·7926 | ·7954 | ·7983 | ·8012 | ·8040 | ·8069 | 5 | 9 | 14 | 19 | 24 |
| 39° | 0·8098 | ·8127 | ·8156 | ·8185 | ·8214 | ·8243 | ·8273 | ·8302 | ·8332 | ·8361 | 5 | 10 | 15 | 20 | 24 |
| 40° | 0·8391 | ·8421 | ·8451 | ·8481 | ·8511 | ·8541 | ·8571 | ·8601 | ·8632 | ·8662 | 5 | 10 | 15 | 20 | 25 |
| 41° | 0·8693 | ·8724 | ·8754 | ·8785 | ·8816 | ·8847 | ·8878 | ·8910 | ·8941 | ·8972 | 5 | 10 | 16 | 21 | 26 |
| 42° | 0·9004 | ·9036 | ·9067 | ·9099 | ·9131 | ·9163 | ·9195 | ·9228 | ·9260 | ·9293 | 5 | 11 | 16 | 21 | 27 |
| 43° | 0·9325 | ·9358 | ·9391 | ·9424 | ·9457 | ·9490 | ·9523 | ·9556 | ·9590 | ·9623 | 6 | 11 | 17 | 22 | 28 |
| 44° | 0·9657 | ·9691 | ·9725 | ·9759 | ·9793 | ·9827 | ·9861 | ·9896 | ·9930 | ·9965 | 6 | 11 | 17 | 23 | 29 |

## NATURAL TANGENTS

| Angle | 0' | 6' | 12' | 18' | 24' | 30' | 36' | 42' | 48' | 54' | 1' | 2' | 3' | 4' | 5' |
|---|---|---|---|---|---|---|---|---|---|---|---|---|---|---|---|
| 45° | 1·0000 | 1·0035 | 1·0070 | 1·0105 | 1·0141 | 1·0176 | 1·0212 | 1·0247 | 1·0283 | 1·0319 | 6 | 12 | 18 | 24 | 30 |
| 46° | 1·0355 | 1·0392 | 1·0428 | 1·0464 | 1·0501 | 1·0538 | 1·0575 | 1·0612 | 1·0649 | 1·0686 | 6 | 12 | 18 | 25 | 31 |
| 47° | 1·0724 | 1·0761 | 1·0799 | 1·0837 | 1·0875 | 1·0913 | 1·0951 | 1·0990 | 1·1028 | 1·1067 | 6 | 13 | 19 | 25 | 32 |
| 48° | 1·1106 | 1·1145 | 1·1184 | 1·1224 | 1·1263 | 1·1303 | 1·1343 | 1·1383 | 1·1423 | 1·1463 | 7 | 13 | 20 | 26 | 33 |
| 49° | 1·1504 | 1·1544 | 1·1585 | 1·1626 | 1·1667 | 1·1708 | 1·1750 | 1·1792 | 1·1833 | 1·1875 | 7 | 14 | 21 | 28 | 34 |
| 50° | 1·1918 | 1·1960 | 1·2002 | 1·2045 | 1·2088 | 1·2131 | 1·2174 | 1·2218 | 1·2261 | 1·2305 | 7 | 14 | 22 | 29 | 36 |
| 51° | 1·2349 | 1·2393 | 1·2437 | 1·2482 | 1·2527 | 1·2572 | 1·2617 | 1·2662 | 1·2708 | 1·2753 | 8 | 15 | 23 | 30 | 38 |
| 52° | 1·2799 | 1·2846 | 1·2892 | 1·2938 | 1·2985 | 1·3032 | 1·3079 | 1·3127 | 1·3175 | 1·3222 | 8 | 16 | 24 | 31 | 39 |
| 53° | 1·3270 | 1·3319 | 1·3367 | 1·3416 | 1·3465 | 1·3514 | 1·3564 | 1·3613 | 1·3663 | 1·3713 | 8 | 16 | 25 | 33 | 41 |
| 54° | 1·3764 | 1·3814 | 1·3865 | 1·3916 | 1·3968 | 1·4019 | 1·4071 | 1·4124 | 1·4176 | 1·4229 | 9 | 17 | 26 | 34 | 43 |
| 55° | 1·4281 | 1·4335 | 1·4388 | 1·4442 | 1·4496 | 1·4550 | 1·4605 | 1·4659 | 1·4715 | 1·4770 | 9 | 18 | 27 | 36 | 45 |
| 56° | 1·4826 | 1·4882 | 1·4938 | 1·4994 | 1·5051 | 1·5108 | 1·5166 | 1·5224 | 1·5282 | 1·5340 | 10 | 19 | 29 | 38 | 48 |
| 57° | 1·5399 | 1·5458 | 1·5517 | 1·5577 | 1·5637 | 1·5697 | 1·5757 | 1·5818 | 1·5880 | 1·5941 | 10 | 20 | 30 | 40 | 50 |
| 58° | 1·6003 | 1·6066 | 1·6128 | 1·6191 | 1·6255 | 1·6319 | 1·6383 | 1·6447 | 1·6512 | 1·6577 | 11 | 21 | 32 | 43 | 53 |
| 59° | 1·6643 | 1·6709 | 1·6775 | 1·6842 | 1·6909 | 1·6977 | 1·7045 | 1·7113 | 1·7182 | 1·7251 | 11 | 23 | 34 | 45 | 56 |
| 60° | 1·7321 | 1·7391 | 1·7461 | 1·7532 | 1·7603 | 1·7675 | 1·7747 | 1·7820 | 1·7893 | 1·7966 | 12 | 24 | 36 | 48 | 60 |
| 61° | 1·8040 | 1·8115 | 1·8190 | 1·8265 | 1·8341 | 1·8418 | 1·8495 | 1·8572 | 1·8650 | 1·8728 | 13 | 26 | 38 | 51 | 64 |
| 62° | 1·8807 | 1·8887 | 1·8967 | 1·9047 | 1·9128 | 1·9210 | 1·9292 | 1·9375 | 1·9458 | 1·9542 | 14 | 27 | 41 | 55 | 68 |
| 63° | 1·9626 | 1·9711 | 1·9797 | 1·9883 | 1·9970 | 2·0057 | 2·0145 | 2·0233 | 2·0323 | 2·0413 | 15 | 29 | 44 | 58 | 73 |
| 64° | 2·0503 | 2·0594 | 2·0686 | 2·0778 | 2·0872 | 2·0965 | 2·1060 | 2·1155 | 2·1251 | 2·1348 | 16 | 31 | 47 | 63 | 78 |
| 65° | 2·1445 | 2·1543 | 2·1642 | 2·1742 | 2·1842 | 2·1943 | 2·2045 | 2·2148 | 2·2251 | 2·2355 | 17 | 34 | 51 | 68 | 85 |
| 66° | 2·2460 | 2·2566 | 2·2673 | 2·2781 | 2·2889 | 2·2998 | 2·3109 | 2·3220 | 2·3332 | 2·3445 | 18 | 37 | 55 | 73 | 92 |
| 67° | 2·3559 | 2·3673 | 2·3789 | 2·3906 | 2·4023 | 2·4142 | 2·4262 | 2·4383 | 2·4504 | 2·4627 | 20 | 40 | 60 | 79 | 99 |
| 68° | 2·4751 | 2·4876 | 2·5002 | 2·5129 | 2·5257 | 2·5386 | 2·5517 | 2·5649 | 2·5782 | 2·5916 | 22 | 43 | 65 | 87 | 108 |
| 69° | 2·6051 | 2·6187 | 2·6325 | 2·6464 | 2·6605 | 2·6746 | 2·6889 | 2·7034 | 2·7179 | 2·7326 | 24 | 47 | 71 | 95 | 119 |
| 70° | 2·7475 | 2·7625 | 2·7776 | 2·7929 | 2·8083 | 2·8239 | 2·8397 | 2·8556 | 2·8716 | 2·8878 | 26 | 52 | 78 | 104 | 130 |
| 71° | 2·9042 | 2·9208 | 2·9375 | 2·9544 | 2·9714 | 2·9887 | 3·0061 | 3·0237 | 3·0415 | 3·0595 | 29 | 58 | 87 | 116 | 144 |
| 72° | 3·0777 | 3·0961 | 3·1146 | 3·1334 | 3·1524 | 3·1716 | 3·1910 | 3·2106 | 3·2305 | 3·2506 | 32 | 64 | 96 | 129 | 161 |
| 73° | 3·2709 | 3·2914 | 3·3122 | 3·3332 | 3·3544 | 3·3759 | 3·3977 | 3·4197 | 3·4420 | 3·4646 | 36 | 72 | 108 | 144 | 180 |
| 74° | 3·4874 | 3·5105 | 3·5339 | 3·5576 | 3·5816 | 3·6059 | 3·6305 | 3·6554 | 3·6806 | 3·7062 | 41 | 81 | 122 | 163 | 204 |
| 75° | 3·7321 | 3·7583 | 3·7848 | 3·8118 | 3·8391 | 3·8667 | 3·8947 | 3·9232 | 3·9520 | 3·9812 | | | | | |
| 76° | 4·0108 | 4·0408 | 4·0713 | 4·1022 | 4·1335 | 4·1653 | 4·1976 | 4·2303 | 4·2635 | 4·2972 | | | | | |
| 77° | 4·3315 | 4·3662 | 4·4015 | 4·4374 | 4·4737 | 4·5107 | 4·5483 | 4·5864 | 4·6252 | 4·6646 | | | | | |
| 78° | 4·7046 | 4·7453 | 4·7867 | 4·8288 | 4·8716 | 4·9152 | 4·9594 | 5·0045 | 5·0504 | 5·0970 | | | | | |
| 79° | 5·1446 | 5·1929 | 5·2422 | 5·2924 | 5·3435 | 5·3955 | 5·4486 | 5·5026 | 5·5578 | 5·6140 | | | | | |
| 80° | 5·6713 | 5·7297 | 5·7894 | 5·8502 | 5·9124 | 5·9758 | 6·0405 | 6·1066 | 6·1742 | 6·2432 | Mean differences not sufficiently accurate. | | | | |
| 81° | 6·3138 | 6·3859 | 6·4596 | 6·5350 | 6·6122 | 6·6912 | 6·7720 | 6·8548 | 6·9395 | 7·0264 | | | | | |
| 82° | 7·1154 | 7·2066 | 7·3002 | 7·3962 | 7·4947 | 7·5958 | 7·6996 | 7·8062 | 7·9158 | 8·0285 | | | | | |
| 83° | 8·1443 | 8·2636 | 8·3863 | 8·5126 | 8·6427 | 8·7769 | 8·9152 | 9·0579 | 9·2052 | 9·3572 | | | | | |
| 84° | 9·5144 | 9·6768 | 9·8448 | 10·019 | 10·199 | 10·385 | 10·579 | 10·780 | 10·988 | 11·205 | | | | | |
| 85° | 11·430 | 11·664 | 11·909 | 12·163 | 12·429 | 12·706 | 12·996 | 13·300 | 13·617 | 13·951 | | | | | |
| 86° | 14·301 | 14·669 | 15·056 | 15·464 | 15·895 | 16·350 | 16·832 | 17·343 | 17·886 | 18·464 | | | | | |
| 87° | 19·081 | 19·740 | 20·446 | 21·205 | 22·022 | 22·904 | 23·859 | 24·898 | 26·031 | 27·271 | | | | | |
| 88° | 28·636 | 30·145 | 31·821 | 33·694 | 35·801 | 38·188 | 40·917 | 44·066 | 47·740 | 52·081 | | | | | |
| 89° | 57·290 | 63·657 | 71·615 | 81·847 | 95·489 | 114·59 | 143·24 | 190·98 | 286·48 | 572·96 | | | | | |

# NATURAL COSECANTS

Subtract Mean Differences.

| Angle. | 0' | 6' | 12' | 18' | 24' | 30' | 36' | 42' | 48' | 54' | 1' | 2' | 3' | 4' | 5' |
|---|---|---|---|---|---|---|---|---|---|---|---|---|---|---|---|
| 0° | ∞ | 572·96 | 286·48 | 190·99 | 143·24 | 114·59 | 95·495 | 81·853 | 71·622 | 63·665 | | | | | |
| 1° | 57·299 | 52·090 | 47·750 | 44·077 | 40·930 | 38·202 | 35·815 | 33·708 | 31·836 | 30·161 | | | | | |
| 2° | 28·654 | 27·290 | 26·050 | 24·918 | 23·880 | 22·926 | 22·044 | 21·229 | 20·471 | 19·766 | | | | | |
| 3° | 19·107 | 18·492 | 17·914 | 17·372 | 16·862 | 16·380 | 15·926 | 15·496 | 15·089 | 14·703 | | | | | |
| 4° | 14·336 | 13·987 | 13·654 | 13·337 | 13·035 | 12·745 | 12·469 | 12·204 | 11·951 | 11·707 | | | | | |
| 5° | 11·474 | 11·249 | 11·034 | 10·826 | 10·626 | 10·433 | 10·248 | 10·068 | 9·8955 | 9·7283 | | | | | |
| 6° | 9·5668 | 9·4105 | 9·2593 | 9·1129 | 8·9711 | 8·8337 | 8·7004 | 8·5711 | 8·4457 | 8·3238 | | | | | |
| 7° | 8·2055 | 8·0905 | 7·9787 | 7·8700 | 7·7642 | 7·6613 | 7·5611 | 7·4635 | 7·3684 | 7·2757 | | Mean | | | |
| 8° | 7·1853 | 7·0972 | 7·0112 | 6·9273 | 6·8454 | 6·7655 | 6·6874 | 6·6111 | 6·5366 | 6·4637 | | differences | | | |
| 9° | 6·3925 | 6·3228 | 6·2546 | 6·1880 | 6·1227 | 6·0589 | 5·9963 | 5·9351 | 5·8751 | 5·8164 | | not | | | |
| 10° | 5·7588 | 5·7023 | 5·6470 | 5·5928 | 5·5396 | 5·4874 | 5·4362 | 5·3860 | 5·3367 | 5·2883 | | sufficiently | | | |
| 11° | 5·2408 | 5·1942 | 5·1484 | 5·1034 | 5·0593 | 5·0159 | 4·9732 | 4·9313 | 4·8901 | 4·8496 | | accurate. | | | |
| 12° | 4·8097 | 4·7706 | 4·7321 | 4·6942 | 4·6569 | 4·6202 | 4·5841 | 4·5486 | 4·5137 | 4·4793 | | | | | |
| 13° | 4·4454 | 4·4121 | 4·3792 | 4·3469 | 4·3150 | 4·2837 | 4·2527 | 4·2223 | 4·1923 | 4·1627 | | | | | |
| 14° | 4·1336 | 4·1048 | 4·0765 | 4·0486 | 4·0211 | 3·9939 | 3·9672 | 3·9408 | 3·9147 | 3·8890 | | | | | |
| 15° | 3·8637 | 3·8387 | 3·8140 | 3·7897 | 3·7657 | 3·7420 | 3·7186 | 3·6955 | 3·6727 | 3·6502 | | | | | |
| 16° | 3·6280 | 3·6060 | 3·5843 | 3·5629 | 3·5418 | 3·5209 | 3·5003 | 3·4799 | 3·4598 | 3·4399 | | | | | |
| 17° | 3·4203 | 3·4009 | 3·3817 | 3·3628 | 3·3440 | 3·3255 | 3·3072 | 3·2891 | 3·2712 | 3·2535 | | | | | |
| 18° | 3·2361 | 3·2188 | 3·2017 | 3·1848 | 3·1681 | 3·1515 | 3·1352 | 3·1190 | 3·1030 | 3·0872 | | | | | |
| 19° | 3·0716 | 3·0561 | 3·0407 | 3·0256 | 3·0106 | 2·9957 | 2·9811 | 2·9665 | 2·9521 | 2·9379 | | | | | |
| 20° | 2·9238 | 2·9099 | 2·8960 | 2·8824 | 2·8688 | 2·8555 | 2·8422 | 2·8291 | 2·8161 | 2·8032 | | | | | |
| 21° | 2·7904 | 2·7778 | 2·7653 | 2·7529 | 2·7407 | 2·7285 | 2·7165 | 2·7046 | 2·6927 | 2·6811 | | | | | |
| 22° | 2·6695 | 2·6580 | 2·6466 | 2·6354 | 2·6242 | 2·6131 | 2·6022 | 2·5913 | 2·5805 | 2·5699 | 18 | 37 | 55 | 73 | 92 |
| 23° | 2·5593 | 2·5488 | 2·5384 | 2·5282 | 2·5180 | 2·5078 | 2·4978 | 2·4879 | 2·4780 | 2·4683 | 17 | 34 | 50 | 67 | 84 |
| 24° | 2·4586 | 2·4490 | 2·4395 | 2·4300 | 2·4207 | 2·4114 | 2·4022 | 2·3931 | 2·3841 | 2·3751 | 15 | 31 | 46 | 62 | 77 |
| 25° | 2·3662 | 2·3574 | 2·3486 | 2·3400 | 2·3314 | 2·3228 | 2·3144 | 2·3060 | 2·2976 | 2·2894 | 14 | 28 | 43 | 57 | 71 |
| 26° | 2·2812 | 2·2730 | 2·2650 | 2·2570 | 2·2490 | 2·2412 | 2·2333 | 2·2256 | 2·2179 | 2·2103 | 13 | 26 | 39 | 52 | 65 |
| 27° | 2·2027 | 2·1952 | 2·1877 | 2·1803 | 2·1730 | 2·1657 | 2·1584 | 2·1513 | 2·1441 | 2·1371 | 12 | 24 | 36 | 48 | 61 |
| 28° | 2·1301 | 2·1231 | 2·1162 | 2·1093 | 2·1025 | 2·0957 | 2·0890 | 2·0824 | 2·0757 | 2·0692 | 11 | 22 | 34 | 45 | 56 |
| 29° | 2·0627 | 2·0562 | 2·0498 | 2·0434 | 2·0371 | 2·0308 | 2·0245 | 2·0183 | 2·0122 | 2·0061 | 10 | 21 | 31 | 42 | 52 |
| 30° | 2·0000 | 1·9940 | 1·9880 | 1·9821 | 1·9762 | 1·9703 | 1·9645 | 1·9587 | 1·9530 | 1·9473 | 10 | 19 | 29 | 39 | 49 |
| 31° | 1·9416 | 1·9360 | 1·9304 | 1·9249 | 1·9194 | 1·9139 | 1·9084 | 1·9031 | 1·8977 | 1·8924 | 9 | 18 | 27 | 36 | 45 |
| 32° | 1·8871 | 1·8818 | 1·8766 | 1·8714 | 1·8663 | 1·8612 | 1·8561 | 1·8510 | 1·8460 | 1·8410 | 8 | 17 | 25 | 34 | 42 |
| 33° | 1·8361 | 1·8312 | 1·8263 | 1·8214 | 1·8166 | 1·8118 | 1·8070 | 1·8023 | 1·7976 | 1·7929 | 8 | 16 | 24 | 32 | 40 |
| 34° | 1·7883 | 1·7837 | 1·7791 | 1·7745 | 1·7700 | 1·7655 | 1·7610 | 1·7566 | 1·7522 | 1·7478 | 7 | 15 | 22 | 30 | 37 |
| 35° | 1·7434 | 1·7391 | 1·7348 | 1·7305 | 1·7263 | 1·7221 | 1·7179 | 1·7137 | 1·7095 | 1·7054 | 7 | 14 | 21 | 28 | 35 |
| 36° | 1·7013 | 1·6972 | 1·6932 | 1·6892 | 1·6852 | 1·6812 | 1·6772 | 1·6733 | 1·6694 | 1·6655 | 7 | 13 | 20 | 26 | 33 |
| 37° | 1·6616 | 1·6578 | 1·6540 | 1·6502 | 1·6464 | 1·6427 | 1·6390 | 1·6353 | 1·6316 | 1·6279 | 6 | 12 | 19 | 25 | 31 |
| 38° | 1·6243 | 1·6207 | 1·6171 | 1·6135 | 1·6099 | 1·6064 | 1·6029 | 1·5994 | 1·5959 | 1·5925 | 6 | 12 | 18 | 23 | 29 |
| 39° | 1·5890 | 1·5856 | 1·5822 | 1·5788 | 1·5755 | 1·5721 | 1·5688 | 1·5655 | 1·5622 | 1·5590 | 6 | 11 | 17 | 22 | 28 |
| 40° | 1·5557 | 1·5525 | 1·5493 | 1·5461 | 1·5429 | 1·5398 | 1·5366 | 1·5335 | 1·5304 | 1·5273 | 5 | 10 | 16 | 21 | 26 |
| 41° | 1·5243 | 1·5212 | 1·5182 | 1·5151 | 1·5121 | 1·5092 | 1·5062 | 1·5032 | 1·5003 | 1·4974 | 5 | 10 | 15 | 20 | 25 |
| 42° | 1·4945 | 1·4916 | 1·4887 | 1·4859 | 1·4830 | 1·4802 | 1·4774 | 1·4746 | 1·4718 | 1·4690 | 5 | 9 | 14 | 19 | 23 |
| 43° | 1·4663 | 1·4635 | 1·4608 | 1·4581 | 1·4554 | 1·4527 | 1·4501 | 1·4474 | 1·4448 | 1·4422 | 4 | 9 | 13 | 18 | 22 |
| 44° | 1·4396 | 1·4370 | 1·4344 | 1·4318 | 1·4293 | 1·4267 | 1·4242 | 1·4217 | 1·4192 | 1·4167 | 4 | 8 | 13 | 17 | 21 |

## NATURAL COSECANTS

Subtract Mean Differences.

| Angle | 0' | 6' | 12' | 18' | 24' | 30' | 36' | 42' | 48' | 54' | 1' | 2' | 3' | 4' | 5' |
|---|---|---|---|---|---|---|---|---|---|---|---|---|---|---|---|
| 45° | 1·4142 | 1·4118 | 1·4093 | 1·4069 | 1·4044 | 1·4020 | 1·3996 | 1·3972 | 1·3949 | 1·3925 | 4 | 8 | 12 | 16 | 20 |
| 46° | 1·3902 | 1·3878 | 1·3855 | 1·3832 | 1·3809 | 1·3786 | 1·3763 | 1·3741 | 1·3718 | 1·3696 | 4 | 8 | 11 | 15 | 19 |
| 47° | 1·3673 | 1·3651 | 1·3629 | 1·3607 | 1·3585 | 1·3563 | 1·3542 | 1·3520 | 1·3499 | 1·3478 | 4 | 7 | 11 | 14 | 18 |
| 48° | 1·3456 | 1·3435 | 1·3414 | 1·3393 | 1·3373 | 1·3352 | 1·3331 | 1·3311 | 1·3291 | 1·3270 | 3 | 7 | 10 | 14 | 17 |
| 49° | 1·3250 | 1·3230 | 1·3210 | 1·3190 | 1·3171 | 1·3151 | 1·3131 | 1·3112 | 1·3093 | 1·3073 | 3 | 7 | 10 | 13 | 16 |
| 50° | 1·3054 | 1·3035 | 1·3016 | 1·2997 | 1·2978 | 1·2960 | 1·2941 | 1·2923 | 1·2904 | 1·2886 | 3 | 6 | 9 | 12 | 15 |
| 51° | 1·2868 | 1·2849 | 1·2831 | 1·2813 | 1·2796 | 1·2778 | 1·2760 | 1·2742 | 1·2725 | 1·2708 | 3 | 6 | 9 | 12 | 15 |
| 52° | 1·2690 | 1·2673 | 1·2656 | 1·2639 | 1·2622 | 1·2605 | 1·2588 | 1·2571 | 1·2554 | 1·2538 | 3 | 6 | 8 | 11 | 14 |
| 53° | 1·2521 | 1·2505 | 1·2489 | 1·2472 | 1·2456 | 1·2440 | 1·2424 | 1·2408 | 1·2392 | 1·2376 | 3 | 5 | 8 | 11 | 13 |
| 54° | 1·2361 | 1·2345 | 1·2329 | 1·2314 | 1·2299 | 1·2283 | 1·2268 | 1·2253 | 1·2238 | 1·2223 | 3 | 5 | 8 | 10 | 13 |
| 55° | 1·2208 | 1·2193 | 1·2178 | 1·2163 | 1·2149 | 1·2134 | 1·2120 | 1·2105 | 1·2091 | 1·2076 | 2 | 5 | 7 | 10 | 12 |
| 56° | 1·2062 | 1·2048 | 1·2034 | 1·2020 | 1·2006 | 1·1992 | 1·1978 | 1·1964 | 1·1951 | 1·1937 | 2 | 5 | 7 | 9 | 12 |
| 57° | 1·1924 | 1·1910 | 1·1897 | 1·1883 | 1·1870 | 1·1857 | 1·1844 | 1·1831 | 1·1818 | 1·1805 | 2 | 4 | 7 | 9 | 11 |
| 58° | 1·1792 | 1·1779 | 1·1766 | 1·1753 | 1·1741 | 1·1728 | 1·1716 | 1·1703 | 1·1691 | 1·1679 | 2 | 4 | 6 | 8 | 10 |
| 59° | 1·1666 | 1·1654 | 1·1642 | 1·1630 | 1·1618 | 1·1606 | 1·1594 | 1·1582 | 1·1570 | 1·1559 | 2 | 4 | 6 | 8 | 10 |
| 60° | 1·1547 | 1·1535 | 1·1524 | 1·1512 | 1·1501 | 1·1490 | 1·1478 | 1·1467 | 1·1456 | 1·1445 | 2 | 4 | 6 | 8 | 9 |
| 61° | 1·1434 | 1·1423 | 1·1412 | 1·1401 | 1·1390 | 1·1379 | 1·1368 | 1·1357 | 1·1347 | 1·1336 | 2 | 4 | 5 | 7 | 9 |
| 62° | 1·1326 | 1·1315 | 1·1305 | 1·1294 | 1·1284 | 1·1274 | 1·1264 | 1·1253 | 1·1243 | 1·1233 | 2 | 3 | 5 | 7 | 9 |
| 63° | 1·1223 | 1·1213 | 1·1203 | 1·1194 | 1·1184 | 1·1174 | 1·1164 | 1·1155 | 1·1145 | 1·1136 | 2 | 3 | 5 | 6 | 8 |
| 64° | 1·1126 | 1·1117 | 1·1107 | 1·1098 | 1·1089 | 1·1079 | 1·1070 | 1·1061 | 1·1052 | 1·1043 | 2 | 3 | 5 | 6 | 8 |
| 65° | 1·1034 | 1·1025 | 1·1016 | 1·1007 | 1·0998 | 1·0989 | 1·0981 | 1·0972 | 1·0963 | 1·0955 | 1 | 3 | 4 | 6 | 7 |
| 66° | 1·0946 | 1·0938 | 1·0929 | 1·0921 | 1·0913 | 1·0904 | 1·0896 | 1·0888 | 1·0880 | 1·0872 | 1 | 3 | 4 | 6 | 7 |
| 67° | 1·0864 | 1·0856 | 1·0848 | 1·0840 | 1·0832 | 1·0824 | 1·0816 | 1·0808 | 1·0801 | 1·0793 | 1 | 3 | 4 | 5 | 6 |
| 68° | 1·0785 | 1·0778 | 1·0770 | 1·0763 | 1·0755 | 1·0748 | 1·0740 | 1·0733 | 1·0726 | 1·0719 | 1 | 2 | 4 | 5 | 6 |
| 69° | 1·0711 | 1·0704 | 1·0697 | 1·0690 | 1·0683 | 1·0676 | 1·0669 | 1·0662 | 1·0655 | 1·0649 | 1 | 2 | 3 | 5 | 5 |
| 70° | 1·0642 | 1·0635 | 1·0628 | 1·0622 | 1·0615 | 1·0608 | 1·0602 | 1·0595 | 1·0589 | 1·0583 | 1 | 2 | 3 | 4 | 5 |
| 71° | 1·0576 | 1·0570 | 1·0564 | 1·0557 | 1·0551 | 1·0545 | 1·0539 | 1·0533 | 1·0527 | 1·0521 | 1 | 2 | 3 | 4 | 5 |
| 72° | 1·0515 | 1·0509 | 1·0503 | 1·0497 | 1·0491 | 1·0485 | 1·0480 | 1·0474 | 1·0468 | 1·0463 | 1 | 2 | 3 | 4 | 5 |
| 73° | 1·0457 | 1·0451 | 1·0446 | 1·0440 | 1·0435 | 1·0429 | 1·0424 | 1·0419 | 1·0413 | 1·0408 | 1 | 2 | 3 | 4 | 4 |
| 74° | 1·0403 | 1·0398 | 1·0393 | 1·0388 | 1·0382 | 1·0377 | 1·0372 | 1·0367 | 1·0363 | 1·0358 | 1 | 2 | 2 | 3 | 4 |
| 75° | 1·0353 | 1·0348 | 1·0343 | 1·0338 | 1·0334 | 1·0329 | 1·0324 | 1·0320 | 1·0315 | 1·0311 | 1 | 2 | 2 | 3 | 4 |
| 76° | 1·0306 | 1·0302 | 1·0297 | 1·0293 | 1·0288 | 1·0284 | 1·0280 | 1·0276 | 1·0271 | 1·0267 | 1 | 1 | 2 | 3 | 4 |
| 77° | 1·0263 | 1·0259 | 1·0255 | 1·0251 | 1·0247 | 1·0243 | 1·0239 | 1·0235 | 1·0231 | 1·0227 | 1 | 1 | 2 | 3 | 3 |
| 78° | 1·0223 | 1·0220 | 1·0216 | 1·0212 | 1·0209 | 1·0205 | 1·0201 | 1·0198 | 1·0194 | 1·0191 | 1 | 1 | 2 | 2 | 3 |
| 79° | 1·0187 | 1·0184 | 1·0180 | 1·0177 | 1·0174 | 1·0170 | 1·0167 | 1·0164 | 1·0161 | 1·0157 | 1 | 1 | 2 | 2 | 3 |
| 80° | 1·0154 | 1·0151 | 1·0148 | 1·0145 | 1·0142 | 1·0139 | 1·0136 | 1·0133 | 1·0130 | 1·0127 | 0 | 1 | 1 | 2 | 2 |
| 81° | 1·0125 | 1·0122 | 1·0119 | 1·0116 | 1·0114 | 1·0111 | 1·0108 | 1·0106 | 1·0103 | 1·0101 | 0 | 1 | 1 | 2 | 2 |
| 82° | 1·0098 | 1·0096 | 1·0093 | 1·0091 | 1·0089 | 1·0086 | 1·0084 | 1·0082 | 1·0079 | 1·0077 | 0 | 1 | 1 | 2 | 2 |
| 83° | 1·0075 | 1·0073 | 1·0071 | 1·0069 | 1·0067 | 1·0065 | 1·0063 | 1·0061 | 1·0059 | 1·0057 | 0 | 1 | 1 | 1 | 2 |
| 84° | 1·0055 | 1·0053 | 1·0051 | 1·0050 | 1·0048 | 1·0046 | 1·0045 | 1·0043 | 1·0041 | 1·0040 | 0 | 1 | 1 | 1 | 1 |
| 85° | 1·0038 | 1·0037 | 1·0035 | 1·0034 | 1·0032 | 1·0031 | 1·0030 | 1·0028 | 1·0027 | 1·0026 | 0 | 0 | 1 | 1 | 1 |
| 86° | 1·0024 | 1·0023 | 1·0022 | 1·0021 | 1·0020 | 1·0019 | 1·0018 | 1·0017 | 1·0016 | 1·0015 | 0 | 0 | 1 | 1 | 1 |
| 87° | 1·0014 | 1·0013 | 1·0012 | 1·0011 | 1·0010 | 1·0010 | 1·0009 | 1·0008 | 1·0007 | 1·0007 | 0 | 0 | 0 | 1 | 1 |
| 88° | 1·0006 | 1·0006 | 1·0005 | 1·0004 | 1·0004 | 1·0003 | 1·0003 | 1·0003 | 1·0002 | 1·0002 | 0 | 0 | 0 | 0 | 0 |
| 89° | 1·0002 | 1·0001 | 1·0001 | 1·0001 | 1·0001 | 1·0000 | 1·0000 | 1·0000 | 1·0000 | 1·0000 | 0 | 0 | 0 | 0 | 0 |

## NATURAL SECANTS

| Angle. | 0' | 6' | 12' | 18' | 24' | 30' | 36' | 42' | 48' | 54' | 1' | 2' | 3' | 4' | 5' |
|---|---|---|---|---|---|---|---|---|---|---|---|---|---|---|---|
| 0° | 1·0000 | 1·0000 | 1·0000 | 1·0000 | 1·0000 | 1·0000 | 1·0001 | 1·0001 | 1·0001 | 1·0001 | 0 | 0 | 0 | 0 | 0 |
| 1° | 1·0002 | 1·0002 | 1·0002 | 1·0003 | 1·0003 | 1·0003 | 1·0004 | 1·0004 | 1·0005 | 1·0006 | 0 | 0 | 0 | 0 | 0 |
| 2° | 1·0006 | 1·0007 | 1·0007 | 1·0008 | 1·0009 | 1·0010 | 1·0010 | 1·0011 | 1·0012 | 1·0013 | 0 | 0 | 0 | 0 | 0 |
| 3° | 1·0014 | 1·0015 | 1·0016 | 1·0017 | 1·0018 | 1·0019 | 1·0020 | 1·0021 | 1·0022 | 1·0023 | 0 | 0 | 1 | 1 | 1 |
| 4° | 1·0024 | 1·0026 | 1·0027 | 1·0028 | 1·0030 | 1·0031 | 1·0032 | 1·0034 | 1·0035 | 1·0037 | 0 | 0 | 1 | 1 | 1 |
| 5° | 1·0038 | 1·0040 | 1·0041 | 1·0043 | 1·0045 | 1·0046 | 1·0048 | 1·0050 | 1·0051 | 1·0053 | 0 | 1 | 1 | 1 | 1 |
| 6° | 1·0055 | 1·0057 | 1·0059 | 1·0061 | 1·0063 | 1·0065 | 1·0067 | 1·0069 | 1·0071 | 1·0073 | 0 | 1 | 1 | 1 | 2 |
| 7° | 1·0075 | 1·0077 | 1·0079 | 1·0082 | 1·0084 | 1·0086 | 1·0089 | 1·0091 | 1·0093 | 1·0096 | 0 | 1 | 1 | 2 | 2 |
| 8° | 1·0098 | 1·0101 | 1·0103 | 1·0106 | 1·0108 | 1·0111 | 1·0114 | 1·0116 | 1·0119 | 1·0122 | 0 | 1 | 1 | 2 | 2 |
| 9° | 1·0125 | 1·0127 | 1·0130 | 1·0133 | 1·0136 | 1·0139 | 1·0142 | 1·0145 | 1·0148 | 1·0151 | 0 | 1 | 1 | 2 | 2 |
| 10° | 1·0154 | 1·0157 | 1·0161 | 1·0164 | 1·0167 | 1·0170 | 1·0174 | 1·0177 | 1·0180 | 1·0184 | 1 | 1 | 2 | 2 | 3 |
| 11° | 1·0187 | 1·0191 | 1·0194 | 1·0198 | 1·0201 | 1·0205 | 1·0209 | 1·0212 | 1·0216 | 1·0220 | 1 | 1 | 2 | 2 | 3 |
| 12° | 1·0223 | 1·0227 | 1·0231 | 1·0235 | 1·0239 | 1·0243 | 1·0247 | 1·0251 | 1·0255 | 1·0259 | 1 | 1 | 2 | 3 | 3 |
| 13° | 1·0263 | 1·0267 | 1·0271 | 1·0276 | 1·0280 | 1·0284 | 1·0288 | 1·0293 | 1·0297 | 1·0302 | 1 | 1 | 2 | 3 | 4 |
| 14° | 1·0306 | 1·0311 | 1·0315 | 1·0320 | 1·0324 | 1·0329 | 1·0334 | 1·0338 | 1·0343 | 1·0348 | 1 | 2 | 2 | 3 | 4 |
| 15° | 1·0353 | 1·0358 | 1·0363 | 1·0367 | 1·0372 | 1·0377 | 1·0382 | 1·0388 | 1·0393 | 1·0398 | 1 | 2 | 3 | 3 | 4 |
| 16° | 1·0403 | 1·0408 | 1·0413 | 1·0419 | 1·0424 | 1·0429 | 1·0435 | 1·0440 | 1·0446 | 1·0451 | 1 | 2 | 3 | 4 | 4 |
| 17° | 1·0457 | 1·0463 | 1·0468 | 1·0474 | 1·0480 | 1·0485 | 1·0491 | 1·0497 | 1·0503 | 1·0509 | 1 | 2 | 3 | 4 | 5 |
| 18° | 1·0515 | 1·0521 | 1·0527 | 1·0533 | 1·0539 | 1·0545 | 1·0551 | 1·0557 | 1·0564 | 1·0570 | 1 | 2 | 3 | 4 | 5 |
| 19° | 1·0576 | 1·0583 | 1·0589 | 1·0595 | 1·0602 | 1·0608 | 1·0615 | 1·0622 | 1·0628 | 1·0635 | 1 | 2 | 3 | 4 | 5 |
| 20° | 1·0642 | 1·0649 | 1·6655 | 1·0662 | 1·0669 | 1·0676 | 1·0683 | 1·0690 | 1·0697 | 1·0704 | 1 | 2 | 3 | 5 | 6 |
| 21° | 1·0711 | 1·0719 | 1·0726 | 1·0733 | 1·0740 | 1·0748 | 1·0755 | 1·0763 | 1·0770 | 1·0778 | 1 | 2 | 4 | 5 | 6 |
| 22° | 1·0785 | 1·0793 | 1·0801 | 1·0808 | 1·0816 | 1·0824 | 1·0832 | 1·0840 | 1·0848 | 1·0856 | 1 | 3 | 4 | 5 | 7 |
| 23° | 1·0864 | 1·0872 | 1·0880 | 1·0888 | 1·0896 | 1·0904 | 1·0913 | 1·0921 | 1·0929 | 1·0938 | 1 | 3 | 4 | 6 | 7 |
| 24° | 1·0946 | 1·0955 | 1·0963 | 1·0972 | 1·0981 | 1·0989 | 1·0998 | 1·1007 | 1·1016 | 1·1025 | 1 | 3 | 4 | 6 | 7 |
| 25° | 1·1034 | 1·1043 | 1·1052 | 1·1061 | 1·1070 | 1·1079 | 1·1089 | 1·1098 | 1·1107 | 1·1117 | 2 | 3 | 5 | 6 | 8 |
| 26° | 1·1126 | 1·1136 | 1·1145 | 1·1155 | 1·1164 | 1·1174 | 1·1184 | 1·1194 | 1·1203 | 1·1213 | 2 | 3 | 5 | 6 | 8 |
| 27° | 1·1223 | 1·1233 | 1·1243 | 1·1253 | 1·1264 | 1·1274 | 1·1284 | 1·1294 | 1·1305 | 1·1315 | 2 | 3 | 5 | 7 | 9 |
| 28° | 1·1326 | 1·1336 | 1·1347 | 1·1357 | 1·1368 | 1·1379 | 1·1390 | 1·1401 | 1·1412 | 1·1423 | 2 | 4 | 5 | 7 | 9 |
| 29° | 1·1434 | 1·1445 | 1·1456 | 1·1467 | 1·1478 | 1·1490 | 1·1501 | 1·1512 | 1·1524 | 1·1535 | 2 | 4 | 6 | 8 | 9 |
| 30° | 1·1547 | 1·1559 | 1·1570 | 1·1582 | 1·1594 | 1·1606 | 1·1618 | 1·1630 | 1·1642 | 1·1654 | 2 | 4 | 6 | 8 | 10 |
| 31° | 1·1666 | 1·1679 | 1·1691 | 1·1703 | 1·1716 | 1·1728 | 1·1741 | 1·1753 | 1·1766 | 1·1779 | 2 | 4 | 6 | 8 | 10 |
| 32° | 1·1792 | 1·1805 | 1·1818 | 1·1831 | 1·1844 | 1·1857 | 1·1870 | 1·1883 | 1·1897 | 1·1910 | 2 | 4 | 7 | 9 | 11 |
| 33° | 1·1924 | 1·1937 | 1·1951 | 1·1964 | 1·1978 | 1·1992 | 1·2006 | 1·2020 | 1·2034 | 1·2048 | 2 | 5 | 7 | 9 | 12 |
| 34° | 1·2062 | 1·2076 | 1·2091 | 1·2105 | 1·2120 | 1·2134 | 1·2149 | 1·2163 | 1·2178 | 1·2193 | 2 | 5 | 7 | 10 | 12 |
| 35° | 1·2208 | 1·2223 | 1·2238 | 1·2253 | 1·2268 | 1·2283 | 1·2299 | 1·2314 | 1·2329 | 1·2345 | 3 | 5 | 8 | 10 | 13 |
| 36° | 1·2361 | 1·2376 | 1·2392 | 1·2408 | 1·2424 | 1·2440 | 1·2456 | 1·2472 | 1·2489 | 1·2505 | 3 | 5 | 8 | 11 | 13 |
| 37° | 1·2521 | 1·2538 | 1·2554 | 1·2571 | 1·2588 | 1·2605 | 1·2622 | 1·2639 | 1·2656 | 1·2673 | 3 | 6 | 8 | 11 | 14 |
| 38° | 1·2690 | 1·2708 | 1·2725 | 1·2742 | 1·2760 | 1·2778 | 1·2796 | 1·2813 | 1·2831 | 1·2849 | 3 | 6 | 9 | 12 | 15 |
| 39° | 1·2868 | 1·2886 | 1·2904 | 1·2923 | 1·2941 | 1·2960 | 1·2978 | 1·2997 | 1·3016 | 1·3035 | 3 | 6 | 9 | 12 | 16 |
| 40° | 1·3054 | 1·3073 | 1·3093 | 1·3112 | 1·3131 | 1·3151 | 1·3171 | 1·3190 | 1·3210 | 1·3230 | 3 | 7 | 10 | 13 | 16 |
| 41° | 1·3250 | 1·3270 | 1·3291 | 1·3311 | 1·3331 | 1·3352 | 1·3373 | 1·3393 | 1·3414 | 1·3435 | 3 | 7 | 10 | 14 | 17 |
| 42° | 1·3456 | 1·3478 | 1·3499 | 1·3520 | 1·3542 | 1·3563 | 1·3585 | 1·3607 | 1·3629 | 1·3651 | 4 | 7 | 11 | 14 | 18 |
| 43° | 1·3673 | 1·3696 | 1·3718 | 1·3741 | 1·3763 | 1·3786 | 1·3809 | 1·3832 | 1·3855 | 1·3878 | 4 | 8 | 11 | 15 | 19 |
| 44° | 1·3902 | 1·3925 | 1·3949 | 1·3972 | 1·3996 | 1·4020 | 1·4044 | 1·4069 | 1·4093 | 1·4118 | 4 | 8 | 12 | 16 | 20 |

## NATURAL SECANTS

| 0' | 6' | 12' | 18' | 24' | 30' | 36' | 42' | 48' | 54' | 1' | 2' | 3' | 4' | 5' |
|---|---|---|---|---|---|---|---|---|---|---|---|---|---|---|
| 1·4142 | 1·4167 | 1·4192 | 1·4217 | 1·4242 | 1·4267 | 1·4293 | 1·4318 | 1·4344 | 1·4370 | 4 | 8 | 13 | 17 | 21 |
| 1·4396 | 1·4422 | 1·4448 | 1·4474 | 1·4501 | 1·4527 | 1·4554 | 1·4581 | 1·4608 | 1·4635 | 4 | 9 | 13 | 18 | 22 |
| 1·4663 | 1·4690 | 1·4718 | 1·4746 | 1·4774 | 1·4802 | 1·4830 | 1·4859 | 1·4887 | 1·4916 | 5 | 9 | 14 | 19 | 23 |
| 1·4945 | 1·4974 | 1·5003 | 1·5032 | 1·5062 | 1·5092 | 1·5121 | 1·5151 | 1·5182 | 1·5212 | 5 | 10 | 15 | 20 | 25 |
| 1·5243 | 1·5273 | 1·5304 | 1·5335 | 1·5366 | 1·5398 | 1·5429 | 1·5461 | 1·5493 | 1·5525 | 5 | 10 | 16 | 21 | 26 |
| 1·5557 | 1·5590 | 1·5622 | 1·5655 | 1·5688 | 1·5721 | 1·5755 | 1·5788 | 1·5822 | 1·5856 | 6 | 11 | 17 | 22 | 28 |
| 1·5800 | 1·5925 | 1·5959 | 1·5994 | 1·6029 | 1·6064 | 1·6099 | 1·6135 | 1·6171 | 1·6207 | 6 | 12 | 18 | 24 | 29 |
| 1·6243 | 1·6279 | 1·6316 | 1·6353 | 1·6390 | 1·6427 | 1·6464 | 1·6502 | 1·6540 | 1·6578 | 6 | 12 | 19 | 25 | 31 |
| 1·6616 | 1·6655 | 1·6694 | 1·6733 | 1·6772 | 1·6812 | 1·6852 | 1·6892 | 1·6932 | 1·6972 | 7 | 13 | 20 | 26 | 33 |
| 1·7013 | 1·7054 | 1·7095 | 1·7137 | 1·7179 | 1·7221 | 1·7263 | 1·7305 | 1·7348 | 1·7391 | 7 | 14 | 21 | 28 | 35 |
| 1·7434 | 1·7478 | 1·7522 | 1·7566 | 1·7610 | 1·7655 | 1·7700 | 1·7745 | 1·7791 | 1·7837 | 7 | 15 | 22 | 30 | 37 |
| 1·7883 | 1·7929 | 1·7976 | 1·8023 | 1·8070 | 1·8118 | 1·8166 | 1·8214 | 1·8263 | 1·8312 | 8 | 16 | 24 | 32 | 40 |
| 1·8361 | 1·8410 | 1·8460 | 1·8510 | 1·8561 | 1·8612 | 1·8663 | 1·8714 | 1·8766 | 1·8818 | 9 | 17 | 26 | 34 | 43 |
| 1·8871 | 1·8924 | 1·8977 | 1·9031 | 1·9084 | 1·9139 | 1·9194 | 1·9249 | 1·9304 | 1·9360 | 9 | 18 | 27 | 36 | 45 |
| 1·9416 | 1·9473 | 1·9530 | 1·9587 | 1·9645 | 1·9703 | 1·9762 | 1·9821 | 1·9880 | 1·9940 | 10 | 19 | 29 | 39 | 49 |
| 2·0000 | 2·0061 | 2·0122 | 2·0183 | 2·0245 | 2·0308 | 2·0371 | 2·0434 | 2·0498 | 2·0562 | 10 | 21 | 31 | 42 | 52 |
| 2·0627 | 2·0692 | 2·0757 | 2·0824 | 2·0890 | 2·0957 | 2·1025 | 2·1093 | 2·1162 | 2·1231 | 11 | 22 | 34 | 45 | 56 |
| 2·1301 | 3·1371 | 2·1441 | 2·1513 | 2·1584 | 2·1657 | 2·1730 | 2·1803 | 2·1877 | 2·1952 | 12 | 24 | 36 | 48 | 61 |
| 2·2027 | 2·2103 | 2·2179 | 2·2256 | 2·2333 | 2·2412 | 2·2490 | 2·2570 | 2·2650 | 2·2730 | 13 | 26 | 39 | 52 | 65 |
| 2·2812 | 2·2894 | 2·2976 | 2·3060 | 2·3144 | 2·3228 | 2·3314 | 2·3400 | 2·3486 | 2·3574 | 14 | 28 | 43 | 57 | 71 |
| 2·3662 | 2·3751 | 2·3841 | 2·3931 | 2·4022 | 2·4114 | 2·4207 | 2·4300 | 2·4395 | 2·4490 | 15 | 31 | 46 | 62 | 77 |
| 2·4586 | 2·4683 | 2·4780 | 2·4879 | 2·4978 | 2·5078 | 2·5180 | 2·5282 | 2·5384 | 2·5488 | 17 | 34 | 50 | 67 | 84 |
| 2·5593 | 2·5699 | 2·5805 | 2·5913 | 2·6022 | 2·6131 | 2·6242 | 2·6354 | 2·6466 | 2·6580 | 18 | 37 | 55 | 73 | 92 |
| 2·6695 | 2·6811 | 2·6927 | 2·7046 | 2·7165 | 2·7285 | 2·7407 | 2·7529 | 2·7653 | 2·7778 | 20 | 40 | 60 | 81 | 101 |
| 2·7904 | 2·8032 | 2·8161 | 2·8291 | 2·8422 | 2·8555 | 2·8688 | 2·8824 | 2·8960 | 2·9099 | 22 | 44 | 67 | 89 | 111 |
| 2·9238 | 2·9379 | 2·9521 | 2·9665 | 2·9811 | 2·9957 | 3·0106 | 3·0256 | 3·0407 | 3·0561 | 25 | 49 | 74 | 98 | 123 |
| 3·0716 | 3·0872 | 3·1030 | 3·1190 | 3·1352 | 3·1515 | 3·1681 | 3·1848 | 3·2017 | 3·2188 | 27 | 55 | 82 | 110 | 137 |
| 3·2361 | 3·2535 | 3·2712 | 3·2891 | 3·3072 | 3·3255 | 3·3440 | 3·3628 | 3·3817 | 3·4009 | 31 | 61 | 92 | 123 | 153 |
| 3·4203 | 3·4399 | 3·4598 | 3·4799 | 3·5003 | 3·5209 | 3·5418 | 3·5629 | 3·5843 | 3·6060 | | | | | |
| 3·6280 | 3·6502 | 3·6727 | 3·6955 | 3·7186 | 3·7420 | 3·7657 | 3·7897 | 3·8140 | 3·8387 | | | | | |
| 3·8637 | 3·8890 | 3·9147 | 3·9408 | 3·9672 | 3·9939 | 4·0211 | 4·0486 | 4·0765 | 4·1048 | | | | | |
| 4·1336 | 4·1627 | 4·1923 | 4·2223 | 4·2527 | 4·2837 | 4·3150 | 4·3469 | 4·3792 | 4·4121 | | | | | |
| 4·4454 | 4·4793 | 4·5137 | 4·5486 | 4·5841 | 4·6202 | 4·6569 | 4·6942 | 4·7321 | 4·7706 | | | | | |
| 4·8097 | 4·8496 | 4·8901 | 4·9313 | 4·9732 | 5·0159 | 5·0593 | 5·1034 | 5·1484 | 5·1942 | | | | | |
| 5·2408 | 5·2883 | 5·3367 | 5·3860 | 5·4362 | 5·4874 | 5·5396 | 5·5928 | 5·6470 | 5·7023 | | | | | |
| 5·7588 | 5·8164 | 5·8751 | 5·9351 | 5·9963 | 6·0589 | 6·1227 | 6·1880 | 6·2546 | 6·3228 | Mean differences not sufficiently accurate. | | | | |
| 6·3925 | 6·4637 | 6·5366 | 6·6111 | 6·6874 | 6·7655 | 6·8454 | 6·9273 | 7·0112 | 7·0972 | | | | | |
| 7·1853 | 7·2757 | 7·3684 | 7·4635 | 7·5611 | 7·6613 | 7·7642 | 7·8700 | 7·9787 | 8·0905 | | | | | |
| 8·2055 | 8·3238 | 8·4457 | 8·5711 | 8·7004 | 8·8337 | 8·9711 | 9·1129 | 9·2593 | 9·4105 | | | | | |
| 9·5668 | 9·7283 | 9·8955 | 10·068 | 10·248 | 10·433 | 10·626 | 10·826 | 11·034 | 11·249 | | | | | |
| 11·474 | 11·707 | 11·951 | 12·204 | 12·469 | 12·745 | 13·035 | 13·337 | 13·654 | 13·987 | | | | | |
| 14·336 | 14·703 | 15·089 | 15·496 | 15·926 | 16·380 | 16·862 | 17·372 | 17·914 | 18·492 | | | | | |
| 19·107 | 19·766 | 20·471 | 21·229 | 22·044 | 22·926 | 23·880 | 24·918 | 26·050 | 27·290 | | | | | |
| 28·654 | 30·161 | 31·836 | 33·708 | 35·815 | 38·202 | 40·930 | 44·077 | 47·750 | 52·090 | | | | | |
| 57·299 | 63·665 | 71·622 | 81·853 | 95·495 | 114·59 | 143·24 | 190·99 | 286·48 | 572·96 | | | | | |

## NATURAL COTANGENTS

Subtract Mean Diffe

| Angle. | 0' | 6' | 12' | 18' | 24' | 30' | 36' | 42' | 48' | 54' | 1' | 2' | 3' | 4' |
|---|---|---|---|---|---|---|---|---|---|---|---|---|---|---|
| 0° | ∞ | 572·96 | 286·48 | 190·98 | 143·24 | 114·59 | 95·489 | 81·847 | 71·615 | 63·657 | | | | |
| 1° | 57·290 | 52·081 | 47·740 | 44·066 | 40·917 | 38·188 | 35·801 | 33·694 | 31·821 | 30·145 | | | | |
| 2° | 28·636 | 27·271 | 26·031 | 24·898 | 23·859 | 22·904 | 22·022 | 21·205 | 20·446 | 19·740 | | | | |
| 3° | 19·081 | 18·464 | 17·886 | 17·343 | 16·832 | 16·350 | 15·895 | 15·464 | 15·056 | 14·669 | | | | |
| 4° | 14·301 | 13·951 | 13·617 | 13·300 | 12·996 | 12·706 | 12·429 | 12·163 | 11·909 | 11·664 | | Mean | | |
| 5° | 11·430 | 11·205 | 10·988 | 10·780 | 10·579 | 10·385 | 10·199 | 10·019 | 9·8448 | 9·6768 | | differenc | | |
| 6° | 9·5144 | 9·3572 | 9·2052 | 9·0579 | 8·9152 | 8·7769 | 8·6427 | 8·5126 | 8·3863 | 8·2636 | | not | | |
| 7° | 8·1443 | 8·0285 | 7·9158 | 7·8062 | 7·6996 | 7·5958 | 7·4947 | 7·3962 | 7·3002 | 7·2066 | | sufficient | | |
| 8° | 7·1154 | 7·0264 | 6·9395 | 6·8548 | 6·7720 | 6·6912 | 6·6122 | 6·5350 | 6·4596 | 6·3859 | | accurate | | |
| 9° | 6·3138 | 6·2432 | 6·1742 | 6·1066 | 6·0405 | 5·9758 | 5·9124 | 5·8502 | 5·7894 | 5·7297 | | | | |
| 10° | 5·6713 | 5·6140 | 5·5578 | 5·5026 | 5·4486 | 5·3955 | 5·3435 | 5·2924 | 5·2422 | 5·1929 | | | | |
| 11° | 5·1446 | 5·0970 | 5·0504 | 5·0045 | 4·9594 | 4·9152 | 4·8716 | 4·8288 | 4·7867 | 4·7453 | | | | |
| 12° | 4·7046 | 4·6646 | 4·6252 | 4·5864 | 4·5483 | 4·5107 | 4·4737 | 4·4373 | 4·4015 | 4·3662 | | | | |
| 13° | 4·3315 | 4·2972 | 4·2635 | 4·2303 | 4·1976 | 4·1653 | 4·1335 | 4·1022 | 4·0713 | 4·0408 | | | | |
| 14° | 4·0108 | 3·9812 | 3·9520 | 3·9232 | 3·8947 | 3·8667 | 3·8391 | 3·8118 | 3·7848 | 3·7583 | 46 | 93 | 139 | 18 |
| 15° | 3·7321 | 3·7062 | 3·6806 | 3·6554 | 3·6305 | 3·6059 | 3·5816 | 3·5576 | 3·5339 | 3·5105 | 41 | 81 | 122 | 16 |
| 16° | 3·4874 | 3·4646 | 3·4420 | 3·4197 | 3·3977 | 3·3759 | 3·3544 | 3·3332 | 3·3122 | 3·2914 | 36 | 72 | 108 | 14 |
| 17° | 3·2709 | 3·2506 | 3·2305 | 3·2106 | 3·1910 | 3·1716 | 3·1524 | 3·1334 | 3·1146 | 3·0961 | 32 | 64 | 96 | 12 |
| 18° | 3·0777 | 3·0595 | 3·0415 | 3·0237 | 3·0061 | 2·9887 | 2·9714 | 2·9544 | 2·9375 | 2·9208 | 29 | 58 | 87 | 11 |
| 19° | 2·9042 | 2·8878 | 2·8716 | 2·8556 | 2·8397 | 2·8239 | 2·8083 | 2·7929 | 2·7776 | 2·7625 | 26 | 52 | 78 | 10 |
| 20° | 2·7475 | 2·7326 | 2·7179 | 2·7034 | 2·6889 | 2·6746 | 2·6605 | 2·6464 | 2·6325 | 2·6187 | 24 | 47 | 71 | 9 |
| 21° | 2·6051 | 2·5916 | 2·5782 | 2·5649 | 2·5517 | 2·5386 | 2·5257 | 2·5129 | 2·5002 | 2·4876 | 22 | 43 | 65 | 8 |
| 22° | 2·4751 | 2·4627 | 2·4504 | 2·4383 | 2·4262 | 2·4142 | 2·4023 | 2·3906 | 2·3789 | 2·3673 | 20 | 40 | 60 | 7 |
| 23° | 2·3559 | 2·3445 | 2·3332 | 2·3220 | 2·3109 | 2·2998 | 2·2889 | 2·2781 | 2·2673 | 2·2566 | 18 | 37 | 55 | 7 |
| 24° | 2·2460 | 2·2355 | 2·2251 | 2·2148 | 2·2045 | 2·1943 | 2·1842 | 2·1742 | 2·1642 | 2·1543 | 17 | 34 | 51 | 6 |
| 25° | 2·1445 | 2·1348 | 2·1251 | 2·1155 | 2·1060 | 2·0965 | 2·0872 | 2·0778 | 2·0686 | 2·0594 | 16 | 31 | 47 | 6 |
| 26° | 2·0503 | 2·0413 | 2·0323 | 2·0233 | 2·0145 | 2·0057 | 1·9970 | 1·9883 | 1·9797 | 1·9711 | 15 | 29 | 44 | 5 |
| 27° | 1·9626 | 1·9542 | 1·9458 | 1·9375 | 1·9292 | 1·9210 | 1·9128 | 1·9047 | 1·8967 | 1·8887 | 14 | 27 | 41 | 5 |
| 28° | 1·8807 | 1·8728 | 1·8650 | 1·8572 | 1·8495 | 1·8418 | 1·8341 | 1·8265 | 1·8190 | 1·8115 | 13 | 26 | 38 | 5 |
| 29° | 1·8040 | 1·7966 | 1·7893 | 1·7820 | 1·7747 | 1·7675 | 1·7603 | 1·7532 | 1·7461 | 1·7391 | 12 | 24 | 36 | 4 |
| 30° | 1·7321 | 1·7251 | 1·7182 | 1·7113 | 1·7045 | 1·6977 | 1·6909 | 1·6842 | 1·6775 | 1·6709 | 11 | 23 | 34 | 4 |
| 31° | 1·6643 | 1·6577 | 1·6512 | 1·6447 | 1·6383 | 1·6319 | 1·6255 | 1·6191 | 1·6128 | 1·6066 | 11 | 21 | 32 | 4 |
| 32° | 1·6003 | 1·5941 | 1·5880 | 1·5818 | 1·5757 | 1·5697 | 1·5637 | 1·5577 | 1·5517 | 1·5458 | 10 | 20 | 30 | 4 |
| 33° | 1·5399 | 1·5340 | 1·5282 | 1·5224 | 1·5166 | 1·5108 | 1·5051 | 1·4994 | 1·4938 | 1·4882 | 10 | 19 | 29 | 3 |
| 34° | 1·4826 | 1·4770 | 1·4715 | 1·4659 | 1·4605 | 1·4550 | 1·4496 | 1·4442 | 1·4388 | 1·4335 | 9 | 18 | 27 | 3 |
| 35° | 1·4281 | 1·4229 | 1·4176 | 1·4124 | 1·4071 | 1·4019 | 1·3968 | 1·3916 | 1·3865 | 1·3814 | 9 | 17 | 26 | 3 |
| 36° | 1·3764 | 1·3713 | 1·3663 | 1·3613 | 1·3564 | 1·3514 | 1·3465 | 1·3416 | 1·3367 | 1·3319 | 8 | 16 | 25 | 3 |
| 37° | 1·3270 | 1·3222 | 1·3175 | 1·3127 | 1·3079 | 1·3032 | 1·2985 | 1·2938 | 1·2892 | 1·2846 | 8 | 16 | 24 | 3 |
| 38° | 1·2799 | 1·2753 | 1·2708 | 1·2662 | 1·2617 | 1·2572 | 1·2527 | 1·2482 | 1·2437 | 1·2393 | 8 | 15 | 23 | 3 |
| 39° | 1·2349 | 1·2305 | 1·2261 | 1·2218 | 1·2174 | 1·2131 | 1·2088 | 1·2045 | 1·2002 | 1·1960 | 7 | 14 | 22 | 2 |
| 40° | 1·1918 | 1·1875 | 1·1833 | 1·1792 | 1·1750 | 1·1708 | 1·1667 | 1·1626 | 1·1585 | 1·1544 | 7 | 14 | 21 | 2 |
| 41° | 1·1504 | 1·1463 | 1·1423 | 1·1383 | 1·1343 | 1·1303 | 1·1263 | 1·1224 | 1·1184 | 1·1145 | 7 | 13 | 20 | 2 |
| 42° | 1·1106 | 1·1067 | 1·1028 | 1·0990 | 1·0951 | 1·0913 | 1·0875 | 1·0837 | 1·0799 | 1·0761 | 6 | 13 | 19 | 2 |
| 43° | 1·0724 | 1·0686 | 1·0649 | 1·0612 | 1·0575 | 1·0538 | 1·0501 | 1·0464 | 1·0428 | 1·0392 | 6 | 12 | 18 | 2 |
| 44° | 1·0355 | 1·0319 | 1·0283 | 1·0247 | 1·0212 | 1·0176 | 1·0141 | 1·0105 | 1·0070 | 1·0035 | 6 | 12 | 18 | 2 |

# NATURAL COTANGENTS

Subtract Mean Differences.

| 0' | 6' | 12' | 18' | 24' | 30' | 36' | 42' | 48' | 54' | 1' | 2' | 3' | 4' | 5' |
|---|---|---|---|---|---|---|---|---|---|---|---|---|---|---|
| 0000 | 0·9965 | 0·9930 | 0·9896 | 0·9861 | 0·9827 | 0·9793 | 0·9759 | 0·9725 | 0·9691 | 6 | 11 | 17 | 23 | 29 |
| 9657 | 0·9623 | 0·9590 | 0·9556 | 0·9523 | 0·9490 | 0·9457 | 0·9424 | 0·9391 | 0·9358 | 6 | 11 | 17 | 22 | 28 |
| 9325 | 0·9293 | 0·9260 | 0·9228 | 0·9195 | 0·9163 | 0·9131 | 0·9099 | 0·9067 | 0·9036 | 5 | 11 | 16 | 21 | 27 |
| 9004 | 0·8972 | 0·8941 | 0·8910 | 0·8878 | 0·8847 | 0·8816 | 0·8785 | 0·8754 | 0·8724 | 5 | 10 | 16 | 21 | 26 |
| 8693 | 0·8662 | 0·8632 | 0·8601 | 0·8571 | 0·8541 | 0·8511 | 0·8481 | 0·8451 | 0·8421 | 5 | 10 | 15 | 20 | 25 |
| 8391 | 0·8361 | 0·8332 | 0·8302 | 0·8273 | 0·8243 | 0·8214 | 0·8185 | 0·8156 | 0·8127 | 5 | 10 | 15 | 20 | 24 |
| 8098 | 0·8069 | 0·8040 | 0·8012 | 0·7983 | 0·7954 | 0·7926 | 0·7898 | 0·7869 | 0·7841 | 5 | 10 | 14 | 19 | 24 |
| 7813 | 0·7785 | 0·7757 | 0·7729 | 0·7701 | 0·7673 | 0·7646 | 0·7618 | 0·7590 | 0·7563 | 5 | 9 | 14 | 18 | 23 |
| 7536 | 0·7508 | 0·7481 | 0·7454 | 0·7427 | 0·7400 | 0·7373 | 0·7346 | 0·7319 | 0·7292 | 5 | 9 | 14 | 18 | 23 |
| 7265 | 0·7239 | 0·7212 | 0·7186 | 0·7159 | 0·7133 | 0·7107 | 0·7080 | 0·7054 | 0·7028 | 4 | 9 | 13 | 18 | 22 |
| 7002 | 0·6976 | 0·6950 | 0·6924 | 0·6899 | 0·6873 | 0·6847 | 0·6822 | 0·6796 | 0·6771 | 4 | 9 | 13 | 17 | 21 |
| 6745 | 0·6720 | 0·6694 | 0·6669 | 0·6644 | 0·6619 | 0·6594 | 0·6569 | 0·6544 | 0·6519 | 4 | 8 | 13 | 17 | 21 |
| 6494 | 0·6469 | 0·6445 | 0·6420 | 0·6395 | 0·6371 | 0·6346 | 0·6322 | 0·6297 | 0·6273 | 4 | 8 | 12 | 16 | 20 |
| 6249 | 0·6224 | 0·6200 | 0·6176 | 0·6152 | 0·6128 | 0·6104 | 0·6080 | 0·6056 | 0·6032 | 4 | 8 | 12 | 16 | 20 |
| 6009 | 0·5985 | 0·5961 | 0·5938 | 0·5914 | 0·5890 | 0·5867 | 0·5844 | 0·5820 | 0·5797 | 4 | 8 | 12 | 16 | 20 |
| 5774 | 0·5750 | 0·5727 | 0·5704 | 0·5681 | 0·5658 | 0·5635 | 0·5612 | 0·5589 | 0·5566 | 4 | 8 | 12 | 15 | 19 |
| 5543 | 0·5520 | 0·5498 | 0·5475 | 0·5452 | 0·5430 | 0·5407 | 0·5384 | 0·5362 | 0·5340 | 4 | 8 | 11 | 15 | 19 |
| 5317 | 0·5295 | 0·5272 | 0·5250 | 0·5228 | 0·5206 | 0·5184 | 0·5161 | 0·5139 | 0·5117 | 4 | 7 | 11 | 15 | 19 |
| 5095 | 0·5073 | 0·5051 | 0·5029 | 0·5008 | 0·4986 | 0·4964 | 0·4942 | 0·4921 | 0·4899 | 4 | 7 | 11 | 15 | 18 |
| 4877 | 0·4856 | 0·4834 | 0·4813 | 0·4791 | 0·4770 | 0·4748 | 0·4727 | 0·4706 | 0·4684 | 4 | 7 | 11 | 14 | 18 |
| 4663 | 0·4642 | 0·4621 | 0·4599 | 0·4578 | 0·4557 | 0·4536 | 0·4515 | 0·4494 | 0·4473 | 4 | 7 | 10 | 14 | 18 |
| 4452 | 0·4431 | 0·4411 | 0·4390 | 0·4369 | 0·4348 | 0·4327 | 0·4307 | 0·4286 | 0·4265 | 3 | 7 | 10 | 14 | 17 |
| 4245 | 0·4224 | 0·4204 | 0·4183 | 0·4163 | 0·4142 | 0·4122 | 0·4101 | 0·4081 | 0·4061 | 3 | 7 | 10 | 14 | 17 |
| 4040 | 0·4020 | 0·4000 | 0·3979 | 0·3959 | 0·3939 | 0·3919 | 0·3899 | 0·3879 | 0·3859 | 3 | 7 | 10 | 13 | 17 |
| 3839 | 0·3819 | 0·3799 | 0·3779 | 0·3759 | 0·3739 | 0·3719 | 0·3699 | 0·3679 | 0·3659 | 3 | 7 | 10 | 13 | 17 |
| 3640 | 0·3620 | 0·3600 | 0·3581 | 0·3561 | 0·3541 | 0·3522 | 0·3502 | 0·3482 | 0·3463 | 3 | 7 | 10 | 13 | 16 |
| 3443 | 0·3424 | 0·3404 | 0·3385 | 0·3365 | 0·3346 | 0·3327 | 0·3307 | 0·3288 | 0·3269 | 3 | 6 | 10 | 13 | 16 |
| 3249 | 0·3230 | 0·3211 | 0·3191 | 0·3172 | 0·3153 | 0·3134 | 0·3115 | 0·3096 | 0·3076 | 3 | 6 | 10 | 13 | 16 |
| 3057 | 0·3038 | 0·3019 | 0·3000 | 0·2981 | 0·2962 | 0·2943 | 0·2924 | 0·2905 | 0·2886 | 3 | 6 | 9 | 13 | 16 |
| 2867 | 0·2849 | 0·2830 | 0·2811 | 0·2792 | 0·2773 | 0·2754 | 0·2736 | 0·2717 | 0·2698 | 3 | 6 | 9 | 13 | 16 |
| 2679 | 0·2661 | 0·2642 | 0·2623 | 0·2605 | 0·2586 | 0·2568 | 0·2549 | 0·2530 | 0·2512 | 3 | 6 | 9 | 12 | 16 |
| 2493 | 0·2475 | 0·2456 | 0·2438 | 0·2419 | 0·2401 | 0·2382 | 0·2364 | 0·2345 | 0·2327 | 3 | 6 | 9 | 12 | 15 |
| 2309 | 0·2290 | 0·2272 | 0·2254 | 0·2235 | 0·2217 | 0·2199 | 0·2180 | 0·2162 | 0·2144 | 3 | 6 | 9 | 12 | 15 |
| 2126 | 0·2107 | 0·2089 | 0·2071 | 0·2053 | 0·2035 | 0·2016 | 0·1998 | 0·1980 | 0·1962 | 3 | 6 | 9 | 12 | 15 |
| 1944 | 0·1926 | 0·1908 | 0·1890 | 0·1871 | 0·1853 | 0·1835 | 0·1817 | 0·1799 | 0·1781 | 3 | 6 | 9 | 12 | 15 |
| 1763 | 0·1745 | 0·1727 | 0·1709 | 0·1691 | 0·1673 | 0·1655 | 0·1638 | 0·1620 | 0·1602 | 3 | 6 | 9 | 12 | 15 |
| 1584 | 0·1566 | 0·1548 | 0·1530 | 0·1512 | 0·1495 | 0·1477 | 0·1459 | 0·1441 | 0·1423 | 3 | 6 | 9 | 12 | 15 |
| 1405 | 0·1388 | 0·1370 | 0·1352 | 0·1334 | 0·1317 | 0·1299 | 0·1281 | 0·1263 | 0·1246 | 3 | 6 | 9 | 12 | 15 |
| 1228 | 0·1210 | 0·1192 | 0·1175 | 0·1157 | 0·1139 | 0·1122 | 0·1104 | 0·1086 | 0·1069 | 3 | 6 | 9 | 12 | 15 |
| 1051 | 0·1033 | 0·1016 | 0·0998 | 0·0981 | 0·0963 | 0·0945 | 0·0928 | 0·0910 | 0·0892 | 3 | 6 | 9 | 12 | 15 |
| 0875 | 0·0857 | 0·0840 | 0·0822 | 0·0805 | 0·0787 | 0·0769 | 0·0752 | 0·0734 | 0·0717 | 3 | 6 | 9 | 12 | 15 |
| 0699 | 0·0682 | 0·0664 | 0·0647 | 0·0629 | 0·0612 | 0·0594 | 0·0577 | 0·0559 | 0·0542 | 3 | 6 | 9 | 12 | 15 |
| 0524 | 0·0507 | 0·0489 | 0·0472 | 0·0454 | 0·0437 | 0·0419 | 0·0402 | 0·0384 | 0·0367 | 3 | 6 | 9 | 12 | 15 |
| 0349 | 0·0332 | 0·0314 | 0·0297 | 0·0279 | 0·0262 | 0·0244 | 0·0227 | 0·0209 | 0·0192 | 3 | 6 | 9 | 12 | 15 |
| 0175 | 0·0157 | 0·0140 | 0·0122 | 0·0105 | 0·0087 | 0·0070 | 0·0052 | 0·0035 | 0·0017 | 3 | 6 | 9 | 12 | 15 |

## Answers to Exercises

### Exercise 1

(1) $011\frac{1}{4}°$, N $11\frac{1}{4}°$ E      (2) $067\frac{1}{2}°$, N $67\frac{1}{2}°$ E
(3) $123\frac{3}{4}°$, S $56\frac{1}{4}°$ E      (4) $202\frac{1}{2}°$, S $22\frac{1}{2}°$ W
(5) $326\frac{1}{4}°$, N $33\frac{3}{4}°$ W

### Exercise 2

(1) N $67\frac{1}{2}°$ E, ENE      (2) S $11\frac{1}{4}°$ E, S by E
(3) S $22\frac{1}{2}°$ W, SSW      (4) N $78\frac{3}{4}°$ W, W by N
(5) N $22\frac{1}{2}°$ W, NNW

### Exercise 3

(1) $033\frac{3}{4}°$, NE by N      (2) $112\frac{1}{2}°$, ESE
(3) $191\frac{1}{4}°$, S by W      (4) $247\frac{1}{2}°$, WSW
(5) $326\frac{1}{4}°$, NW by N

### Exercise 4

(a) (1) $012\frac{1}{2}°$    (2) $136\frac{1}{4}°$    (3) $237\frac{1}{2}°$    (4) $290°$
     (5) $140°$
(b) (1) N $41°$ E    (2) S $51°$ E    (3) S $50°$ W
     (4) N $15°$ W    (5) S $35°$ E

### Exercise 5

(a) (1) $3°$ E    (2) $1°$ W    (3) $1\frac{1}{2}°$ W    (4) $1°$ E
     (5) $3\frac{1}{2}°$ E
(b) (1) N $25\frac{1}{2}°$ E    (2) N $79°$ E    (3) S $6\frac{1}{2}°$ E
     (4) S $68\frac{1}{2}°$ W    (5) N $56\frac{1}{2}°$ W

## Exercise 6

| | True Direction | Var. | Mag. Direction | Dev. | Comp. Error | Comp. Direction |
|---|---|---|---|---|---|---|
| 1 | | | 070° | | 5° W | 065° |
| 2 | 325° | 10° W | 335° | | | |
| 3 | 310° | | | 20° W | | 320° |
| 4 | | 10° W | | 30° E | | 220° |
| 5 | 315° | | | 5° E | 10° E | |

## Exercise 7

(a) 280° Comp., 82 n. miles; 208½° Comp., 77 n. miles; 13·3 n. miles rounding C
(b) 125° Comp., 84 n. miles
(c) Total distance 257 n. miles; Steaming time 25 h 40 min

## Exercise 8

(a) 122° G, 18 n. miles
(b) Set 357° T, Drift 6½ n. miles
(c) Rate 1·8 knots
(d) 262° T, 34 n. miles, 9·7 knots

## Exercise 9

(a) 134° G, 15 n. miles     (b) 233° T, 262° Comp.
(c) G/S 9·2 knots, E.T.A. 0449 hours
(d) 228° T, 257° Comp.

**Exercise 10**

(a) 191° T, 31½ n. miles        (b) 183° T
(c) 172° T, 30¼ n. miles


**Exercise 11**

(a) 218° T and 278° T    (b) 098° B, Dist. 17 n. miles


**Exercise 12**

(a) 034° E, Dist. 19 n. miles
(b) Dev. 3° W, Error 33° W


**Exercise 13**

(a) Dev. 5° E                (b) Dev. 5° W


**Exercise 14**

(a) 1 n. mile                (b) 0° 56·5′


**Exercise 15**

19·55 n. miles


**Exercise 16**

(1) 51·45 min    (2) 60° 47′ W    (3) 175·7 n. miles
(4) 39 min       (5) 58° 02½′


**Exercise 17**

(1) 071° T, 46 n. miles      (2) 34° 50′ S 173° 36′ E
(3) 51° 03·5′ N 4° 15·8′ W   (4) 52° 28′ N 2° 37·1′ W
(5) 037° 51′, 152 n. miles

## Exercise 18

(1) S 48° 49′ W, 2931·4 n. miles
(2) S 79° 40′ E, 4592 n. miles
(3) N 49° 38′ E, 2809·5 n. miles
(4) N 64° 53′ E, 1428¼ n. miles
(5) (a) N 70° 03′ E, 3803 n. miles
    (b) 3593·5 n. miles, S 72° 08′ E

## Exercise 19

(1) 31° 34·2′      (2) 62° 05′       (3) 68° 04·75′
(4) 74° 10′        (5) 58° 56·6′     (6) 50° 27·85′

## Exercise 20

(1) 34° 42′ S      (2) 9° 30·4 N     (3) 10° 27·8′ S
(4) 26° 58·5′ N    (5) 36° 13′ N

## Exercise 21

(1) 1st Az. N 84° E, 1st Int. 8·4′ away
    2nd D.R. Posn. 47° 26·6′ N 59° 24·4′ W
    2nd Az. S 20° E, 2nd Int. 11·1′ away
    Final Position 47° 35′ N 59° 38½′ W
(2) 1st Az. N 18·5° E, 1st Int. 3·1′ away
    2nd D.R. Posn. 4° 29·4′ N 63° 21·2′ E
    2nd Az. N 34° W, 2nd Int. 7′ towards
    Final Position 4° 30′ N 63° 09½′ E
(3) 1st Az. N 59½° E, 1st Int. 7′ away
    2nd D.R. Posn. 41° 10′ S 93° 23·4′ E
    2nd Az. N 49° W, 2nd Int. 3·3′ towards
    Final Position 41° 12½′ S 93° 14·8′ E
(4) 1st Az. S 61½° W, 1st Int. 6·5′ towards
    2nd Az. S 82° E, 2nd Int. 7·6′ away
    Position 34° 30·5′ N 160° 01′ E
(5) 1st Az. N 49½° E, 1st Int. 8′ away
    2nd Az. N 61½° W, 2nd Int. 6·2′ away
    Position 43° 28′ S 35° 30′ W

### Some Books for Further Study

*The Admiralty Manual of Navigation*, Vols. I, II and III. H.M.S.O.

*Nicholls's Concise Guide*, Vol. I (for Second Mates) and Vol. II (for Mates and Masters). Brown, Son and Ferguson, Glasgow.

*The Elements of Navigation*, by C. H. Cotter. Pitman.

For the mathematics of navigation:

*Mathematical Notes and Examples for Second Mates*, Parts 1 and 2, by A. C. Gardner. Brown, Son and Ferguson, Glasgow.

# Index